THIRD WORLD THEOLOGIES

D0556149

THIRD WORLD THEOLOGIES

COMMONALITIES AND DIVERGENCES

Papers and Reflections from the Second General Assembly
of the Ecumenical Association of Third World Theologians,
December, 1986, Oaxtepec, Mexico

Edited by
K. C. Abraham
for the Executive Committee
of the Ecumenical Association of Third World Theologians

ORBIS BOOKS

Maryknoll, New York 10545

The Catholic Foreign Mission Society of America (Maryknoll) recruits and trains people for overseas missionary service. Through Orbis Books, Maryknoll aims to foster the international dialogue that is essential to mission. The books published, however, reflect the opinions of their authors and are not meant to represent the official position of the society.

Library of Congress Cataloging-in-Publication Data

Ecumenical Association of Third World Theologians. General Assembly
 (2nd : 1986 : Oaxtepec, Mexico)
   Third World theologies : commonalities and divergences : papers
 and reflections from the Second General Assembly of the Ecumenical
 Association of Third World Theologians, December 1986, Oaxtepec,
 Mexico / edited by K.C. Abraham for the Executive Committee of the
 Ecumenical Association of Third World Theologians.
     p. cm.
   Includes bibliographical references.
   ISBN 0-88344-681-2
   1. Theology, Doctrinal—Developing countries—Congresses.
 2. Theology—20th century—Congresses. 3. Developing countries—
 Church history—20th century—Congresses. 4. Librarian theology—
 Congresses. 5. Christianity and culture. I. Abraham, K.C.
 II. Ecumenical Association of Third World Theologians. Executive
 Committee. III. Title.
 BT30.D4E28 1986
 230'.09172'4—dc20
                                                    90-34760
                                                      CIP

Contents

Preface

Third World Theologies: Conversion to Others

Maria Clara Lucchetti Bingemer

To celebrate ten years of its progress and work, EATWOT (Ecumenical Association of Third World Theologians) organized a general assembly of its members in Oaxtepec, Mexico, from 7 to 14 December 1986. The choice of Mexico as a venue was extremely fortunate and full of significance: standing at a confluence of ancestral, colonial, and modern cultures; a crossroads between indigenous Aztec and Maya religious experience and the cradle of Christian evangelization of the continent of Latin America, Mexico offers the ideal geographical environment and intellectual climate for an exchange and meeting of all the varied currents of theology emanating from the various regions of the Third World.

Preceded by an international meeting of women theologians, from 1 to 6 December, the assembly was solemnly opened on the evening of 7 December, with the delegates being set the task of examining the theme: "Commonalities, Divergences, and Cross-fertilization among Third World, Theologies."

The attempt to make this appraisal in common did not pass off smoothly. As the assembly progressed, there were difficulties and conflicts, produced by divisions and misunderstandings within our number. In the end, however, the high quality of the papers presented and the common desire to resolve the tensions so as to achieve a fruitful exchange won through, and the assembly must be reckoned an important stage in the growth of the association.

Dealing with the elements common to and the divergences among the three continents (Africa, Asia, and Latin America) and the North American minorities, and pondering and evaluating the cross-fertilization that can

This essay originally appeared in *Concilium* 199 (1988), pp. 116–23. It is reprinted with permission from T&T Clark, Edinburgh.

result from these, the participants emerged more clearly aware of their own identity, and determined to live and develop their theological mission as a contemplative commitment, in which methodology, choice of subject matter, and systematic examination of the experience and struggles of the oppressed will combine to produce a real experience of God and proper attention to the God of others. Seeing the revelation of God shining in the faces of others, those who are different from us, we all, as theologians, felt called to conversion and to make our theology too an effective and gratuitous instrument of conversion.

THE COMMONALITIES OF THE THEOLOGICAL ENDEAVOR

The Oaxtepec meeting showed that the Christian churches of the Third World today share a common theological purpose. They are churches that reflect on their Christian faith, and on the experiences this faith produces, in a particular context, with its particular characteristics. This reflection shares common elements, which gives the theologies of the Third World an aspect of brotherly and sisterly solidarity and helps them to see each other as close to one another and part of the same overall purpose.

Third World theologies are theologies born out of a *spiritual experience.* All the churches of the Third World are demonstrating an awakening and a new appreciation of the importance of spirituality. The peoples of the Third World—basically Christian in Latin America and among the minorities in North America, pluralist in Africa and above all in Asia—are going through, against the background of their situation of oppression, a deep and rich religious experience. A theology seeking to be of service to these peoples must necessarily be a theology that starts from a meeting with God, a meeting that takes place within a situation of challenge, a situation that awakens Christians to a *contemplative commitment.*[1] In this contemplative, committed endeavor, Third World theologians are reliving the paschal mystery of Jesus Christ at every moment. Their theologies are born of the suffering and humiliations of their peoples, of their painful experience of poverty, of hunger, of genocide, of death, and at the same time of their longing for dignity and liberation based on the victory already won by Jesus Christ.[2]

More specifically, they are theologies born out of a context of injustice and oppression. This is why they are organized and expressed as rebellion against domination and exercise of power. Listening to one another at Oaxtepec, the theologians there clearly felt they all came from countries under attack: on the economic, social, political, ideological, and cultural fronts. This cross weighing on the shoulders of their peoples leads them to ask who the God they adore and serve is: the God of life or the golden idol[3] hidden behind the masks of racism, sexism, or naked capitalism.

Because they arise in such contexts, Third World theologies are, by nature, *combative* theologies. They attempt to introduce theological discourse within the movement of peoples organizing themselves for their liberation. Their theory takes account of the praxis of these peoples, which, in its turn, leans heavily on theory. Its starting-point is experiencing and describing historical reality from both analytical and intuitive standpoints, including struggles for change to the benefit of the oppressed. Our theologies recognize that the most important thing is not their theological discourse and the words they use, but the liberation that has to take place, in the process of which theology has a part to play and a specific identity. The struggle of Third World theologies is eschatological—while these theologies understand that the Reign of God will not be fully manifest until the final coming of Christ, they struggle to bring the Reign into being now, and take on all the sufferings involved in the fight against the anti-Reign. Liberation and the struggle to bring it about form the common theme; and the central experience, common to these theologies and the peoples they serve, has until now been oppression of every sort.

Third World theologies are also *ecclesial* theologies. They need to retain and maintain their common basis in the churches, despite differences among the churches, of denomination and regional and cultural expression in the various locations in which they work, of involvement in theology and the process of liberation, of response to the situations that challenge and call out to them. Third World theologians accept and proclaim their belonging to these churches, experiencing this belonging as a reference and sometimes as a challenge. But they share a common feeling that "the church of Christ is God's instrument for the liberation of the human spirit and for demonstrating the first fruits of God's Reign."[4] The way Third World theologians are rooted in their churches, their resolve to do theology from within the church, in accord with the longings and aspirations of the people of God, is something they share in common, and something that marks them out as servants of these humiliated and downtrodden peoples, praying that they may, individually or collectively, become instruments of the Reign of God on earth.

These commonalities are counter-balanced by a series of wide divergences. Bringing out these divergent points, though it produced some shocks and even battles at the assembly, overall proved a source of great enrichment.

THE QUEST FOR IDENTITY THROUGH DIFFERENCES

Observing one another in this beautiful Mexican valley, the Third World theologians could see differences in their faces that reflect the diversity of the faces of their peoples. The Oaxtepec assembly proved an excellent opportunity for reflecting on one's own identity through one's differences from others. EATWOT has always seen itself as different from the cultures and theologies of the First World, but this time it was the differences and contrasts within itself, among its own members, that came to the fore. Even the influence of colonialism has made itself felt in different ways in the various continents, and still more among the minority peoples of the United States.[5]

The contributions from *Asia* brought out particular differences from other parts, as well as aspects in common with them. With its special privilege of being the cradle of the most ancient cultures and the birthplace of all the great world religions, cultures, and religions that are still alive and deeply influential on the continent, Asia provides a strong challenge to Christian theology. Besides this, the existence of so many different races, ethnic groups, tribes and — in India — castes, gives this continent a special individuality and an almost magical power of fascination. There are also some problems common to the three continents which are seen at their starkest in Asia. The one that cries out loudest is undoubtedly the domination of women, who are exploited in the home, at work, in social life, devalued as human beings to an extreme degree.

In view of this complex panorama, Asia presents challenges not found to the same degree on the other continents, such as how the Judeo-Christian revelation should enter into dialogue with the ancient religions of the East. How are the basic truths of revelation — the mystery of the incarnation, the Holy Trinity, the eschatological destiny of humankind — to be regarded within the framework of Eastern philosophies, of the sacred books of India and China? And how, on the other hand, do we, in dialogue with non-Christian religions, both teach and learn from them when dealing with concepts so basic and dear to Third World Christian theology as the integral liberation of human beings, the development of social justice, and so on?

Africa, besides the elements it shares with the other continents, also has its own characteristics, giving the oppression its peoples suffer from its own identity. This identity, paradoxically, appears as a threat to the identity of the continent, which suffers from excessive linguistic fragmentation, founded on the fragmentation brought about by colonization: French-, English-, Portuguese-, and Arabic-speaking Africa is still crushed and subjugated by these outside cultures telling it what it should say and think. Besides this, Africa still suffers, in the apartheid regime of South Africa, from one of the worst racist scandals in the history of humanity, ranking with Nazism and blind anti-Semitism in its horror and tyranny.[6]

On the basis of these exceptional factors, African speakers at Oaxtepec developed the concept of *anthropological poverty*. This means more than poverty on the material level; it seeks to give an account of the exploitation and slavery to which the black peoples were subjected, and of the way in which they themselves have interiorized the patterns, values, and models of the slave-owning powers. In the face of this anthropological poverty, Western Christendom is called to pronounce a humble "mea culpa," confessing its sin of complicity in European colonization and of omission in failing to denounce the abuses of power that took place on the continent. This theme of anthropological poverty, dear and proper to Africa and distinguishing it from the other Third World continents, branches out into two main channels: that of the *inculturation* of Christianity, which must take on the particular forms of the native cultural matrices if it is to live and proclaim the gospel and the apostolic tradition; and that of *liberation* on the social, economic, and cultural levels as the means of overcoming the pervasive anthropological poverty. The centrality of culture in African concern is steering the theology being developed there toward a humanism based on solidarity, ancestor worship, and a mystique of life that includes the dead, thereby bringing the rites and customs and the whole rich panoply of African culture within a theological framework.

Latin America generally continues its theological development of the theme of social, economic, and political liberation. The Christian churches of the continent that produced the list of faces taken by poverty, in the Puebla Final Document—the faces of young children, of young people, of the indigenous peoples, the peasants, laborers, the underemployed and unemployed, marginalized and overcrowded urban dwellers, old people[7]— are gradually opening out the fan of this vision of the poor as the privileged recipients of theology and the agents of the struggle for their rights, their dignity, their liberation. Latin American theological thought is incorporating a mass of pedagogical reflection: on the means of working with the people in terms of popular education, community meetings, Bible study groups. The theology produced on the continent has, in turn, moved out from academic circles into the streets, informal discussions, the press, and the communications media.

Latin America is also witnessing the emergence of three large groups, previously marginalized and now coming forward to challenge the Christian churches and their theology in a way that is bound to bring deep questioning and change. They are: first, the *blacks*, who previously organized themselves in separate councils and brotherhoods, but are now looking to find their own place within the main body of the church, in the fields of ministry, liturgy, and theology itself; then, the *Amerindians*, who are regaining their own tradition and dignity in the sphere of the churches, interlinking religious renewal with the struggle for the indigenous cause, the recognition of their tribal lands, the preservation of their culture; finally, *women*, who are rising up and making a new voice heard, a voice different in tone and content, producing a new way of doing theology.

The *North American minorities*—Indians, blacks, and Hispanics—are the oppressed and discriminated against presence of the Third World in the heart of the most typical country of the First: the United States. Poor— trying to carve out a place in a society that has no room for them—these North American minorities are now daring to try and create something new, expressed in black theology,[8] in the richness of the religious experience of the Hispanic peoples, and now emerging as a significant presence in EATWOT.

CROSS-FERTILIZATION

The first piece of cross-fertilization that can be reported concerned the question of methodology. We found that it is in the struggle for fuller life that we meet the God of life and so discover our method of doing theology. Our theologies are not great principles to be applied to reality, but an orientation to clarify our commitment and practice, to establish new relationships and a new lifestyle.

Among the great themes of theology, Christology is one that is greatly enriched by the cross-fertilization brought about by the meeting of Third World theologies. The continent of Asia above all teaches us how to safeguard the originality of Jesus over against other forms of manifestation of the word of God, how to unite the Jesus of history and the cosmic Christ in a richly pneumatic Christology and a cosmo-theandric vision of reality.

Cross-fertilization also took place on the level of our understanding of our mission as *church*. In Oaxtepec, representatives of the different continents and religions were able to question one another on the quality and relevance of their ecclesial mission of evangelization, and on their churches' understanding of themselves as disciples among disciples, seeking a greater and better participation in God's truth.

CONCLUSION: CONVERSION TO OTHERS

The great lesson that came from this assembly was the need for us, as an association, to be activated ever more deeply and persistently by a profound movement of conversion to others. Despite the moments of tension and polarization we experienced, the final outcome of the assembly was our discovery of the possibility of moving beyond these differences and reaffirming reconciliation in truth and love.

The work of Third World theologians is directed toward a global view of humanity. Challenged by the differences we found among ourselves, we have come out of this assembly more open and better disposed to stimulate dialogue and exchange, to allow ourselves to be reached and influenced by difference and otherness. In this way we — speaking from the powerlessness and fragility of the situation of the Third World — feel more capable of daring to devise and create something new.

May the Creator Spirit, who at the dawn of time hovered over original chaos and drew creation from it, come down on and act in the work of these theologians, allowing them to move in the direction of conversion to others and experience of the God of others, to take on together their enriching differences and—in the five years till the next general assembly of their association—produce a new theology for the whole world.

Translated by Paul Burns

NOTES

1. See what L. Boff says on this subject of "committed contemplation," in "A teologia do terceiro mundo," *REB* 49 (1986), p. 848: "... a contemplation that mobilizes for transforming action and ... an action that requires contemplation. ..."

2. See the statement in part 8, below, no. 15.

3. Ibid., no. 16.

4. Ibid., no. 17.

5. For example, Latin America is the most Westernized continent and serves to show how complex the phenomenon of Western European Christianity is.

6. See the African Report, below.

7. P. Scharper and J. Eagleson, eds., *Puebla and Beyond* (Maryknoll, N.Y.: Orbis, 1979), nos. 31–39.

8. See J. Cone, *A Black Theology of Liberation*, 2d ed. (Maryknoll, N.Y.: Orbis, 1987).

Introduction

The Executive Committee

The Ecumenical Association of Third World Theologians (EATWOT) started its journey in 1976 in Dar-es-Salaam, Africa. It reached its tenth anniversary at Oaxtepec, after passing through Delhi in 1981. Dar-es-Salaam, Delhi, and Oaxtepec are all important milestones in that journey. They were occasions to deepen and reaffirm our commitment to do theology in solidarity with the poor.

The purpose of Oaxtepec was to deepen the dialogue between different partners in EATWOT—Africans, Asians, Latin Americans, and U.S. minorities. The theme chosen was "Commonalities, Divergences, and Cross-fertilization among Third World Theologies." Each continental group and the U.S. minorities prepared a document on the theme, and those documents were circulated earlier for study and comment by other partners. They served as the main body of the material for discussion. In this volume we have reproduced them. Brief presentations were made at the plenary session by representatives of each group on each of the three segments of the theme: commonalities, divergences, and cross-fertilization. Slightly edited versions of these presentations are given here. We also asked some of our participants to make evaluative reports of the conference, and they are published in this volume. There is also a statement giving the highlights and the main trends of the discussion. This was originally drafted by one of the participants but has been revised and abridged by the executive committee. All these materials together will provide the reader with a synoptic view of the Oaxtepec conference.

One of our commentators called the body of these materials "a splash of colors." Indeed, it is a splash of colors that can excite our imagination and provoke us to think. If we succeed in doing that about the process of theologizing from the perspectives of the poor, then we are more than satisfied.

We want to thank all our contributors. Many of our members were involved in preparing the background papers, and we remember with gratitude their contributions.

Our thanks are due to Orbis Books for its willingness to publish these materials; and for their help and encouragement we particularly wish to thank Robert J. Gormley, Robert Ellsberg, and Eve Drogin.

The editing has been a collective work of the executive committee of EATWOT. The members are Maria Clara Bingemer (Brazil), Virgil Elizondo (United States), Virginia Fabella (Philippines), Simon Maimela (South Africa), Sergio Torres (Chile), Teresa Okure (Nigeria), and K. C. Abraham (India).

President's Report

Emílio de Carvalho

Between EATWOT's meetings in New Delhi (1981) and in Oaxtepec (1986), we celebrated our tenth anniversary, a decade of abundant and valuable contribution to theological reflection and praxis in our continents.

That five year span was marked by an intensive concentration on regional activities, aimed at promoting EATWOT in our regions, following the recommendations from the first general assembly held in New Delhi, from 17 to 19 August 1981, that "concrete steps be taken in the regions in order to pursue the local efforts of contextualization, towards a more relevant theology for the Third World."[1] The main purpose would then be "to shift the focus of our work from the international level to the local and regional levels at the same time keeping the links at the international level on the ongoing dialogue with other regions of the Third World."[2]

In keeping faith to that New Delhi mandate and program, four continental coordinators were appointed within the regions, with the specific responsibility of coordination of the theological work of the association in the areas. Allow me to thank Engelbert Mveng, Julio de Santa Ana, Tissa Balasuriya, and James Cone for their performance in these capacities. Continental meetings as well as working commissions meetings were held during the five years on specific themes for research, publication, and action.

I participated in a number of those events held or sponsored by EATWOT, in the following order: (1) I attended the preparatory and planning meetings, and the executive committee meeting from 14 to 18 January 1982, in Geneva, Switzerland, to organize the theological dialogue between EATWOT members and First World theologians and representatives. (2) I participated in the Dialogue between Third and First World theologies, held in Geneva, Switzerland, from 5 to 13 January 1983. The main theme was "Doing Theology in a Divided World," and discussions centered on how to formulate theologically the task of Christians in our divided world. (3) While in Hong Kong for the executive committee meeting of the association, I also attended as an observer the Second Asia Theological Conference, from 2 to 11 August 1984. (4) I participated in the African EATWOT members' meeting in Cairo, Egypt, from 24 to 28 August 1985, and in the executive committee meeting held in conjunction with that assembly in the Egyptian capital.

Regretfully I was unable to be a part of the China trip in May 1986, but as I read James Cone's fine report, I cannot but acknowledge the need for more unity among ourselves toward the creation of a unique "Third World theology" in the future. Also I was not present at a number of other regional events, both due to my heavy responsibilities as a church administrator and lack of invitation from the organizers. I certainly would have been delighted to attend if only invited to be an integral part of those interesting consultations.

Among other correspondence, I issued a letter to all EATWOT members on the seventh anniversary of EATWOT, on 31 August 1983. My letter to Cardinal Willebrands on the "liberation" of our brother Leonardo Boff was sent to that member of the Vatican secretariat. Other letters to the newly incoming members of EATWOT were also sent on behalf of the association, and I want to thank all those who acknowledged receipt of the same.

All of us celebrate the increase in membership in our association, namely the increase in female membership (thirty-five new members in 1985). See, for example, the increasing adherency of women theologians in Latin America, Asia, and Africa. I salute 16 June 1982, when the EATWOT Indonesian group was formed under the leadership of Marianne Katoppo. Other outstanding events were: (1) The 1984 dialogue with theologians from South Africa on "The Church and Black Theology in South Africa," which took place in Yaoundé, Cameroun, from January 24 to 28, (2) the consultation on "Black Culture and Theology in Latin America," held in Nova Iguaçú, Rio de Janeiro, Brazil, from 8 to 12 July 1985. This later event came as an answer to a long-time concern raised over and over again in our association, on the need to stress and make more visible the importance of the contribution of black people both to religion and life in Latin America, and to the lack in the Latin American theological reflection of such a valuable contribution. Let me say "better late than never."

Concluding, let me reiterate that contextual Third World theologies need no longer to be affirmed. What is at stake today is the continuity or discontinuity of the Ecumenical Association of Third World Theologians (EATWOT) as a "tricontinental association" more and more rooted in each of our continents. This I am sure will be the focus of this second general assembly. As individual members of EATWOT living and doing theology in contexts where EATWOT has no organic structures or relationships whatsoever with existing similar and continentwide ecumenical organizations, we are facing a daily challenge for survival and relevance. On the other hand, the lack of some kind of structural link between EATWOT members spread all over the world makes it difficult for us to feel any connectionalism between or among ourselves, unless we come to meetings such as this.

As we come here "to deepen the dialogue and trust among our continents," let us face the truth and confess with James Cone, that after a decade of doing theology together, we have not yet been able to cement our relationships. We are still far from producing "a genuine Third World theology" that will "include the particularities of all" and "that we all can support."[3]

Will it happen that after examining very seriously our "commonalities and our divergences" we may be able to come down to a common theology which represents "all in one"?

I hope so.

NOTES

1. See *Proposals for the Future of EATWOT* (1981–1986).
2. Ibid., p. 2.
3. See *EATWOT Visits China: Some Theological Implications* (2–13 May 1986).

THIRD WORLD THEOLOGIES

PART I

REGIONAL REPORTS

1

Asian Report

I. SOCIO-ECONOMIC AND POLITICAL REALITIES

A. Asia

1. Of all the regions of the world, Asia is perhaps the most difficult about which to make generalizations.

1.1. Geographically, it is vast, and it is made up of countries covering large territories of land, for example, China and India, and many countries that are archipelagic in character and disconnected from each other and from the Asian "mainland" by equally large bodies of water, e.g., the Philippines, Indonesia, and Japan.

1.2. Demographically, the most populous countries in the world are in the Asian region, namely, China and India—the former with over one billion persons and the latter with over 700 million. When the population of the rest of the countries is added to these, Asia clearly holds within its ambit 58 percent of the world's population. Thus, Asia has the largest labor force and is potentially the largest market for finished products.

1.3. Economically, the region is made up of countries that have achieved wide disparities of economic growth and development, with some countries like Japan reaching a level of economic and technological progress that is on the level and competitive with the First World, on the one hand, and some countries like Bangladesh that are considered among the poorest in the world, on the other.

1.4. Politically, it is also a region with a wide variety of systems of political rule. There are countries that are governed according to the basic forms of liberal, parliamentary democracies, for example, Japan; others are ruled along authoritarian lines that approximate the national security state; and still others are within the ambit of socialist regimes, namely Burma, China, Laos, Vietnam, Kampuchea, and North Korea.

1.5. Despite this variety that poses difficulty in delineating commonalities, we think that our theological task must be addressed to and situated

3

in the context of a number of basic socio-economic and political realities that may be described under a number of thematic issues.

2. There is, first of all, the continuing reality of the scandalous and pervasive *poverty and misery* in which masses of people live in each country alongside the abominable luxury and opulence which a relatively small number of people enjoy. The level of poverty and the degree of disparity between the rich and the poor vary from country to country:

2.1. Japan has reached a level of economic growth and productivity in such a way that the percentage of the "poor" is relatively lower than in most Asian countries, and the income levels and standard of living of people in general are likewise relatively higher than in most Asian countries.

2.2. The so-called economic miracles that have occurred in South Korea, Hong Kong, Singapore, and Taiwan have also increased the gross national products and per capita incomes in these countries.

2.3. There are countries of "medium range" economic growth, such as Indonesia and Malaysia, where vast natural resources have generated appreciable growth and lowered the level of poverty in recent times.

2.4. India, though still poor, is already the tenth industrial producer in the world.

2.5. There are countries in which economic growth has been quite slow with very large poverty-stricken portions of their population. In both the Philippines and Bangladesh, for example, rough estimates show 80 percent of the people living below the poverty level.

2.6. China is on a different plane. While the per capita income remains low, it has nevertheless achieved a very high parity of economic standard among its large population and has been successful in delivering basic needs and services to its people, while preventing large-scale inflation.

3. When one reflects more closely on these facts, however, one discovers that there is only an average of about 10–15 percent of the total population of Asia who live fairly comfortably, with the rest still living in scandalously poor conditions. The massive and grinding poverty of large numbers of people despite presumptuous claims of economic progress and economic miracles attests to these basic socio-economic facts: the enormous disparity and the glaringly unequal distribution of wealth and power, the widening gap between the rich and the poor, and the endemic consequences which this entails in the social, economic, and political life of Asian nations.

4. There is, in the second place, the continuing *control of the economies* of Asian countries by imperialistic powers, e.g., the United States, principally through the operation of transnational capital and the intensified incursion of multinational corporations.

5. The experience of colonialism varied among the Asian countries.

5.1. Most countries — e.g., Indonesia, Malaysia, and India — became subject to the direct political control of a major Western power.

5.2. Others, like the Philippines, went through successive and alternate control and occupation by two Western powers.

5.3. Still others, like China, were "carved up like watermelons"; they were never really taken over by one Western power, but their territories were divided among Western powers, both European and North American.

5.4. Still others, for example Korea, were colonized by another Asian country, like Japan.

5.5. Only Japan and Thailand were never taken over or colonized by any foreign powers.

6. Given the variety of colonial experience, Asian countries at present are mostly neocolonial economies, structurally and materially controlled and manipulated by the economic superpowers.

6.1. The countries that have achieved so-called economic miracles, such as South Korea, Singapore, Hong Kong, and Taiwan, have relatively fragile economies, very much dependent upon the vagaries of the international market and the fluctuations of international trade.

6.2. There are countries that are under severe debt crises and are dependent upon and subject to the dictation of the international financial institutions, such as the International Monetary Fund and the World Bank. The Philippines and South Korea are examples of those who suffer from this predicament.

6.3. Export-oriented production is a trend in most of the countries, and "export processing zones" have proliferated in many countries with generally adverse social and economic consequences in the internal life of these countries.

6.4. The level of unemployment is very high in some countries so that the exportation of labor and the migration of workers have been heavy within the region and into other parts of the world. The Philippines is one of the largest exporters of labor.

7. As a result of these factors, few countries in Asia can claim economic sovereignty and fewer still can sustain productive growth and economic stability without having to rely on the beneficence and "assistance" of outside and more powerful countries.

7.1. Japan may be considered an exception in this regard. It has in fact become a "semi-imperialistic" country, extending both economic and technological assistance to other countries and in some ways being able to control the economies of others. The rest of Asia has virtually become the marketplace of Japanese industry and commercial interest.

7.2. China may also be considered an exception to this fact. Its socialist construction has provided the structural foundations for and the material basis of a relatively self-reliant and self-sustaining economic life.

8. There is, in the third place, the continuing general *exclusion of the masses* from any meaningful participation in the decision-making processes of society and the political structures of the nations.

8.1. There are countries that are under liberal democratic regimes and which therefore maintain a semblance of parliamentary rule, e.g., Japan and India.

8.2. The general trend and overall common feature, however, is for the rise of the "omnipotent state," exercising centralized and authoritarian powers, usually supported by North American hegemony, which serves largely the interests of social, economic, and political elites.

8.3. Expressions of the national security state system operate in very many countries of the region in which military and technocratic elites control the political system toward presumed quick economic growth and development.

8.4. The result is the perpetuation of political repression from within and imperialistic dictation from without so that "democratic space" is narrow and the presumed achievement of political independence is largely a farce. Authoritarianism, political structures of oppression and dominance, the violation and restriction of basic human rights and civil liberties, foreign intervention, and the absence of authentic democratic political institutions through which popular will and sovereignty can be expressed are the dominant political realities of the region.

9. In the fourth place, *militarization* continues to be entrenched not only as a mode of political rule but also as a way of life in the region.

9.1. There are countries that are under direct military rule, e.g., Indonesia, South Korea, and Taiwan.

9.2. There are countries that have presumably shed off "martial rule," like the Philippines, but the "democratic space" that has been achieved remains relatively narrow and fragile.

9.3. Military budgets have risen in recent years in most if not all of the Asian countries.

9.4. The increasing predominance of military in positions of political power is a common phenomenon in most Asian countries.

9.5. Of extreme importance to the region is the revival of militarism and nationalism in Japan. Japan has quietly rearmed and raised a very powerful army and is engaged in the manufacture of military armaments. The revival of Japan's imperial and militaristic tradition has surfaced prominently in recent times.

10. Beyond these very direct expressions of militarization, however, there is the process whereby military values, ideology, and patterns of behavior continue to achieve a dominating influence on the political, social, economic, and external affairs of the state. It is a process which has begun to seep not only into the political life but also into the structures of social, cultural, and educational life of Asian countries. Violations of human rights, subjugation of popular movements and organizations, suppression of dissent and opposition, summary arrests, and even summary killings have become almost standard operating procedure in the political life of most Asian societies. The values of obedience, subservience, and "cooperation," which are predominant in the military ethos, are equally becoming inculcated in the cultural and educational life of Asian societies.

11. These socio-economic and political realities have exacerbated and provided new ingredients to the traditional sources of *social conflict,* such as the suppression of minorities, the tension between religious groups, and the rivalries between ethnic and tribal loyalties within the countries of the region.

12. Commonalities and divergences in this regard are many: India has to face the increasing militancy of the Sikhs. Sri Lanka has the Sinhala and Tamil issue, which has reached very violent proportions lately. The Philippines faces major problems relative to strong urgings for autonomy and even secession by minority cultural groups in the North and the Muslims in the South. Indonesia continues to face the Timorese issue. Malaysia has very sensitive issues of race born out of the conflict between the Chinese and Malay components of its population. Even highly industrialized Japan faces the internal problems and tension that grow out of its treatment of a minority Korean population within.

13. There are finally the intense *ideological rivalries* and the rivalries between the superpowers that have their peculiar flavor in the Asian region and within each of the countries.

13.1. The Asian region holds a string of U.S. military bases and facilities that extend from the northern to the southern portions of the area. From the Pacific Ocean, to the South China Sea, on to the Indian Ocean, these military bases and facilities have been set up to maintain an arc of defense of the "free world" against the aggression of the "communist world."

13.2. The Vietnam War, which has been one of the most intense wars in the post–Second World War period, gained for the Soviet Union a military foothold within the Southeast Asian region.

13.3. The "red scare" is intense in many countries of the region, e.g., in the Philippines, South Korea, and Indonesia.

13.4. The emergence of socialist societies has caused political divisions in a number of countries, e.g., Korea, so that the question of division and reunification constitutes a major preoccupation that has ideological, as well as political, economic, and social components.

13.5. The "communist question" has led to or precipitated various kinds of "coups" that have involved the "extermination" of large numbers of people, e.g., in Indonesia. Here, ideological and ethnic issues and animosities brought about one of the more violent manifestations of internal political conflicts that could be seen anywhere.

13.6. In the Philippines, a people's war is being waged that has very clear ideological components. The embers of communist insurgency remain in many Asian countries.

13.7. The challenge of the socialist models is present in the Asian region not only in theory but in the actual existence of socialist societies.

14. Amidst the persisting structures of economic poverty and dependence, uneven development within and among the various countries of the region, political repression and dominance, ideological conflict and foreign incursion, there are *popular movements* of social transformation and political change that have grown in varying degrees and importance in different countries. These also constitute a major component of the socio-economic and political landscape of the region.

14.1. In the urban centers, there are workers' struggles and movements for justice and equity. In varying degrees, the workers' struggles continue to prosper in various Asian countries despite all the controls imposed upon them.

14.2. There are organized movements of peasants in the countryside which also continue to grow, seeking the dismantling of age-old systems of feudal landholdings and demanding a control of the fruits of their labor.

14.3. Organized religious groups, involving Christians and people of other living faiths, in solidarity with the poor have expressed commitment to the struggle for liberation.

14.4. There is the rising consciousness and movements of women in various societies against the injustice that has been heaped upon them and for full participation in the life and transformation of the social order.

14.5. There are movements of ethnic and cultural minorities putting into question the injustice and inequity of the larger society in which they live.

14.6. There are organized movements of consumers that point out the most elementary violation of human rights, which is the deprivation of basic goods and services for survival.

14.7. There are movements of students and teachers for better and more people-oriented education and for the emancipation of their societies from militaristic, autocratic, and imperialistic control.

14.8. There are movements for nationalism and against foreign domination in various areas of social, economic, political, and professional life.

14.9. There are movements against nuclearization and for peace in and independence of the region.

14.10. There are movements for human rights and political freedoms and directly against militarization.

14.11. There are movements for the maintenance of ecological and environmental balance that would maintain a more healthy natural surrounding for human growth and preserve the integrity of creation.

14.12. There are, finally, organized movements for national liberation, in some areas like the Philippines waging armed struggle, and in other areas engaging in various forms of political work to enhance national freedom and the authentic democratization and transformation of economic, social, and political life.

15. In short, within certain common socio-economic and political realities, there are divergences that occur within each of the countries of the region that emerge out of peculiar historical, cultural, and other factors. It is clear, however, that within these commonalities and divergences, the socio-economic and political life of the region is in a situation of great stress and unrest that is born out of the continuing and intensifying entrenchment of structures of repression and dominance, on the one hand,

and the rising movement and organization of popular struggle, on the other. It is within this context of stress and contradiction that theological reflection must take place.

B. Comparison with Other Third World Regions

16. Commonalities and divergences with the other Third World regions seem generally obvious. The experience of colonialism and neocolonialism is common, although the specific historical shape which this has taken among the countries and the regions may have divergences. The reality of poverty is common, but the levels and degrees of disparity between the rich and the poor may vary. The phenomenon of a major industrial and economic power like Japan interacting with its regional neighbors in a way that regionalizes imperialistic incursion may be peculiar to Asia, although there are indications that similar situations may be on the rise in the other regions as well. The phenomenon of city-states that have progressed quite well economically is peculiar to the Asian region.

17. The continuance and entrenchment of political systems of repression, e.g., the national security state, is common, but again the specific expressions of this may vary. The Vietnam War and the Korean War are military conflicts that so far are not duplicated in their magnitude and in their consequences in the other regions. The degree and the form of direct military presence of foreign powers, e.g., the United States, vary considerably in and among the regions of the world. Asia has considerable presence of military facilities and personnel of the United States, which is not true in the other regions. This creates certain social, political, and economic issues which are not experienced in those regions or countries where this military presence is not felt.

18. The ideological question represented by the socialist challenge is present in all, but the peculiar political manifestation of this issue in the political division of countries such as Korea is peculiar to Asia. The degree of military conflict and confrontation this has generated may have also been more intense in Asia than anywhere else. The religious component of social and political conflict may be more dominant in Asia than in the other regions. The racial component of social and political conflict is present in Asia, although it may in general not be as dominant as it is in South Africa.

II. RELIGIO-CULTURAL REALITIES

A. Asia

19. Asia is the home of some of the world's most ancient cultures and the source of all the great world religions. The religions and many of the cultures are still alive today and are active influences in the Asian countries.

20. The cultures and religions are related and intermingled. Some relig-

ions are present in many cultures. Some cultures are open to several religions. The complexity of Asia's religio-cultural reality is reflected in the
following overview:

20.1. *Buddhism, Islam, and Christianity,* which are missionary religions,
are present in many cultural backgrounds. Buddhism, spreading from North
India, is the main religion in Sri Lanka, Burma, Thailand, Laos, Kampuchea, and Vietnam and has numerous followers in China, Korea, and Japan.
Islam spread from West Asia to Pakistan, Bangladesh, Malaysia, and Indonesia. Christianity is in most countries of Asia as a small percentage; only
in the Philippines is it the religion of the vast majority (92 percent) of the
population.

20.2. *Hinduism* is mainly in India and where peoples of Indian origins
are. India has religionists—such as Hindus, Moslems, Sikhs, Christians, and
Jains—sharing in the general Indian culture.

20.3. *Confucianism, Taoism, and Shintoism* are the main philosophical
and religious influences among the Chinese, Japanese, and Korean peoples.

20.4. Thus multiplicity and crisscrossing of cultures and religions are
understandable in a continent which represents about 58 percent of the
human race and has the longest living memory of organized religions.

21. Asia is also characterized by the presence of diverse *races, ethnic
groups, tribes,* and, in the Indian subcontinent, *castes.* These are often dis-
tinguished by language and cultural traits and sometimes by religion. These
groups have their own community interests, and they strive to maintain
their identity, rights, and privileges. Many of the conflicts within Asian
countries are of an ethnic, racial, tribal, or caste nature. These conflicts
cannot be reduced to economic interests alone, though economic factors
also have a vital impact. The conflicts of Hindus and Sikhs in India, of
Sinhala and Tamil in Sri Lanka, and of the Moros struggling for autonomy
in the Philippines, have an ethnic character in a background of different
religions.

22. Throughout Asia's millennial history, *women* have been treated as
the inferior sex. They have been exploited in the home, at work, and in
social life. This is true of almost all the racial and ethnic groups, cultures,
and religions.

23. In all the Asian countries there are *folk religions* that evolved from
among the peoples over generations. They are based on an effort to cope
with the unknown, the imponderables, and the joys and tragedies of the
human predicament. They deal with sickness, birth and death, fears,
dreams, rivalries, the evil eye, the spirits, propitiation to the gods, the
weather, good and bad fortune, harvests, etc.

23.1. These cults have their regular votaries and practitioners, priests
and performers of ritual. The people have recourse to them in their needs
and have evolved elaborate rituals for diverse occasions, e.g., Shamanism
in Korea.

23.2. Many aspects of the developed religions have been influenced by the practices of these folk religions, e.g., folk Christianity in the Philippines. This explains partly why and how the different religions coexist among the people. Persons of all religions pay homage at certain shrines because these answer their need for the ministrations of religiosity in different circumstances of life.

24. The *organized world religions,* such as Hinduism, Buddhism, Christianity, Islam, and the religio-philosophical approaches like Confucianism, have a long tradition of spiritual ministration to the Asian peoples.

25. They have their sacred writings which have both a deep philosophical reflection as well as teachings on spiritual advancement of persons. The philosophical schools have their own system of logic and explanations of human life and destiny in relation to the transcendent values of God and/ or spiritual fulfillment. The writings, such as the Vedas and Upanishads, come down from ancient times and have been handed down and commented on by several generations of learned seers. They include the words of the Buddha, Confucius, and Lao Tse, the Bible, and the Koran.

26. The religions have their great founders like the Buddha, Jesus, and Mohammed, who were great religious reformers and prophets in their day and for successive generations. In more recent times there have been other great spiritual leaders—the best known of whom is Mahatma Gandhi.

27. The Asian religions have a tradition of both scholarship and mysticism. In all the religions there is an accent on personal purification and inner liberation.

27.1. Buddhism and Hinduism emphasize self-realization through meditation and right action in a cycle of birth, death, and rebirth in several lives.

27.2. In Hinduism there is an underlying tradition of union with God the Absolute, who is regarded as the source of all being, all goodness and truth.

27.3. The Confucian ethic lays an accent on right conduct and on sincerity and honesty in personal and public life.

27.4. Christianity and Islam are more concerned with human life in community and teach that eternal salvation depends on one's present life here on earth.

28. The Asian religions have a common humanizing core of teachings concerning personal, moral, and social life. They all stress the value and need of unselfishness and detachment from material things. They teach compassion, concern for the other, sharing of possessions, love for the family, respect for the elders, care of nature, and right conduct in personal and public life. These present occasions for self-purification and for serving human beings in their needs. This core of common values can be the basis for integral human liberation and for cooperation in building human communities in our pluralist societies of Asia. In working for the common human concerns, basic human communities or action groups can deal with issues as they arise in society.

29. The impact of the *religio-cultural factors* is notable in Asia. While the basic motivations of the Asian religions and cultures are other-centered and liberative, there are also harmful and enslaving aspects of these religions and cultures.

29.1. They can lead persons and groups to selfishness and narrow communalism, whether the groups be of a cultural, religious, linguistic, ethnic, tribal, or caste nature. The others can be considered aliens and even competitors and enemies. Cultural prejudices, stereotypes, and myths buttress such narrow, chauvinistic attitudes.

29.2. In the relationship of the sexes, the religions have had both liberative and oppressive aspects. In all the religions there is some understanding of both the male and female as sharing in the life of the Absolute or as capable of ultimate self-realization. However all the religions have discriminatory attitudes toward women. In most religions, they are debarred from decision-making roles and participation as clergy.

29.3. The religions influence the psychology of peoples. Some of them encourage human action for the transformation of the universe. But by and large they foster a passive and fatalistic attitude toward nature and development, life and death, social relations and structures. They tend to bring up successive generations in the attitude of conformism and subordination to the powers that be, be they feudal, capitalistic, colonial, or neocolonial. This can have the impact of legitimizing political, social, and economic powers and male domination.

29.4. The Asian cultures have been powerful means for the perpetuation of the oppressive relationships and structures in society by bringing about an internalization of the consciousness of inferiority and weakness in the dominated sex, castes, tribes, and ethnic groups. The collective consciousness of both the dominant and the dominated is thus strengthened and handed down from generation to generation in a way that oppression is legitimized within even the oppressed. In order to achieve integral liberation people need an inner personal and group psychotherapy to help them to be freed of such inhibitions, fears, and myths.

29.5. The religions have been powerful critiques of injustice, inequality, corruption, and authoritarianism. The religions have also a culture of protest and of resistance to such abuses, as was seen in the Indian Independence movement led by Mahatma Gandhi, in the revolution in Iran led by Ayatollah Khomeini, in the human rights struggles in South Korea, and in the protest action of the Filipino people against Marcos.

30. Due to the influence of modern science and technology and the unification of world trade, travel, and the flow of communications, certain *trends* in the cultures and religions in Asia can be noted toward:

a. a modernization of lifestyles, practices, and relationships in family and society;

b. a fundamentalism which leads to a closing in of cultures and religions and a defense of one's privileges against others, and even an attack on other religions and cultures;

c. a renewal of religions by a scientific study of their sources and a return to the best inspirations of their foundation; an approach of openness to other cultures while developing what is good in one's own culture;

d. interfaith ecumenism which transcends the limitations of doctrine and meets in dialogue around basic core values and fundamental inspirations, thus contributing powerfully toward integral human liberations and the fulfillment of persons and peoples.

31. The relationship between *ideologies and Asian religions* needs to be considered. The Asian states relate differently to the Asian religions and cultures:

31.1. Those which are capitalistic and for free enterprise encourage freedom in the religions, but try to entice them toward supporting the capitalistic value system. These countries are open to cultural influences from outside, especially the rich Western countries. Consumerism is spread through trade, aid, education, and development policies. These have their good and bad effects. The latter include abuses such as drug addiction, prostitution, corruption, and the undesirable influence of the mass media. Religions are generally bought by being offered freedom and the material advantages of the system.

31.2. The socialistic states under Marxist regimes were first opposed to the religions and even persecuted them. They tried to build a counterculture different from both the traditional conservative values, as of Confucianism in China, and the modern Western lifestyle. But recently they have become more tolerant of religions and are opening up to the modern culture of the industrialized countries, with China as an example of such a process.

31.3. Some states, like India, have adopted a largely secular philosophy without having any state religion. Others, like Pakistan and Iran, have made Islam the state religion. Both of these face different types of problems in trying to satisfy the demands of the majority and minority cultural and religious groups within their countries.

31.4. The world powers through their impact on economic, political, and military issues have an influence on the cultures and even on the religious attitudes of the Asian peoples.

32. The Asian religions and cultures are complex social realities that pose issues for their peoples as they open up to the modern world. They likewise pose deep issues for Christian theological reflection.

B. Comparison with Other Third World Regions

33. In African and Asian societies, *culture* plays a predominant role in the formation of the community, in shaping the personality, and in the continuity of past and future. African society gives more emphasis to the initiation process, the role of dance in community celebration, and respect for ancestors. However, Eastern Asia too has respect for ancestors linked to the religious traditions of Confucianism.

34. A commonality shared by the three continents is that they all were invaded and colonized by Western powers and their cultures were attacked or depreciated.

34.1. In Latin America, the attack on the cultures resulted in an almost complete disappearance of the original native cultures from the mainstream of public life. There was an imposition of Spanish and Portuguese culture, language, and Catholicism on the native peoples who survived the sword of the conquistadors. A similar process took place in the Philippines.

34.2. In Africa, the cultures have generally survived and have been reasserted since political independence from the colonizers. Primal cultures, which were marginalized because of the incursion of organized world religions such as Christianity and Islam, are now being revived, renewed, and reevaluated.

34.3. In Asia, cultures and religions suffered much humiliation but have survived the attack of Westerners. Nevertheless the cultures evidence traces of influences of modernization and Westernization. In the Philippines, Christianity has influenced the way of life of the vast majority of the people — except among the cultural minorities and where Islam was the established religion, as among the Moros.

35. Asia has all the great *world religions.* Out of these world religions Africa has mainly Islam and Christianity, and Latin America almost exclusively Christianity.

36. Asian religions have a long tradition of written scriptures while Africa has mainly an oral tradition, except in North Africa. In Latin America the present written tradition is from Western Europe.

37. Africa, Asia, and the ancient South American native religions have a belief in a supreme, transcendent being, with the significant exception of Theravada Buddhism.

38. In all three continents, Christianity has been considered as a foreign religion. It came earliest to Asia, as far back as the early Christian era, then to the African continent, and very much later, in the fifteenth century, to Latin America.

39. In all three continents, all other religions were attacked by Christians as "pagan." In Latin America and Africa the primal religions have been largely marginalized, despised, and brought to a point of disappearance in many places. Islam held its own and is advancing in Africa. In Asia, despite the attempts of missionaries to establish Christianity, the other world religions have maintained their dominance. Christians have remained a minority of less than 3 percent, except in the Philippines.

40. The *domination of women* by men has been universal in all three continents. It is only in recent years that there have been movements for women's emancipation; these movements are gradually making an impact in all three continents. The socialist societies have been more conscious of the equality of women and men in society. China under Chairman Mao carried through very wide reforms for women's equality and dignity.

III. THEOLOGICAL ISSUES ARISING OUT OF SOCIO-ECONOMIC, POLITICAL, AND RELIGIO-CULTURAL REALITIES

A. Asia

41. The issue of a theology of social change, in general, and of struggle, in particular, that would deal with the following matters:

a. the significance of struggle as a means of social and political change and as a critical instrument in bringing about a purification and renewal of Christian theological reflection and spirituality;

b. the religious and theological significance of affirming that the people, the poor, or the oppressed are the subjects of social and political change, and the meaning of Christian solidarity;

c. where and in what form we encounter or locate the presence of God in the present struggle for social, economic, and political change;

d. the varieties of struggle and the theology or ethics of violence and nonviolence;

e. what these would mean in terms of the pastoral action of the church and of Christian discipleship.

42. The issue of a new hermeneutic of the Christian tradition and the Bible in the light of a new hermeneutic of our present history:

a. how and in what ways we discover "people" as the subjects of history;

b. how we reread and reinterpret the biblical narrative and the whole history of Christian tradition and mission, in such a way that we discover the liberational and transformational dimensions of faith.

43. The issue of a new understanding of the sovereignty of the people that raises the following points:

a. the democratization of social, economic, and political life;

b. the stewardship of God's creation and the redistribution of the ownership of the means and benefits of production;

c. the critique of imperialism and neocolonial relationships.

44. The issue of theology and ideology that would deal with the following matters:

a. a critical examination of the meaning of ideology and the ideological options that the Christian may take;

b. a critical recognition of the ideological function of theology as legitimation and rationalization of the present orders and powers of society;

c. a constructive discovery of the role of theology as a critical discipline of and reflection upon the liberating and transformative praxis in the present.

45. The issue of Christian spirituality and justice that would give attention to the following:

a. the social and political content of spirituality;

b. the discovery and inculcation of liberational and transformative dimensions in "popular" spirituality and religiosity.

46. The issue of ecclesiology that would give attention to the following matters:

a. the transformation of the church in such a way that it serves rather than obstructs the struggle for liberation and social transformation;

b. the shape, structure, leadership, and role of a transformed church in a transformed society; the social and political shape of the church in the future;

c. how to deal with grace, spirituality, and power in the church.

47. Finally, a key Christological question: Who is Jesus Christ to those who are engaged in the political and social struggle, and what does it mean for them and for us to believe in him?

48. In summary, the theological task in relation to Asia's politico-economic reality has to do with the articulation of how and in what manner the popular struggle for liberation and social transformation meets and coincides with the purpose of God. Such an articulation becomes a critical "principle" by which the life of the church is assessed, including its "traditional" understanding of theology and spirituality. Such an articulation would as well clarify critically the issue of who does theology and for what purpose, and would redefine the meaning of Christian praxis and pastoral action in the world.

49. In relation to the Asian cultures, there is a need to deal with the following issues:

a. a critique of the cultures, distinguishing the liberating and enslaving aspects of each;

b. the extent and way of inculturation:

—in language, art, music, architecture

—in lifestyle, in identification with the poor

—in relating culture to the struggle of the oppressed for liberation and self-realization

—in transforming male-dominant relationships to partnership and participation

—in helping resolve cultural and ethnic conflicts, transcending narrowness of communalism (loyalty to a socio-political grouping based on religious affiliation).

50. The theological issues arising from the relationship of Christianity to other religions include:

a. openness to and tolerance of other religions;

b. acceptance of the other religions and working with them as partners in community building;

c. expressing Christian revelation in and through the philosophical and religious concepts of the Asian peoples and religions;

d. working for the purification of Christianity and the other religions so that all could share in the struggle for human liberation in Asia; linking up the positive liberative elements of the religions;

e. rethinking the Christian concept of revelation: how far and in what way God can be communicating a message to Asian peoples through the other religions—through their founders, leaders, scriptures; the place of the Bible—reevaluating whether it is normative, final, unique, universal; rereading the Bible from this newly grounded perspective;

f. the understanding of sin, redemption, and grace (soteriology), and the role of Jesus the Christ in the divine plan of salvation/liberation;

g. problems of Christology, in the context of other religions: Does the divinity of Jesus impede God from other manifestations of incarnations of the divine?

h. an evaluation of the traditional construct of Western theology: How far is it universal or culture-bound?

i. an understanding of the reign of God and of the church and the mission of church in the Asian countries in relation to other religions; our theology to be more God- and human-centered rather than church-centered; church authority and its relationship to the task of building the community according to values of the reign of God which are beyond the church's control.

51. The doing of theology in Asia within its religious and cultural realities faces the following challenges:

a. purification of Christian theology;

b. relating the core of the gospel of Jesus to core values of other religions and ideologies;

c. participating in building human relations and human community in truth, love, justice, and peace;

d. developing a spirituality of commitment and contemplation of the One God along with all others inspired by the traditional schools and practices of spirituality; developing inner liberation and a social psychotherapy to heal the damage done to the collective psyche.

52. The following issues need to be raised in relation to the sexes:

a. rereading the Bible from the feminist perspective, and accordingly rethinking the message of Jesus and Christology;

b. critique of the teaching and practice of the church concerning women-men relations within the church, especially regarding ministry, authority, liturgy, etc.;

c. questions of morality, sexuality, biogenetics, the control over human life, the human body;

d. cooperation among women of different religions for the purification of all religions of sexism and its consequences.

B. Comparison with Other Third World Regions

53. In comparison with the other Third World regions, we perceive the following commonalities and divergences:

53.1. In Africa, as in Asia, there has been a general tendency for Christian theology not to give adequate consideration to the local religions. These were considered, at best, as complementary to the biblical revelation to the Jews and as later understood by the Christians. As in Asia, there was even a depreciation of the local values, customs, and rituals.

53.2. Present-day theological reflection is, however, beginning to question such attitudes, with some African writers raising issues similar to those being asked in some Asian writings. Questions are raised as to the uniqueness and universality of the Bible and the possibility of God's revelation to different African peoples. From these follow questions of Christology, the personality of Jesus, the nature and mission of the church, what conversion to Christianity should entail, etc. In this, a similarity is being realized at the level of theological interrogation and elaboration in Africa and Asia.

53.3. The rise of the African Independent Churches is an indication that the mainline churches have failed to respond to many of the issues raised by African society, such as the explanation of dreams, sickness, polygamy, the acceptance of dance, and peoples' participation in the liturgical services. This is not a predominant feature in Asia.

54. African theological responses have been in two main directions during the past decade.

54.1. In the countries which are independent the emphasis is on the relation of Christian theology to African culture, African religions and religiosity, and African spirituality. New and radical thinking is emerging. Christian theologians are raising the issues of what it is to be an African man or woman disciple of Jesus Christ. In this process, issues concerning the whole content of theology, the nature of mission, teachings concerning the moral life, and the role of the church are coming up.

54.2. In Southern Africa, the present accent is on liberation from the oppressive white regime that continues the exploitation of the blacks and of the region. African theology is on the march and is likely to be most fruitful in the decade.

55. In the recent decades Latin America has seen a flowering of theology. It began with an analysis and critique of society and a presentation of social liberation from a Christian point of view. This went alongside a rereading of the Bible from the perspective of the poor and a development of a method of doing theology in relation to commitment to social transformation. In the process there was a rethinking of the role and mission of the church and of Christian spirituality in relation to their social mission of human liberation. The emerging Philippine theology of struggle contains many similar elements.

56. In recent years, Latin American theologians have become more conscious of the feminist movement, of the "black" pressure in Latin America, and of the culture and religiosity of the native peoples of these regions. These are only small beginnings. As they advance they are likely to lead to a greater cross-fertilization in relation to African and Asian theologies.

57. In all these continents, theological reflection needs to be complemented by an overall study and strategizing in relation to world capitalism,
the socialist countries, and directions of the churches as a whole. The
continental approach being generally used may not bring out adequately
the global dimensions of the contemporary challenges to the peoples of the
Third World and to their doing theology today.

IV. COMMON AND DIVERGENT METHODOLOGIES OF EATWOT

58. Methodology is central to theology. In all doing of theology a methodology is explicitly or implicitly adopted. It relates to issues such as:
 —sources of theology
 —assumptions and presuppositions in doing theology
 —context and perspectives from which theology is done
 —the subject, or the one doing theology
 —process, or the way of doing theology
 —the medium of expressing one's theology
 —content of theology
 —consequences of different methodologies and their contribution to the
development of theology.
  Only a few of the above aspects are dealt with in relation to the methodologies described in this section.
  59. This section will deal first with a general methodology with references
made to other regions and then with a short description of four prevailing
methodologies being developed in the Asian context.
  60. For the most part, Asian theologians accept what is valuable in the
general advances made by liberation theology concerning committed Christians as the subjects doing theology, commitment as the first act of theology,
social analysis as an indicator of the signs of the times, the process of doing
theology by action-reflection-action, the medium of expressing theology
through the arts, and the spirituality of commitment to integral human
liberation.

A. Historico-contextual Methodology, with Reference to the African and
Latin American Regions

  61. Theological methodologies are ways of doing theology on biblical
grounds and sources, in relation to historical contexts, that is, in commitment or response to the struggles of oppressed peoples in the Third World.
Two topics point to the basic historico-contextual methodology that is common in EATWOT theologies: (1) historico-contextual starting points and
themes; and (2) problems of biblico-Christological grounding. They bring
to light the question of relating biblical text and contexts.
  62. The methodological principle of a historico-contextual way of doing
theology has been implied or explicated in European modern theology.

However, the uniqueness and revolutionary character of EATWOT theologies lie in particular historico-contextual starting points and in the option for the oppressed poor peoples of the Third World (and the oppressed minorities in the United States); the uniqueness and character of these theologies also stem from the particular themes that are born of their critiques of Western ecclesio-theological and cultural domination and tradition.

63. The starting points and themes require a radical transformation of the structures of Western domination which are in contradiction to God's righteousness and reign. EATWOT theologies are thus of a particular historical character, and yet of a universal significance.

64. In spite of the fact that the contexts of our three continents are so divergent historically, religio-culturally, radically, and ethnically, all these divergent realities stand under the common fate of Western and modern capitalist domination, and, therefore, have the common theme of liberation. This is a most remarkable, common contextual theme of EATWOT theologies.

65. EATWOT, however, has not yet explored the divergent religio-cultural thoughts, myths, and symbols of other faiths in the three continents, in relation to the common theme of liberation. A coherent methodology for articulating this relationship is still lacking. In the way of interpreting these religio-cultural factors on a biblical basis, there are divergent theological stances—even among EATWOT members—which are not yet explored.

66. Also it is not certain whether EATWOT members are agreed or not as to the direction and way of political and socio-economic liberation. In view of the basic, common starting points and theme of liberation, we can point out some further commonalities and divergences, in terms of common concerns and problems. Commonalities and divergences exist not just among the three continents but within each continent and even among EATWOT members themselves.

67. Marxist political and socio-economic analysis has been used in doing theology.

67.1. Latin American liberation theology has been exemplary in its use of Marxist political and socio-economic analysis and critique of the capitalist world structure, which is now the major instrument of domination and oppression. Marxism has been discussed positively in relation to Christianity in the West, and yet the discussions and positive assessments remain ineffectual within the West.

67.2. The very Third World peoples—the oppressed poor, the minjung, the blacks, and women—who are the victims of dominating capitalist powers also contain within themselves the dynamic of revolution and liberation. Marxism is perhaps the best tool for them to become liberated and to revolutionize toward a new, humane, just world order.

67.3. Marxist socio-economic analysis and influence are also presupposed in various African and, to a greater degree, in Asian peoples' or minjung movements and struggles against Western and Japanese dominations.

67.4. As for China and North Korea, Marxism has become an integral part of their social contexts, although this factor is not yet meaningfully accounted for in Asian theology.

68. Two common problems are to be noted here:

68.1. We are not sure yet how far EATWOT members are agreed about the extent of the validity and presupposition of Marxist elements in EATWOT concerns. Unless this question be explored, it is not possible, in this respect, to identify commonalities and divergences among the three continents. The contexts or peoples' concerns are divergent and complicated within themselves. Two specific questions are to be asked here: Firstly, how can African concern for African anthropology-cosmology be meaningfully related to the Marxist socio-economic analysis and critique toward a new society and world. Secondly, how can Asian religio-cultural heritages be related to the question of the socio-economic liberation of the peoples? These questions must be explored and clarified.

68.2. The use of Marxism implies a future political option for a socialist order. However, this question is not clarified among EATWOT members. At any rate, presupposing the option, there are certain points to be mentioned. Christian appropriations of Marxist socialism or communism imply something of a "third way" beyond the divided worlds, the capitalist and socialist systems as they are. A "third way" does not mean the Christian Democratic Party line of Chile or elsewhere, oscillating between them and after all becoming part of Western Christendom and culture. A "third way" points to the ultimate ground and source of the oppressed people's liberation, the ground and source, that is, of God as such, who is not identical with capitalism or socialism as such, although the latter can be a means to overcome the former. A "third way" is to be taken as that of overcoming the capitalistic West and Christendom, interpreting Marxism on a theological basis toward an eschatological reconciliation of the whole world and the coming of the reign of God.

69. In Western domination over colored peoples, in the enslavement of the blacks, and the genocide of Indians in the past, there lie the historical crimes of white racism, with which Western Christendom and mission were linked. Although the oppressed races are caught up in modern capitalist domination, racism is an older and deeper element of oppression than the socio-economic factor. Perhaps the motif of racial revolt is stronger in African liberation movements than the motifs of socio-economic liberation. The problem of racism must be tackled in connection with that of socio-economic domination by the whites.

70. The religio-cultural heritages of Third World peoples of other faiths are another contextual factor to be accounted for theologically for the liberation of peoples. These heritages include in themselves elements that are oppressive, conflicting, and exclusive. Nevertheless, they are the marks of the people's continuing existence and spiritual identity. The heritages are also caught up in capitalist forces, and yet they are dimensions different from the socio-economic factors.

71. Third World theologies can derive new theological languages from the heritages provided they are reinterpreted on biblico-theological ground. In other words, the experience of God's presence and action in the historical religio-cultural contexts can be articulated in their language, symbols, myths, and images, in service of the struggling people and in service of their liberation movements.

72. In order for the religio-cultural heritages to become liberative languages, they must be critically reinterpreted and reappropriated in relation to their own historical problems or limitations, and also in relation to Third World political and socio-economic problems. Otherwise they become ahistorical in the sense that they continue to exist as if unrelated to their historical contexts and problems, and become even antihistorical in the sense that they play ideological roles for existing capitalist, oppressive power structures.

73. We may note four lines of interpretation and problems:

73.1. Asian religio-cultural thoughts and images, myths and symbols contain spiritualities that are different from Western Christian spirituality and richer than the latter in their penetration into the spiritual dimensions of human and cosmic natures, which are now largely lost under the influence of the aggressive materialistic spirituality of the latter. Over against the latter, the spiritualities of other religious traditions have often come alive, for instance in nationalist-minjung liberation movements. However, the problem of the spiritualities lies in the fact that they, by and large, continue to exist unrelated to given political and socio-economic problems, as if they were transhistorical or ahistorical spiritualities. They must be reinterpreted, on the one hand, in their historical and present political, socio-economic contexts and within the context of people's struggles for liberation; on the other hand, they must be reinterpreted in the light of biblical faith in the Holy Spirit.

73.2. Other religions and cosmic-human spirits and images can be integrated into Christian spirituality and worship forms, reinterpreted on the basis of biblical faith in the Holy Spirit. They are not identical with the Spirit. They can be interpreted as creaturely spiritualities. The spirits and images, or myths and symbols, understood in the light of the freedom of the Holy Spirit, can be summoned up in oppressed people's liberating symbolic acts, for example, in the case of the American Indian ghost dance over against white Americans, and also in the case of shamans. However, unless set in the present political and socio-economic contexts, the spirits and images or myths and symbols cannot become the languages of the liberation of the people who are politically and socio-economically oppressed.

73.3. A holistic theology, as asserted in South Asia, points to a synthetic vision of the totality of religio-cultural spiritualities, both of Christianity and of other faiths, a vision of human-cosmic, transcendental, spiritual wholeness. The intention is similar to that of a theology of religion-culture, as is attempted in Korea. We may assume the same line of theological efforts in Chinese religio-cultural settings. An inherent danger in this longing and effort for a holistic vision is abstraction from the problematic, conflicting historical particularities of religions, and from political and socio-economic problems and human guilt, in the face of which any holistic vision of religious spiritualities and thoughts breaks down. Every religion longs for holistic vision and spirituality, and yet breaks down in the face of historical processes. Indeed, one synthetic whole of religious spiritualities may become fulfilled eschatologically by the Holy Spirit of God, in Jesus Christ. However, any religious spirituality must be tested in historical processes, in relation to people's socio-economic life, problems, and struggles, toward the perfection of material reality and order. In fact, profound Asian religious spiritualities have been rendered impotent in the face of Western colonialism and capitalism. The failures and guilts of religious spiritualities, both Christian and otherwise, African and Asian, are to be tested in their relations to historico-contextual problems and critiques, and thus to undergo divine judgment toward their salvation and wholeness.

73.4. The practice of religious poverty in the renunciation of worldly possession in Asian religions, especially in Hinduism and Buddhism, is interpreted in South Asia as having a spiritual and liberational potential over against Western capitalist greed. It is asserted that a political and socio-economic critique is not enough for human liberation. What is necessary for overcoming capitalist materialist greed is the practice of a spiritual poverty which is in accord with Christian evangelical poverty and freedom. Asian religious poverty can be interpreted in this sense indeed. However, though profound, the practice of religious poverty alone is not enough for overcoming socio-economic problems. The methodological question is then how to relate the practice to socio-economic critique and revolutionary praxis in history.

74. The problem of *biblico-Christological grounding* deals with relating Third World historical contexts, oppressed peoples' liberational struggles and movements, and their religio-cultural heritages, to biblical text, source, and norm.

75. The formal principle of biblical hermeneutical method, circular between text and context, is typically explicated by Bultmann and his school, and the methodological principle is much adopted and discussed by Latin American theologians, although the context in the latter case is quite new to Europeans, the context being that of oppressed Third World peoples, standing over against the Western context.

76. According to the circular principle of hermeneutics, text and context are the co-determinative norm and source in doing theology. Here lies a serious problem. If text and context are co-determinative, biblical witness

to God's lordship in history, God's revelatory redeeming, eschatological act in Jesus Christ, and the event of Jesus Christ as such are relativized. In this case, one can easily say, with the Bultmannian existentialist theologian Herbert Brown, that Jesus is the variant and human existence is the constant.

77. To say otherwise means that Jesus can be easily taken as a symbol of existence (as in the case of Friz Buri), or as an exemplification of the principle of historical revolution, as is implied in the emphasis on the historical Jesus by Latin American liberation theology, or as a religious, spiritual symbol, as in the case of the theology of religion-culture in Asia or in Korea. Such a revolutionary exemplification may become superseded by other revolutionary figures. Such a religio-cultural symbol may become lost in the multitude of other symbols, images, myths, and spirits.

78. In order to ward off this danger, the priority and uniqueness of Jesus Christ that are grounded in God's eschatological redemptive act are to be maintained, as is typically explicated by Karl Barth. The priority of biblical norm and source for doing theology is grounded in its witness to God. Under the presupposition of God's priority, the co-determinative or circular relation of text-context can be maintained. This priority is the very core of the Christological Trinitarian tradition, which needs now to be reinterpreted in Third World contexts. The Christological core, though formulated traditionally in metaphysical concepts, points to God as such as the acting subject in Jesus Christ in history. In Third World theologies and in North American feminist theology, the general tendency of taking the historical Jesus over against Christological tradition, as being metaphysical or speculative and as being abstracted from history, is similar to the situation of nineteenth-century liberalism and the Historical Jesus School, in which the revelatory, eschatological dimension of Jesus Christ was reduced to the historical Jesus as a religio-cultural or religio-moral symbol. Third World theologies today contain a problem similar to the Historical Jesus School.

79. The same kind of problem is to be observed in Western Christological tradition, in which the divine priority and lordship of Jesus Christ was, maybe still is, identified with Western Christendom-culture. So, Christian missions for Third World peoples meant, in fact, their Westernization or their subjection to Western Christendom-culture. This was closely linked to the un-Christological and unevangelical soteriological belief that Christian whites and their converts from among "heathens" are saved in heaven while the majority of unbelieving heathens are condemned to hell. Western Christendom and mission have thus misrepresented the Christian gospel, as if they were the criteria of salvation. Jesus Christ's priority and lordship in history mean that all humankind stands in direct relationship to him. There are no "heathens"; no one is excluded.

80. In conclusion, two points to be mentioned are: First, Jesus Christ's priority and lordship mean to the dominating West the divine judgment that is now represented by Third World people's liberation movements.

Second, in acknowledgment of his priority and lordship and of the priority of the biblical source for doing theology, the religio-cultural spiritualities of other faiths can be reinterpreted and appropriated in historical processes as creaturely dimensions and sources for doing theology.

B. Four Emerging Methodologies in Asia

81. Minjung theology derives its name from the Korean term *minjung,* which means, in general, common people or the masses of Korean people, who are deprived of basic human rights, both political and socio-economic. Minjung theology arose in Korea in the 1970s out of theological commitment to the people's movement for human rights, democratization, and social and economic justice. Minjung theology has proposed a method of describing and uncovering minjung stories or minjung biography, in critique of the Western logical way of theologizing. Among the youth the concept of minjung has now assimilated within itself the concept of Marxist social revolution. The youth stand against national and international oppressive powers, such as the military system of Korea-United States-Japan alliance, and the domination of the Korean economy by the United States and Japan. Minjung theology is challenged to account for this minjung movement. The question is, then, how and to what extent Marxism can be appropriated theologically.

82. A "theology of the people" in Korea must be mentioned here; this is a theology that is specifically concerned for Korea's unification. Firstly, this theology includes also the concept of minjung and yet takes the whole Korean people as the subject of the unification. Further, the people as theological theme poses the necessity of national liberation from international, dominating powers, such as the United States and Japan. Secondly, the concept of Korean people linked with the concept of minjung poses the necessity of social change. However, the task of unification and social change toward an egalitarian society cannot be posed as an option simply in Marxist terms. The concept of the "third way," as stated above in theological terms, is related specifically to the task of unification and, at the same time, the task of social change.

Furthermore, the concept of minjung implies class division among the Korean people. However, Korea's unification cannot be achieved only by one part of the people or by the minjung alone, although the people as the subject of history must take the question of minjung into serious consideration toward a unified Korea and a new society in the future. The question of Korea's unification is not to be taken only as a Korean problem. Korea's division reflects the problem and evils of divided world powers and ideologies, under which the Third World suffers and struggles toward liberation and the transformation of the whole world. This universal, common problem has taken a peculiar form in Korea's division. Methodologically, there remains the question of how to reinterpret the concept of the Korean people and other peoples in their respective religio-cultural heritages and histories.

83. The methodology of a theology of struggle emerging in the Philippines has the following characteristics:

a. commitment which entails ongoing involvement with the people's struggle is the starting point for theological reflection today;

b. economic-political and socio-cultural-religious analysis of the concrete historical context is a second vital element;

c. our faith heritage (Bible, church tradition, other elements of a people's living faith) impels us to discover, uncover, and reveal the creator and lord of history's liberating action. This revelation judges, illumines, challenges, and inspires our action;

d. the experience of God's presence and action in the historical context is articulated in new language, symbols, myths, images, and new liturgy understandable and relevant to the struggling people;

e. tentative theological conclusions are made communally, subject to the critique of the main participants in the liberation process, i.e., the poor and oppressed and those who cast their lot with them.

84. The wide plurality of Asian societies impels us toward a methodology that tries, on the one hand, to purify religions and ideologies of their inadequacies and aberrations, and, on the other, goes to the deeper core values which are positive and fulfilling for all. This is a method that in Latin America implies openness to humanism, secularism, and Marxism, and the same is true for Europe and North America. In Asia and Africa it implies a deeper rethinking of the spiritual content of the religions and cultures, all of which require purification also. A theology that is adequate to the Asian context must be purified of the religious fundamentalism and revivalism that are suspicious of and antagonistic to other religions. It must be a genuine religious renewal that seeks to serve all human beings irrespective of differences of race, sex, creed, caste, and culture.

84.1. The elaboration of such a theology needs much sensitive listening to others, frank dialogue, disinterested service, and humble witness to one's own convictions without ulterior motives of advancing one's own religion at the expense of others. Thus interreligious dialogue is also an aspect of this method of doing theology. The dialogue with secularism, humanism, atheism, and Marxism is also connected with such a method both because such schools of thought are present in these countries, and also because the ancient religions have varied philosophical and spiritual traditions that have affinities to their positive values.

84.2. Within this perspective the following approach is recommended:

a. accepting pluriform sources of revelation;

b. purifying theology through the discernment of whatever degrades and insults sections of humanity and the excising of their root causes in the given theological constructs;

c. seeking through frank dialogue the core values of Jesus and Christianity and of other religions and ideologies and working together actively for the realization of those values in given societies;

d. simplifying theology so that in real-life situations it can be more faithful to Jesus and the reign of God he preached.

84.3. These imply a hermeneutic that can have a profound impact on theology if applied with rigorous discernment and deep contemplative conviction and commitment. Jesus and his message need to be liberated from their captivity within dominating theological constructs and from those who claim to have control over him and his message. The foregoing methodology indicates a process for such a liberation, which is needed in our pluralist societies.

2

African Report

INTRODUCTION

The theme of our general assembly is "Commonalities, Divergences, and Cross-fertilization among Third World Theologies." In dealing with the theme of commonalities and divergences, we will consider three points: (1) commonalities and divergences in the political, economic, religious, and cultural challenges; (2) commonalities and divergences in methodologies; and (3) commonalities and divergences in issues and orientations.

Such an approach presupposes a comparative study continent by continent. So a preliminary investigation embracing all the continents would be needed. Such an ambition exceeds the limits of what we want to do here. With regard to the African continent, it seems more appropriate to emphasize what is its specificity in all fields considered here. When compared with the situations of the other continents, the picture will thus automatically bring out the common features and differences between research in Africa and in the other continents.

In the very terms of the topic, it is worthwhile to draw our attention to the fact that our concern is Third World theologies in general, and not only the way of "theologizing" within EATWOT. Therefore, it will not be a surprise to notice in our statement the intervention of theologians who are not members of our association.

CHALLENGES

Among the Third World continents, Africa appears essentially as a land of domination and exploitation, quartered, torn apart, divided, atomized, trampled underfoot. It is the continent where frequently the people have no dignity, no rights, and no hope. These challenges are becoming more intolerable considering that natural catastrophes—which are desperately repeated—are added to evils caused by human mischief and injustice.

28

A. Political Challenges

First of all, Africa appears as a puzzle made up of fifty-five countries, thousands of ethnic groups and dialects, and arbitrary boundaries inherited from the period of colonization. Despite twenty-six years of independence, Africa is still a pure product of European colonization. One of the main obstacles to its political unity comes from its linguistic fragmentation, which itself largely stems from its colonial division. So we have a French-speaking, an English-speaking, a Portuguese- and an Arabic-speaking Africa. Africa is defined as the negation of a proper identity, lack of a given entity, irremediably subjugated to foreign powers which impose on it what to say and what to think.

Africa is also the only continent which is subjected to the most anachronistic colonial system. Political independence is refused to Namibia, which constitutes a real South African challenge to the world. In the West Sahara, in Northern Chad, and in Southern Sudan, people are still struggling for national liberation and independence. With regard to South Africa, it is the only area in the world where the most hideous racism—formerly condemned in Nazism—imposes a bloody terror managed by the Western great powers. Apartheid is one of the greatest scandals in the history of humanity, ranking with the blindest Nazism or anti-Semitism.

Furthermore, neocolonialism is added to the colonial challenge. It consists first of all in the division of Africa between the ideological groups which dominate the world. In Africa, there is evidently no country which is completely nonaligned. Neocolonialism mostly walks under the guise of technical assistance and the mask of cooperation. It forges bonds of economic dependence, the heaviest of which is the debt system imposed on the Third World. In short, neocolonialism develops and puts in place a complete dependence machinery for the effective control of all areas of political, economic, and cultural life.

The state crisis is one of the most striking political challenges. Africa seems to have been caught unprepared for independence. Of course people have fought and continue struggling for political independence, but nobody seems to have really thought about how to manage this independence. Nobody seems to have thought about any conception of state, about any model which would correspond to the particular situation of Africa, or about the needs of the people and what should be the true capacities of a well-organized political power in our specific context. We purely and simply copied foreign models, particularly the worst and those which are farthest from African realities. An absurd totalitarianism manipulated by the foreign hegemonic blocs prevails over nearly all of the continent. It matters little that this totalitarianism is Jacobinic here and Marxist-Leninist there. Having no means for either its pseudo-ideologies, its defense, or its cultural, social, and economic development, the state in Africa finally and totally handed itself over to its new masters. These masters assist it, protect it, guide it, tame it, exploit it, get it into debt, indoctrinate and rule it much more than during colonial times.

The crisis regarding the state brings about immediate consequences. First is the crisis of national unity. For the last twenty-five years, very few countries in Africa have escaped the often bloody calling in question of their very frail unity. Yesterday it was Nigeria, Zaire, Federation of Mali, etc. Today it is Ethiopia, Sudan, Uganda, Chad, Angola, Mozambique, and so on. . . .

The national unity crisis is related to the crisis of African unity. Since its creation in 1963, the Organization of African Unity (OAU) has challenged disunity without solid foundation, without force of persuasion, without financial means and real authority. How much further today are Kwame Nkrumah's dreams for a unified Africa, a central government, a continental army?

African unity is especially hindered by the situation whereby Africa lives in a permanent state of military, cultural, economic, political, and ideological occupation by the most antagonistic powers of the world. The present map of Africa is pulled to pieces into Cuban, Soviet, U.S., British, and French zones of influence. If we add the zones of a Khadafi, we will see that African unity is not yet born.

The military coups d'état represent one other aspect of the present crisis of governments in Africa. Military systems of government took over power in Libya, Niger, Mali, Burkina Faso, Guinea, Liberia, Togo, Benin, Nigeria, Equatorial Guinea, Congo, Zaire, Burundi, Uganda, Sudan, Ethiopia, etc. The African armies are turned mostly against their own fellow citizens as internal opponents rather than against external armies.

The militarization of African states opens wide the door to a new type of neocolonization. All those in power in Africa are real hostages at the mercy of foreign powers through the mechanisms of military assistance. The weapons trade in Africa is dominated by foreign powers. The United States of America is first with an annual weapons sale amounting to 5,360 million U.S. dollars. The Soviet Union comes second with weapons sales amounting to 3,940 million U.S. dollars per year. Next come France (1,450 million U.S. dollars), Great Britain (650 million U.S. dollars), Italy (530 million U.S. dollars), and West Germany (220 million U.S. dollars).

We can better understand the absurd nature of military expenditure when we realize that this is given more importance than education and health in countries such as Burundi, Chad, Ethiopia, Malawi, Morocco, Mozambique, Somaliland, Uganda, Zambia, Zimbabwe, etc.

The misuse of power is another aspect of political challenge in Africa. Almost everywhere in Africa, we hear the groanings of common people who say that independence is worse than colonization. In some countries, there is practically no limit to the excesses of certain tyrants wild with power. Human rights, legal processes, and justice are trampled underfoot with fanatical arrogance.

Government policies are often not geared toward public service but rather are set up as a machinery of oppression and domination. That explains an arbitrariness coupled with the complete impunity of public civil servants. In many countries, corruption and venality have become institutions.

Facing these plagues which threaten the political survival of Africa, it would be unfair and scientifically inexact to ignore the lively forces of eternal Africa. During their history, African blacks have learned how to face suffering, humiliation, misery, and oppression. In the past, they have known how to overcome them through a deep-rooted reserve of spiritual energy. The danger of death which threatens postcolonial Africa is probably the most formidable in the whole history of our continent, for it is the danger of self-destruction. Africa, which has withstood all the external challenges, could well give way, consumed by its internal canker.

That is why in our analysis, we must consider seriously that Africa which refuses to die. The traditional values that colonization tried to destroy are coming back everywhere, which is a vivid sign and guarantee of vitality. The ancestral virtues of courage, fortitude, integrity, and pride were the only effective weapons enabling defenseless populations to triumph over colonialism in many countries. Nowadays, Africa still remains one of the few lands where revolution — according to the moral sense — holds the sway. Faced with the corruption which threatens our continent, there is an invincible revolt by life-giving forces which comes from the deepest wombs of Africa and which will finally triumph over the forces of death. The African soul was frustrated in its quest for freedom for five hundred years, but freedom is now its deepest aspiration. That is why in Africa it is true to say that the future, the real future of African peoples, is based on democracy. Of course, we speak of African democracy, not its caricature in disguised despotism. Attempted democracies in Tanzania, Senegal, and now in Cameroon, certainly open paths to the future.

B. Economic Challenges

Africa appears to be a continent of misery when we glance through the "economic" literature. Nevertheless, all those engaged in earth resources exploration declare, with proof, that Africa has a huge pool of raw materials. Despite the aridity of the Sahara, Kalahari, and Sahel, the rest of the African continent feeds a great part of the world with its cocoa, banana, coffee, tea, palm-oil, etc. The African subsoil's abundant mineral and petroleum resources are fabulous: gold, diamonds, oil, gas, coal, uranium, iron, bauxite, manganese, etc.

Africa also has some of the most abundant sources of energy in the world to draw on. Only one great dam on the Congo River would be sufficient to supply North America with electricity. What can we say then if we add the huge potentials of the rivers Niger, Nile, and Zambezi?

The great paradox is that, despite its huge wealth and its relatively modest population, Africa remains a continent of misery. Statistics of UNESCO and of the World Bank show this very clearly. First of all, Africa is sparsely populated. The unequal distribution of population varies from 1.5 inhabitants per square kilometer (Botswana and Namibia) to 490 inhabitants per square kilometer (Mauritius). Life expectancy is between forty and fifty years and there are about twenty thousand inhabitants for one medical doctor in most countries. This number may go up to seventy thousand (Burkina Faso) and even eighty thousand (Ethiopia). On average, below 50 percent of the adult population is able to read and write. Many countries have only 10 percent of adults capable of reading and writing (Niger, Senegal), and others go down to 5 percent (Burkina Faso). The income per inhabitant is the lowest in the world, showing a disparity which depicts the socio-economic paradoxes of our continent. Chad and Ethiopia have an average income of U.S. $140 per inhabitant while Libya has the fantastic income per inhabitant of U.S. $9,000. Per capita income for Gabon is U.S. $4,500; for Reunion Island: U.S. $3,900; for South Africa: U.S. $2,300; and for Algeria: U.S. $2,200. The other countries vary between U.S. $200 and U.S. $1,800 per capita. Therefore, Africa appears to be the continent of unequal opportunities.

These statistics have some use, but they do not show the total reality. They only present a Western and distorted picture of African misery. In Senegal, for instance, the literacy rates do not take into account the Koranic schools. So those rates are very much distorted. If we consider the local culture, there are many more educated persons in several African countries. Further, the incomes per inhabitant often correspond to very little in reality. The black tribes of the Libyan desert do not have an annual income of even U.S. $100; the same is true of the half-starved peasants of Gabon. The statistics arbitrarily divide by the number of inhabitants a fortune exclusively owned by a few rapacious persons. So we arrive at U.S. $2,300 per inhabitant in South Africa by dividing its fortune by its twenty-five million inhabitants. But in reality, the whole South African goldmine belongs to four million white inhabitants who oppress and exploit twenty-one million black people.

In order to explain African misery, an indefinable concept is used called *underdevelopment*. But the underdevelopment of the Third World, particularly that of Africa, is artificially created by the pauperization of some as a result of the enrichment of others. It is not a secret to anybody that our underdevelopment develops the developed countries. First of all, this is because our economy is located on the periphery, with the North and the West being the center. Our whole wealth is intended for rich countries. The subsoil's resources and the agricultural products are exploited, their extraction and their production being a prime concern of the developed nations. Products for local consumption are mostly imported, whereas the food-producing farms are sacrificed for agribusiness. The situation gets worse with the notorious deterioration in the terms of exchange. Prices of raw materials are fixed by the developed countries without taking into account the real needs of African workers.

The world monetary system is a skillful machinery for exploitation, domination, and systematic pauperization of the Third World countries. Is it necessary to mention here the protests of several African countries against the neocolonialism of the World Bank? Getting Third World countries into debt is the way chosen by that new colonialism. In some countries, the rate of debt per inhabitant is more significant than the income per inhabitant. For instance in Congo the income per inhabitant was U.S. $1,110 while the debt per inhabitant was U.S. $1,230 in 1984–85. The banking system and most of the credit systems of our governments are simply appendices of the foreign systems. They practically put before the citizen an insurmountable obstacle which makes credit inaccessible except to important personalities, and discourages any serious national investment. We might say that foreign countries manage and control our money and have it at their disposal.

We very often have the impression that the assistance system to African countries creates its raison d'être by developing a real industry of misery. For underdevelopment, poverty, and misery are necessary in order to generate assistance. To suppress them would surely eliminate assistance. The debt is then a means to perpetuate misery, and consequently assistance.

The problem of the Third World's mounting debt is a criterion which will enable us to distinguish whether the developed countries really aim at the development of Third World countries or not. How can you save poor persons while making them get into debt? Concerning Africa, a true analysis of our countries' economic situation shows that the current situation is a direct result of colonization. It is the former colonial countries which should pay African countries after having ruined them. Facing such a situation, who can prove that there is a moral obligation for African countries to accept and to pay back their debt? And if they refuse to do it, what other reason than that of violence would prevail against them? The African countries' mounting debt is a scandal to be denounced. The developed countries that really want to help Africa must start abolishing the system which burdens Third World countries with debts.

C. Social Challenges

The crisis in African society before and after independence is one of the most dangerous challenges which threatens our continent.

This crisis comes directly from the colonial system. In fact, whichever system was adopted by colonial powers, whether direct rule as in the French colonies or indirect rule as in the British colonies, the common aim of all the colonial powers was to make native societies dependent by transforming them into simple tools of the colonizing powers. Native societies were viewed as having no aims of purposes in themselves. They were obliged to destroy or to weaken all institutions capable of calling the colonization into question: the family, chieftainships, traditional associations, etc. The religious foundations of African society were profaned and even destroyed. This is the why and the wherefore of the chasing away of secret societies and brotherhood associations. Traditional political power was emptied because it was humiliated and enslaved. The traditional African family was attacked by the administration and churches, then broken up.

That is why the underdevelopment of independent Africa is a social underdevelopment. A people without spiritual leaders, without soul, has been surprised by independence. This people has also been abandoned to the demagogy of politicians. The independent African countries are facing questions as vital as those concerning goals of society. The modern African family status has become a real standoff between traditional stagnation and a caricature of the foreign models. Meanwhile, marriage, stability, children's education, all break down as a result of the powerlessness and even the lack of awareness of established powers.

In their refusal to die, the people struggle more and more desperately in their quest for salvation. This causes the elite to return to anachronistic forms of traditionalism: secret societies, sects, and new solidarity networks not controlled by the establishment. Traditional Christian models in the West are often subjected to an indigenization which worries the officials of orthodoxy.

It must be understood that social problems in Africa are death or life problems. The African family is a sacral structure for the transmission of life. Faced with insolvable problems brought on by the Western models of marriage and family, African Christians find compromise solutions where their Christianity accepts a peaceful coexistence with some pre-Christian African values.

Confronted with unemployment and living-wage problems, even the mystical escape through charismatic associations is no longer sufficient. What to reply then to these poor people when a charismatic leader or a demagogue arises with utopian promises? What magic do words like *revolution* and *change* convey, even if the awakening may lead to a disaster, as in Ethiopia?

African youth are another dilemma. The young people escape more and more from the families' guardianship, and governments have neither means nor power to ensure their total development. The situation becomes even more absurd when we consider that the governments claim monopoly of education and employment.

Faced with famine, drought, and disease, plus a shortage of medical doctors and hospitals; confronted by the indifference of churches; unaware of certain important social centers of established governments which minimize or are the web of the people's life, their projects, and their hope, the people have managed themselves—literally—with the available means and especially with reference to those who speak and understand their languages.

What may be understood is that nowadays African society is disabled. Churches and established governments are also disabled. Society, which is losing everything, struggles for survival. The main question to ask is: What can churches and existing governments do to save society?

The social underdevelopment of Africa represents a fundamental aspect of the anthropological pauperization of the African person. If we define pauperization as the fact of becoming or making poor, namely being deprived of all that we have acquired, all that we are and all that we can do, we shall recognize that Africa is subjugated to structures which result in complete pauperization: political, economic, and social. When it is not a matter of being deprived of all that we own, but rather of all that we are—our human identity, our social roots, our history, our culture, our dignity, our rights, our hopes, and our plans—then pauperization becomes anthropological. It then affects religious and cultural life at its very roots.

D. Cultural Challenges

It is in the cultural area that the anthropological pauperization of Africans attacked the deepest roots of their awakened and fierce instinct of self-defense.

In Africa, culture is only secondarily defined by manifestations of the people's creativeness. First of all and essentially, culture is a conception of the human being, the world, and God. It is this global view which is expressed through the achievements of the Negro-African genius. This is expressed through the inexhaustible resources of social, critical, economic, and religious institutions which have countless means for expression of the African soul through arts, techniques, beliefs, systems of thinking with their different expressions, language and tongues, and the huge heritage of oral tradition.

In the colonial system, the most effective means for destroying Africans was to destroy their culture. Several methods were used to accomplish this aim: assimilation here, segregation there, vandalism everywhere, and especially the practice of "tabula rasa" and systematic negation. School has thus been a huge industry for cultural demolition, depersonalization, and anthropological pauperization. Stripped of their identity, their history, their language, their social, economic, and political institutions, their dignity, their creativeness, the Negro-Africans have been reduced to complete "destitution as human beings," to a real state of near annihilation.

The greatest tragedy of Africa resides in the permanence of this state of annihilation following independence. More than twenty-five years after colonial times, most African countries have recovered neither their languages, their history, their art, nor the huge wealth of their spiritual heritage. Nowadays, in some African families, children come into the world with neither a language nor a village. They do not even know their fore-fathers. Many of those children are but ghosts of Africans, speaking only foreign languages and begging from imported cultures for their food, their clothing, their mental structures, their thought categories, and the carica-tures of their life schemes and their social structures. They continue to be emptied of their life by their schooling. Schools continually turn out uprooted, unemployed workers, who are even foreigners in their own coun-try. In many countries, they are taught in school neither African languages, nor African history, nor African art.

More serious is what is called contemporary African art, mainly music and the show-business art. Present-day African art is most often merely a subproduct of foreign agencies which are more preoccupied with making money from exotic products than with expressing the real message of the deeper Africa.

It is here that we note the pernicious and damaging effects of anthro-pological pauperization. The African stars are often victims of a new type of slave trade. Isolated, uprooted, and far away from their country, most of these stars are at the mercy of firms which exploit them, sell them, and support them in the backbreaking hubbub of theaters and tours.

When we think that our mass media are nourished, teleguided, and controlled by foreign countries, we shall not be surprised at the kind of culture presented by our televisions, our radios, and our cinemas.

The cultural crisis represents a real danger of death for the African soul. It is without doubt the reason why the people's soul, in its refusal of death, reacts insurrectionarily in its last convulsive movements of self-preservation. A careful analysis of contemporary African history and society shows that culture has been and still remains the only efficient weapon for the liber-ation struggle of Africa. The true African revolution has been cultural. It is African culture which has saved the black American identity. It is also this same culture which has radically called the whole colonial system into question. Many superficial critics have not understood very well the deeper meaning of a movement such as Negritude. Nevertheless, it is Negritude which has driven the colonizer out. Within this century, the African culture has taken legal proceedings against racial segregation in South Africa and now gives a death verdict against the apartheid system.

Neither oppression, exploitation, war, torture, corruption, school, nor assimilation has ever succeeded in completely abolishing African languages, beliefs, rites, traditional systems of solidarity, the arts, and the ancient tradition of African wisdom.

It is solely in the cultural area that Africa has inflicted crushing defeats on the Western countries. Knocking the colonial Jericho walls down, Afri-can art, just at the moment when the colonial system was at its peak, has succeeded in making a tremendous impact upon Western countries. African art went so far as to win over the cold academicism of European art to the African model.

Two world festivals of black arts (Dakar 1966 and Lagos 1977) illustrated the cultural vitality of our continent for all the world to see. Of course, there have been some people to shout: it is disproportionate. But no other continent has ever tried to organize such a huge enterprise. The reason is that, when it is culture, Africa finds its real chance for survival. It is also in culture that Africa looks for weapons for its liberation from anthropological pauperization.

That is why the cultural struggle for liberation cannot content itself with being defensive. It must be offensive and even aggressive. We must push the opponent into a corner. Such is the task for modern African artists and writers. We are wrong to ask them to write in African languages, because their task requires the use of Western languages for the moment. Meanwhile they have to struggle for the birth of a literature in national languages. Two cultural events of recent years illustrate that glorious fight. I mean Leopold Sedar Senghor's election at the French Academy and the choice of Wole Soyinka as Nobel Prize winner for literature.

At the outset, it must be recognized that among the efforts engaged in by Africa for the past fifteen years, culture has an honorable place. We have mentioned the Dakar (1966) and Lagos (1977) festivals. The Algiers festival, organized under the aegis of OAU (1969), is not less important. These festivals have given an impetus to a cultural new deal. When we prepared the first festival of Dakar, around the years 1963–65, we could find art schools only in very few African countries: in Ghana, Zaire, Uganda, and Ethiopia. Today, this number has been practically quadrupled. That is not enough, but we have to think of our people's identity crisis mentioned above in order to realize that it is a sudden burst of life.

We may notice also that Africa has become aware of the seriousness of its cultural situation, and it has started reacting. From the Algiers festival (1969) has come a cultural charter of Africa which was finally ratified by the OAU. It is that charter which has inspired another, ten years later — the Lagos Plan, a real pan-African effort to face the economic death threatening Africa.

So it is not an exaggeration to say that culture is the key to the survival of Africa. Africa must devote all its energies to the defense of that heritage. It concerns as well the survival of humankind. Since the crisis of this century is a human crisis par excellence, the African man and woman are in the center of this crisis. Their survival is a guarantee and a hope for all people all over the world.

That is why, at a time which Pope John Paul II calls an "opposition mentality toward life," and a foolish run to death is developed in the West, the message which African culture proclaims is the landslide victory of life over death.

At the beginning of 1986 the greatest Negro-African scholar of present days died in Dakar: Cheikh Anta Diop. Mathematician, physician, and philosopher, he had given over his life neither to making weapons nor bombs, but to reviving the history and the creative genius of black peoples. His struggle was mainly cultural, in order to save the black person's dignity from historical death, to proclaim the primacy of human values in the scientific jungle of this twentieth century as it draws to a close, and to prove that science is and must be an instrument for life, and not a weapon for death.

It is easy now to understand why, on the purely religious plan, gospel education is for us the priority of priorities.

E. Religious Challenges

Ethnologists are all agreed in proclaiming that traditional Africa is principally religious. When we consider modern Africa, however, opinions begin to differ. But an objective analysis of modern African life must recognize that the African, today as yesterday, remains principally religious. A superficial glance is enough to be convinced. A journalist tells the story of an African head of state, one of the greatest and most modern, who one day called the diplomatic corps to reveal that he had just discovered a plot against his government. As sole proof, he presented them a casket containing some ancestors' bones, and declared that his private soothsayer, after having consulted these bones, had revealed to him the plot and its authors. The story is told of one of the greatest African nationalists of modern times who was surprised and killed in his maquis, alone, betrayed by his former comrades, having as a security guard only his old witch.

Another aspect of modern African life is sports. It is no secret that soccer matches in Africa are prepared for by celebrations of the mass and evening gatherings in graveyards.

In present day Africa, the religious phenomenon still controls the subconscious life of all social classes. That is why the religious challenges weigh heavy on the life of individuals and the masses.

In mentioning traditional religions today one often speaks of the awakening of those religions. In fact, they were neither dead nor asleep. Without doubt, evangelization in many situations has provoked a radical break in the converted person. In many situations also, that break has not extended to abolishing the ancestral order. A few years ago we met in a fetish-nunnery of the now Republic of Benin, a mother abbess who was considered a "fair catholic" and who managed a nunnery of a very pagan rite. She seemed perfectly at ease, for that convent was a part of her ancestral heritage.

The new deal of traditional religions is due to a purely simple phenomenon. The Christian faith, as transmitted by missionaries, is completely coated in its Western cultural straitjacket. Too intellectual, too judicial, too much of a stranger to day-to-day life problems, the revived doctrine becomes a Sunday dress worn to church. At home, at the farm, on the job, we put on once more our ordinary dress for current business. Those day-to-day problems are sickness, infertility of wife or cattle, a neighbor's jealousy, scarce or abundant rainfall, the drought which burns farms, luck in hunting, success in business, a victory over an enemy, bad luck, all kinds of poisons, wizards, soothsayers, healers, etc. Now, regarding all that, we find little or nothing in the Roman Ritual. What do we do then? We have to live and try to solve all those problems. In the traditional religions all that is provided for; there are rites and formulas for everything.

Confronted by these necessities of day-to-day life, the most elaborate theology, the most eloquent apologetics, and the most militant atheism are helpless. Traditional religion recovers its rights, for it speaks to the people in their language and proposes replies to their questions.

The reawakening of traditional religions appears in different ways. That reawakening is but rarely aggressive. On the contrary, while it is very efficient, it is also discrete, conciliatory, and calls on faith in God and in the action of ancestors in a way that satisfies everybody, and seldom compromises anybody.

In general, it is syncretism that characterizes the new forms of traditional religions. African syncretism is a reduction of the Holy Bible and of the ritual into African categories and rites. It is the opposite of the missionary's type of conversion, for it converts the Bible's religion into the forefather's religion.

It is not simply a strange mixture of ideas, but a very organized and selective rereading of the language of the Western countries' faith. The fact is that the Bible was but a clumsy attempt by Western countries to express traditional African theogonies and cosmogonies. We had better understand the strange wealth of the syncretist myths and rites.

It is within sects that syncretism finds its place of expression and appearance. The truly African sects date from the colonial period. They have given space of liberty and self-recovery to populations pressed and emptied of their cultural identity. We have noticed that the areas in Africa where sects spread corresponds to the zones where the colonial system has socially, culturally, and politically been the most dehumanizing.

New sects have invaded Africa since the period of independence. These sects are imported products, cleverly introduced to perpetuate the domination of Africa by foreign powers. We can divide these sects into several categories. Pseudoreligious sects from Europe or mostly from America borrow a certain vocabulary from rituals in the Holy Bible or in Christian churches and use it in a distorted and bizarre way. Their commonalities are the fact that they exploit the emptiness left in the African soul by the sudden suppression of most of the traditional secret societies during the colonial period. Basing themselves on the propensity of the African soul for esotericism, they offer it plenty of initiation rites, uses of incense, talismans, prohibitions, and fabulous promises of success here below and in the world to come. These sects have formulae for everything: for healing, for procreating, for becoming powerful in policy-making, for earning money, for charming women, for getting rid of enemies, for making one's self immune to the opponent, etc.

The invasion of these so-called modern sects is significant. A recent inquiry conducted by some young researchers of the Yaoundé University reveals the existence of more than thirty-seven sects introduced within the past fifteen years in the city of Yaoundé alone. Sickness and healing are among the meeting fields for ancestral traditions and modern sects. African traditional medicine has received recognition of its scientific aspect today. For a thousand years, African healers have studied, selected, and classified certain plants with curative qualities.

Their competence and expert evaluation in that field impress even the most demanding and skeptical scientists. But that therapeutic quality is often linked to complicated rituals. European missionaries have considered these rites demoniacal and forbidden Christians to use them. But because of the noticeable effectiveness of such therapy, urban as well as rural populations — be they Christian or not — regularly return to these "demoniacal" rites. In order to satisfy that quest for healing which is widespread in all social levels, several modern charismatic sects are pleased not only to operate publicly with great publicity in the laying on of hands and use of holy water, but also to fight against the use of any kind of organized, traditional, or imported medicine.

Now we understand better why a healing ministry to the sick has become a necessity in today's Africa. Churches cannot exist only in order to condemn or forbid. Moreover nobody takes them seriously. African theologians have opened up in that domain a huge field of research where they act as pioneers. To research and publication, they often successfully join the practice of a true healing ministry. Rev. Fr. Meinrad Hegba of Cameroon and the more famous Archbishop of Lusaka, Mgr. Milingo (now living in exile in Rome), are well-known examples: Bishop Milingo successfully continues his healing ministry, which attracts pilgrims from all over the world to his Roman sanctuary.

In the reawakening of traditional religions as well as in the charismatic movement and healing ministry, women often play an important role, a role which was precisely their own within the ancient African tradition. In Olamza, in the Cameroon-Gabon frontier, it is a woman who presides over the curing rites of Eboga, attracting to that formerly unknown village people from all areas of Central Africa. It would be too long to enumerate all the women that we meet in Benin, hurling the Homa's malediction upon the former oppressive government, gathering the whole country, and driving out the previous government. Others are met in Nigeria, Congo, Zaire, and Southern Africa, electrifying people by their charismatic magnetism.

So we may come back, once more, to the secret societies. If some of them were abolished under the colonial system, others survived. Urbanization and the breakdown of traditional society have deprived them of much of their prestige and effectiveness. But atavistic needs, despite the control of social structures, are present in the soul of the young generation. It is at this level that secret societies from abroad intervene, with their political and economic aims. Their promoters have, for a long time, studied the contours of the African soul, and the emptiness created in it by the structures of anthropological pauperization. The new secret societies—for instance Masonry or the Rosicrucians—recruit politicians and businessmen. The program of those societies is clear and precise. To their followers, these societies promise money, political power, and a world network of secret solidarity. These societies boast of their accomplishments: they make or break people as they wish—heads of state, ministers, African lords of finance and trade. They classify all the human values of our countries, and, in darkness, work to promote some and to hinder others.

Secret societies with political or economic goals are a true challenge to the gospel. Through hidden and subtle forms, these secret societies undermine the foundations of faith. Their targets are principally the elite and the powerful. Well-informed people say that many African heads of state are followers of Freemasonry or the Rosicrucians.

This situation is so worrisome because the ideology which animates these secret societies comes from *the most rigid form of international capitalism,* which is also the least open to the idea of the poor, weak, and oppressed peoples' liberation, particularly Third World peoples.

F. Islam

Islam is today the majority religion in the African continent. According to statistics of 1985, out of a population of 529,386,814 in Africa, 217,527,174 are Muslims, that is 41.09 percent. The total number of Christians was then up to 149,318,991, or 28.20 percent. Muslims remain in the majority even in comparison to the followers of traditional religions, who number only 162,540,689, or 30.70 percent. African Islam has its own characteristics. First of all, it is noticeable for its capacity to be adaptable. Many observers find in this the very secret of its huge success on our continent. It is also an Islam of brotherhood associations: Mouridism in Senegal, Tidjaniya and Quadriy in Western Africa, Mahdism in the Nile Valley and in Eastern Africa.

African Islam now presents a very complex picture, for it brings together almost all the different experiences of Islam around the world. Traditionally, Africa was everywhere considered to be a land of tolerance, and the example of Ethiopia, a Christian empire, receiving the first Muslim refugees just at the moment when Islam appeared, is always cited. Today, some countries, such as Morocco, want to be considered the heirs of that tradition of tolerance. We also find this tradition in black Africa, for instance in the Bamoun Islam on the high plateau of Western Cameroon.

But contemporary African Islam also experiences fundamentalism, with its crisis of intolerance and bloody fanaticism. Egypt, Sudan, Northern Nigeria, without mentioning Libya, are examples.

From the political viewpoint, African Islam offers the same variety and forms, with some little success, which flow from the political tendencies found in the Muslim world. In Africa, we find governments of a traditional pattern which have a feudal tendency, as in Morocco; we also meet with some attempts at Muslim socialism, as in Libya; we find, too, some so-called secular states, as in Nigeria; and finally we find the reformist tendency, as in Morocco.

Whatever the face adopted by African Islam, it continues to spread all over the continent, with sometimes indiscreet proselytism, which even threatens the other religions. This proselytism uses all available means: some political leaders take advantage of their position to impose Islam on entire areas. Sometimes admission to public service is conditional to conversion to Islam. Fanatical groups burn Christian schools and churches. Huge sums of money are used to build mosques, win followers, and give students grants for Islamic studies.

It would be an error to conclude then that Africa lives in a state of religious war. On the contrary, the dialogue between Christians and any other religion takes up the question of how to respond to the African's deepest aspirations. The challenge is economic, for religious proselytizers have huge financial means at their disposal. The challenge is also at the level of dialogue between religions. Condemned to live together, often within the same family, Christians and Muslims must work together for the common good of the people. They also ought to do it as a testimony of their faith.

G. Challenges to Churches

The general situation of Africa that has been described above offers many challenges to churches in Africa.

Of course, the first thing which catches the attention of foreign observers is the extraordinary expansion of the African churches: 63,672,410 Catholics in 1985, and 85,646,541 Protestants and Orthodox Christians; that is, a total of 149,318,951 African Christians, representing 28.20 percent of the whole African population. These figures become impressive when we consider the increase year by year. According to the *Roman Pontifical Yearbook*, there were 50,000 Catholics in Africa in 1800; 377,000 in 1840; 750,000 in 1907; 13 million in 1950; 36,400,000 in 1970; 63,672,410 in 1985. When we recall that there were less than 30 million Catholics in Africa during the independence period in 1960, we shall see that this number has more than doubled during the past twenty-five years. Now it was during that period that the church was indigenized in Africa, and the responsibility for evangelization was given to the African hierarchy.

The clergy's increase is even more spectacular. There were 1,400 major seminarians in 1957. There were 6,231 in 1985. There were 281 African priests in 1938; 6,359 in 1985. In 1930, the only African bishop was in Ethiopia. In 1939, we had 3 Negro-African bishops; they became 40 in 1960; 140 in 1970; and 338 in 1985. There was only one African cardinal in 1960; they became 7 by 1970; and in 1985, they numbered 14.

These figures testify to the vitality of the church in Africa, and justify the optimism of all estimates. They predict for the year 2000, 132 million African Catholics; 148 million Protestants (over the 75 million of today); 21 million Anglicans (over today's 10 million); 54 million followers of the Independent churches (over today's 24 million); 37 million Christians in the Ethiopian and Egyptian Orthodox churches (over today's 23 million).[1]

A great effort at coordination has brought about the creation of continental organizations. Catholics have the Symposium of Episcopal Conferences of Africa and Madagascar, whose headquarters is in Accra, Ghana. Protestants, Orthodox Christians, and Anglicans have the Conference of the Churches of Africa, whose headquarters is in Nairobi, Kenya. Independent churches have the Organization of Independent Churches in Africa, whose headquarters is also in Nairobi.

So, the general situation of Christianity clearly calls for hope. The role to be played by the church is evident because human conditions and institutions of the period subsequent to colonization are deteriorating fast. It would not be too much to say that the church appears to be the only solution to the general distress in certain African countries. However, it would be childish to fall straight forward into self-satisfaction. Although the mission of the church in Africa is great, the real situation of the church, on the other hand, is dramatic. For the African church is intimately tied to the future of the African continent, which is now about to drown. If Africa sinks, the African church will sink with it. The assertion of that reality is the major mission of the African church. In its declarations, the Symposium of Episcopal Conferences of Africa and Madagascar has been trying, for almost twenty years, to present that fragile situation. Those declarations simultaneously sounded like the predictions of Jonah in the streets of Nineveh and the call of John the Baptist in the desert.

The themes of those declarations put emphasis on the political, economic, social, cultural, and religious challenges which we cited above. Confronted with the hugeness of the problems, the church has become aware of its *fragility*. Africans, who by vocation are the church in Africa, are deeply affected in all the roots of their being by the *fragility at the core of Africa*. Now, it is with the African that we have to build the African church. *Evangelization* is henceforth *human promotion*, salvation of the whole man and woman in their world condition first, for the sake of God's Reign. Before the challenges of a breakdown in society, of pauperization by the economic system, of a culture which refuses to die, of a political city often adrift, what weapons, what means, do the African churches have? Fighting against persecution as in Burundi or in South Africa, the churches experience their multiple fragility, and yet, at the same time, they experience within themselves the strength of the Spirit which animates all Yahweh's servants.

That is why, for the churches in Africa, *evangelization*—the announcement of the liberating good news to the poor, the oppressed, and the weak—is the priority of priorities. That is why that evangelization is called *inculturation*: it is a matter of *cultural redemption,* culture being the foundation of our identity, our historical path to salvation, and the best African vehicle for the gospel. That is why such evangelization is also called *human promotion,* a struggle for fundamental human rights, and for political, economic, social, and cultural liberation.

It is in this context that African theology was born. This context explains why all the African theologians, whatever their roots, their language, their geographical situation, speak the same language; it is the language of *liberation,* liberation and evangelization of the Africans and their culture. That theology speaks, first of all, the people's language—about their needs, their worries, their hopes (even if this language is not yet the people's tongue). That same theology deals with sickness and health problems (Mgr. Milingo, Rev. Fr. Hegba); it deals with politics and economics (Jean Marc Éla); it deals with our tradition and with inculturation (John Mbiti); it deals with the churches' life in Africa (Penekou); it opens the African ways of understanding the African context better (Bimwenyi, Ngindu, Mveng . . .); it calls out to God's people, the churches' institutions, individuals, for a conscientization in the struggle against forces of oppression (as in the Kairos documents, South Africa).

The challenges to African churches also come from *abroad.* The pauperization situation that affects the African weighs heavily upon the churches. Domination relationships on the one hand, and dependence on the other hand, which have characterized centuries of interaction between Africa and Europe, have met once more within churches. So it is normal that tensions have appeared. However, the source of those tensions must not be located solely within the African churches. Those who wish to locate the source of such tensions within the African episcopacy cite the famous conflict which would have confronted the Vatican and the African episcopacy. They cite African bishops' declaration in the 1974 Roman Synod; they cite an article of Mgr. Ndayen, Archbishop of Bangui, in *Concilium.* They particularly cite an article of Achille Mbembe in *Le Monde Diplomatique,* no. 378 (September 1985), on tensions between Rome and the African churches. In fact, there is probably no other episcopacy more obedient than the African episcopacy. Let us add that, among different churches coming from the European missionary movement, there is no other church more grateful than the African churches. If there have been some Independent churches, they have resulted from the missionary churches' refusal to accept a cultural expression of the faith other than their own. And today's tensions, where they exist, are the result of the refusal to accept a certain number of questions, which seem strange to the European Christians, but are very important because of the church expansion (development). Such are the cases of the healing ministry, of polygamous Christians' pastoral care, of the matter of the eucharist, of an African ritual and liturgy. Before further development of Christianity in Africa can take place, the African Council Project for African Theologians appears as an evident necessity. It is only surprise which leads certain circles in the West to find fault with that project.

The challenges which come from abroad concern mostly the missionary staff and the financial realm. The sudden drop in vocations in Europe is not caused by the Third World, or by Africa. This breakdown creates a need for relief to Africa. Despite a few examples of countries which no longer render it easy for missionaries to arrive, the whole of Africa remains an example for its welcoming spirit. So the problems are not due to a "moratorium" blocking the way of the non-African missionaries. But we are obliged by the facts to rely more and more on ourselves for our own relief. So, the old countries of Christendom ought to understand this and help the African churches more in their work. The liberation of our churches from financial servitude should be the concern of all the churches, and Christians all over the world. Financial assistance from the European and American churches puts the African churches under a tutorship regime which is not only humiliating, but also hinders evangelization in some areas. The funding agencies impose their programmers, their options, and their orientations on the local churches. There is a parallelism, and even a shameful confusion, between the technical assistance system in former colonial countries and the assistance of missionary churches to the local churches. We really think that it is time to change the anachronic formulae of assistance by a true evangelical sharing of staff and materials.

One other aspect of the challenges to African churches concerns the experience of individuals and of African communities in the Christian life. We have mentioned the extraordinary vitality of African Christianity. Meanwhile, the sole African models for true Christian holiness offered by the official churches are martyrs: those from Uganda or the Anwarite from Zaire. Those models are the most eloquent, of course, for they show the extent to which Africa has followed Jesus Christ. But there are other little-known models, whom African historians and theologians regard more: they are the thousands of African holiness models who are not recorded in books, but who have lived with day-to-day heroism and fidelity. Too much has been written and still is being written on the African "Lapsi," those Christians who have fallen back into polygamy or paganism. We ought to speak more of those thousands of men and women who have not turned back whatever the sacrifice demanded. What can be said about those polygamous chiefs who, in order to be baptized, have separated themselves from their ten, twenty, . . . fifty wives? Today, there are some people who wonder whether Christ really asked them not only to drive away fifty women, some of them aged, and without hope and future, but also to destroy the huge

network of intertribal relationships created by those marriages which were
so many ethnic alliances (unions).

What can be said about those Christian marriage partners who have
heroically lived their fidelity till death? There are young women and young
men who, faced with sickness, all kinds of obstacles or temptations, have
lived with fidelity to Jesus Christ, in a simple African way. And what can
be said about the African priests, monks, and nuns who, in modesty and
with a self-effacing manner, have given an integral and often radical testimony to the gospel?

For a very long time, unreal models have been presented to our Christians. Those models are disconcerting because they present people whose
lives and virtues are unrelated to Africans' day-to-day experience. It is time
now to prove the existence of a purely African holiness: the beatitudes'
holiness lived in an African context.

The African churches' challenges are the same as our people's challenges. And the challenge which sums up all of them is the call that Africa
sounds to the church to be truly, for our discouraged continent, a messenger
of the good news of salvation and liberation.

II. METHODOLOGICAL APPROACHES

We have to remember here that any method is conceived according to
the target. So, we cannot apply any method to any object. With regard to
theology, the African context, which we have just seen, represents such a
complexity and variety that we are obliged to invent or remake our tools
of analysis. The African reality, within the Third World, has its own pecu-
liarity. While reflecting the oppression, misery, and sufferings of the other
continents, Africa does not only and purely reproduce the others' experiences. On the contrary, it carries them to the point of paroxysm, and often
under so many new forms that any comparison becomes faulty. At the very
core of Africa, situations are so different that it will be no use looking for
a universal tool which could be applied to any case.

Meanwhile, a relationship of solidarity links together all the African
theologians, because whatever their own experiences, they work for the
same aim: the African's salvation and liberation. They all draw from the
same sources, their cultural roots which are their common opportunity for
liberation and survival.

That is why we speak of an African theology. It is African because it is
different from any other theology. It is African by definition, by its object,
and by its roots.

Like all Third World theologies, African theology is contextual. It is
located in space, in time, within the living and lived human society. It is
there, in that context, that African theologians try to decipher the message
of Jesus' good news addressed to them and to their people. As in all Third
World theologies, the methodological approach of African theology is on

three levels: (1) the context analysis; (2) sources and foundations; (3) and the conceptual tools.

A. Analysis of the African Context

This analysis must find its basis and aim in the African reality itself. And we have just seen how complex is that reality. In approaching it, we necessarily start by locating this reality in time and space. Our first approach is therefore historical.

For Africans, there is no liberation without their historical presence, since they have been expelled from the field of history by their oppressors. Liberation, if true, must be historical liberation; if not, there is no liberation. This makes it clear why, whenever the question of the African peoples' liberation is raised, its supporters always start with historical rehabilitation. So did the French pioneers Schoelcher and Abbe Gregoire during the first century of the struggle. So even now do all those who, with the famous African scholar Cheikh Antoiop, struggle for the same cause.

The historical approach is also the best way for a better consideration of different aspects of the African context. The present situation of Africa results from the past five centuries of African history, which have imposed on Africa the present situation, which may appear as only a phenomenon of alienation caused by Western capitalism. Then one could conclude that a Marxist analysis should give the key to the modern African situation, even more so when we face situations like racism in South Africa, or colonial oppression in Namibia. Maybe such an analysis could clarify some aspects of these situations, or even suggest some ways toward final liberation; however, we must always keep in mind the fact that Marxist analysis was conceived and developed by people who belonged to capitalist, European society, and that analysis was developed to combat the abuses of that society. And it was that same society which questioned itself and made its own revolution. The historical experience of modern Africa is totally different. Considered from within by the Africans themselves, the problem is not merely capitalistic alienation, but rather historical annihilation and genocide. In such a context, not only is African society questioned, but it is totally destroyed by foreign powers in such a way that self-questioning and revolution become impossible. In Africa, the situations are still rare where the praxis of "historical materialism" causes real, social-class struggles. Our struggle is a struggle for life, and it is the struggle of all classes. The liberation concept, in that context, becomes much more global — and radical — than the concept of revolution. This is the reason we use a methodological approach which is more anthropological. When we consider the human condition in Africa, we discover that under the slavery and oppression of colonial regimes, the oppressors did not intend to physically destroy the black Africans, as they did with the American natives; but rather, they tended toward the political, economic, and cultural destruction of the black man and woman, while preserving their physical labor power, which was considered a precious raw material for the enrichment of whites. The black man and woman deprived of any identity, any personality, were reduced to the state of brutes, to becoming simple machines for production. African independence has brought no liberation to the black man and woman. New structures of oppression—under the mask of assistance—make them politically, economically, and culturally poorer and poorer and more and more dependent. We call this whole system: an anthropological pauperization system. If pauperization consists in making persons poorer and poorer by depriving them of what they have, what they are, and what they do, pauperization becomes anthropological when persons are deprived of their identity, dignity, essential rights, culture, history.... This system of pauperization characterizes today's North-South relationship; it causes our heads of state to become real hostages, and our political regimes simply puppet shows. This situation explains the different forms of assistance, be it from the East or the West, from the North or the South. In this field, oppressive systems, socialist or capitalist, are all the same.

The majority of African socialist systems have come to a catastrophic end, of course! ... except in very rare cases, like Tanzania, which refused to become a copy, or satellite, of foreign systems. The African experience, unfortunately, leads to the conclusion that the pauperization structure is both capitalist and socialist.

These pauperization systems feed on the misery of Third World peoples. They do not tend to end, but to increase misery and poverty. They are real poverty-making industries, run by colossal multinational enterprises.

An analysis of the pauperization system provides the key to the dark mystery overshadowing our continent. It becomes possible to discover destabilization and satellization structures imprisoning almost all the African states. Powerless and forceless, these states are politically poor. They are forced to beg for their subsistence from their tutors, who become their true masters. Then, their political pauperization becomes permanent.

The structures of economic pauperization are more rigid and more effective, since they arrange, manipulate, and maintain the systems which make the poor become poorer, and the rich become richer. The deterioration of the exchange system and involvement in debt express this situation most cynically.

Cultural pauperization structures are both multifarious and subtle. They deprive the whole people of their history, languages, arts, techniques. They totally wash their brain of any creativity, any ambition, any attempt to search, imagine, or achieve any solution adapted to their needs. Moreover, they cause such an economic, social, and cultural bareness that the most dynamic ideas are condemned to die fruitlessly. Then they arrange an appropriate space for the implantation of a cultural misery-making industry maintained by so-called "technical assistance," "technologies transfer systems," and other multinational enterprises for anthropological pauperization.

There exist other structures even more destructive, because they attack the very ethical basis of a people and individual freedom, responsibility, and sovereignty. They launch their steamrollers over any moral values, any traditions of integrity, dignity, responsibility; they negate love of fellow human beings and of country; they negate solidarity, dedication, self-abnegation. They crush them, they dig them up as prehistorical remnants of ignorant ages. In this moral and spiritual wilderness, crowded with wandering, empty-minded, unaware, and irresponsible ghosts, comes and settles the huge monster of corruption. Money then becomes omnipotent over any moral value, and venality and jungle law become omnipotent.

It is quite possible to go on taking apart the structures of different pauperization systems, the spiritual pauperization, for instance, with its horrifying consequences, when people sink desperately into the dark stream of superstition, sects, and secret societies. . . .

We have already mentioned these things. The important point is to dismantle the structures of the African's systematic pauperization.

B. Sources and Foundation

First of all, African theological language has its source and foundation in the Bible, the word of God addressed to all people in all places and at all times. Therefore, the Bible is addressed to us, today, in our place, as well as it was addressed to other people, in different times, in their own places. Some from Asia and America have received the word of God in their own places, in their own time. They have deciphered the message, in order to understand what the message says to them.

The church, as custodian of the word of God and warrant of its integrity, has transmitted it from country to country, from generation to generation, as it does for us today. So throughout the history of humankind, each people has received the word of God, has deciphered in it the good news of salvation, has welcomed or rejected it with full responsibility. The Jews' welcome was not the same as that of the Greeks'; nor was the Romans' welcome the same as the Gauls', nor the Gauls' welcome the same as the slaves'. No people, in answering the message of God, plays another people's role. Nobody becomes the disciple of Christ by proxy. It is time now for Africa to answer the call addressed to it, through the message of the good news. Nobody else can either play its role or take its place.

It is clear therefore that the primary task of any African theologian is to decipher the message of God for Africa today. We call that task the African way of reading the Bible.

It would be too long to go through the implications of such a way of reading the Bible, in fields like history, exegesis, spirituality, and liturgy. The Jerusalem Congress on the Bible and Black Africa has proved that in all these domains, there is still much to be done, and Africa can bring to the Christian tradition, as a whole, its unique contribution.

The second source of African theology is African culture. For us black peoples of Africa, our culture makes us stand as partners in dialogue with God. This culture characterizes us as persons standing in the presence of God. It teaches us how to speak and how to listen. It is through it that God speaks to us.

We have largely proven the importance of culture in our life. Our experience of both the Christian way of life and the message of God needs the categories of our world view and the African cultural language to make the message of God clearly intelligible to the African. The task of inculturation consists in enabling our world views, our categories, and our languages to convey the message of the word of God. It is not merely a school exercise, nor even an academic topic. Inculturation means a living experience of the gospel in an African way, by African people before God. It has been said and repeated that this way of experiencing the gospel is the same as evangelizing the culture. But to evangelize a culture presupposes the existence of that culture. It therefore is impossible to speak of African theology where there exists no African culture. Inculturation demands Africans, African theologians particularly, to be reborn in their own culture, in order to prepare them to receive the gospel. Once evangelized, African theologians then become evangelizers—messengers of the word of God to their own people, in their tongue and language, that is to say, in the culture of their people. African culture is therefore the necessary raw material for any attempt to elaborate an African theological system.

The third reference source of African theology is the living experience of African communities. Theology is but a rational articulation of this experience. The true subject of theology is the people of God who, in historically experiencing their encounter with God, transmit the same experience from generation to generation. What is called, in different contexts, "Christian tradition," is exactly the same experience carried on in communion with our ancestors in faith. The Christian tradition is neither closed, nor achieved, nor fixed. It is continuously in the making, and through it the gospel becomes historically incarnated in a people. From its sources flow any theological elaboration which is an articulation of the lived experience of the faith of the people of God, hic et nunc.

C. Conceptual Tools

The role of African culture in elaborating an African theological system requires also bringing to that system suitable conceptual tools. These tools derive from the world view and the conception of the human person proper to that culture. They are said to be both cosmological and anthropological. When we accurately examine these categories, we finally discover that, if cosmos means the creation by God as a whole, what we call cosmological or anthropological is basically one thing.

For the Negro-African world view, the whole creation is defined as a life-death conflict. We do not have a genuine concept of being, as did the Greeks. The whole structure of the phenomenal world is characterized by that conflict. The world of our experience is a real battlefield where life and death confront one another. Each creature is an agent either of life or death. From there, traditional medicine, rites, cults, and technologies have their explanation. The life-death conflict also gives meaning to any political or social institution. Law and justice are but an expression of the life forces organized against the death forces. Here lie the foundations of any ethical law or institution. Considered from that point, power, authority, common welfare, and even states appear as ethical values in all respects.

It is not only to the external world that the life-death conflict gives significant meaning. It does so particularly to the human being in all its dimensions. Moreover, in this respect, the human being appears as tragically torn between life and death. But the extraordinary meaningfulness of human life consists in the fact that human beings are bound to achieve the victory of life over death. Just because of that conflict, because human existence is torn between life and death, it is defined as a *fatum*. But the existence of humankind is also a destiny because the human being's existence is bound to overcome death and to bring about the victory of life. As individuals, human beings are simply subject to the *fatum*. By love, humankind achieves a destiny, being born again with double dimension, as both man and woman. Then the human being becomes person, community, history. Promoted by love, the human being becomes a tridimensional person, as father-mother-child. Then those persons become society and people. The individual, as such, is bound to death; community and society, as such, are life overcoming death. When we affirm that the cosmological and the anthropological dimensions are basically one, we simply affirm the interrelationship of humankind and cosmos both as *fatum* and as destiny; their common solidarity in the life-death conflict, and in the final victory of life over death. Humankind and cosmos are inseparably bound in struggle, in death and in life.

These concepts bring with them many theological implications, for many mysteries of our faith—like creation, redemption, incarnation, "salvation economy," church and the sacramental celebration of the mystery of salvation, the edification of the secular city as being the body of the city of God—may be translated into the language of African culture as being an actualization, in "spirit and truth," of the mysteries of life and death. So myth and symbol, which are properly a cultural language, may promote the fragility of their enunciation, by sharing the incommunicable truth of the word of God which no culture could exhaust, or imprison, or monopolize.

It is not possible, in this short paper, to explore all the domains concerned with the conceptual tools of African culture. We just wanted to mention them here. Those who read African theologians may better understand the specificity of their approach.

III. ISSUES AND ORIENTATIONS

For a better understanding of issues and orientations of modern African theology, we have at our disposal several sources of information.

First of all, we have the schools of theology. There exist in Africa many flourishing theological institutions for the training of Catholic and Protestant pastors. The number of their students is increasing every year. However, we must recognize the fact that these institutions are the fortress of a very rigid traditionalism. Any theological research system in a modern sense, and particularly any research concerning any modern African theologizing system, are totally absent from these institutions.

The faculties of theology, as well as the universities' institutions for religious studies and research, play a very significant role. A great number of African universities belonging to the Anglo-Saxon tradition have institutes of religious studies. Many prominent African theologians belong to these institutions; I mention only John Mbiti (Makerere, Uganda) and Kwesi-Dickson (Legon-Accra, Ghana). More recently some faculties of theology have been founded in Francophone Africa, for example, Lovanium in Zaire (1957). There is also the Catholic Institute of West Africa (ICAO, Abidjan, 1975). Two more faculties have been created in Anglophone Africa: the West African Catholic Institute of Port Harcourt (Nigeria, 1981), and the East-African Catholic Institute of Nairobi (Kenya, 1984).

From the theological faculty of the University of South Africa (Pretoria), some African lecturers are members of the Ecumenical Association of Third World Theologians (EATWOT), Professor S. Maimela, for example, or Professor Bongajalo Goba.

Besides these theological institutions, let us mention also some theological bulletins and reviews:

—*AFER* (African Ecclesiastical Review), P.O. Box 908, Eldoret, Kenya.

—The *Revue de Clergé Africain* (Mayidi, Zaire), the first African theological bulletin, which is no longer published.

—*Africa Theological Journal,* Lutheran Faculty of Theology, P.O. Box 3033, Arusha, Tanzania.

—The *Revue Africaine de Théologie,* published by Faculte de Théologie Catholique de Kinshasa, P.O. Box 1534, Kinshasa, Zaire.

—*The Bulletin of African Theology,* organ of the Ecumenical Association of African Theologians, P.O. Box 823, Kinshasa XI, Zaire.

—*TELEMA,* African Review of Spirituality, P.O. Box 3277, Kinshasa-Gombe, Zaire.

These are only a few specimens out of the sixty-five titles mentioned by the *Directory of Theological Institutions in Africa.* Among all these publications, *The Bulletin of African Theology,* as official organ of the Ecumenical Association of African Theologians, is considered to contain the best writers on the modern African way of doing theology. The reason is simple: because this bulletin is, in a certain way, the vehicle or channel of the authentically African theological movement that is reviving the movement of the preindependence period. From the latter movement have originated all the issues and orientations of modern African theology. A Belgian missionary, Rev. Fr. Placide Tempels, who published in 1948 his famous *Bantu Philosophy,* and a group of African priests, who published in 1956 (in Présence Africaine, in Paris) a collective book entitled *Des Prêtres noirs s'interrogent,* are considered the pioneers of the movement. The collective book mentioned deals with the fundamental issues of *liberation* and *inculturation.* The publication of that book was really the birth of the *African theology of liberation,* long before the development of liberation theology in Latin America and other continents. It therefore is quite normal that the cradle of modern Third World theology is located in Africa:

1976: Foundation of the Ecumenical Association of Third World Theologians in Dar-Es-Salaam (Tanzania).
1977: Foundation of the Ecumenical Association of African Theologians in Accra (Ghana). The same year, in Abidjan (Ivory Coast), during the colloquium on black civilization and the Catholic church, the project of an African council was adopted and publicized.

For a better understanding of the main issues and orientations of African theology, it is necessary to follow the evolution of what is known now as the African theology movement. Its chronological development is clear enough:

1948: Rev. Fr. Placide Tempels, a Belgian Franciscan missionary in Congo, published a famous book: *Bantu Philosophy.*
1955: Colloquium organized in Accra, by Protestant churches, on the theme "Africa and Christianity."
1956: Publication, by Présence Africaine, in Paris, of essays written by black African priests under the title: *Des prêtres noirs s'interrogent* (black African priests question themselves). This book is considered today as the starting point of the *African theology movement,* because it deals with the fundamental issues of African theology, the issues of liberation and inculturation.
1960: The first theological week of Kinshasa, on the theme: "African Theology and Africanization."
1966: Colloquium organized at Abadan (Nigeria) by the All Africa Conference of Churches (AACC), on the theme: "African Traditions and Christian Faith."
1969: The fourth theological week of Kinshasa on "African Theology."

1975: At the University of Jos (Nigeria), international colloquium on "Christianity in Post-colonial Africa."

1976: Foundation of the Ecumenical Association of Third World Theologians in Dar-Es-Salaam (Tanzania).

1977: Foundation in Accra (Ghana) of the Ecumenical Association of African Theologians (20 December 1977).

1977: Colloquium organized by Présence Africaine in Ivory Coast (Abidjan), on the theme: "Black Civilization and the Catholic." The project of a pan-African council was adopted by that colloquium.

1979: Publication of the first issue of the *Bulletin of African Theology,* official organ of the Ecumenical Association of African Theologians.

1986: Publication of the Kairos documents on the new commitment of the churches in South Africa.

One could also mention other theological meetings like the colloquia in Bonake (Ivory Coast); in Cotonou (organized by Présence Africaine) on the theme "Religions as Sources of African Civilization"; in Lomé (Togo), on "Black Civilization and Protestantism"; one could even mention the general assemblies of our association in Yaoundé (1981) and in Nairobi (1984), or the theological weeks of Kinshasa, which occur almost every two years; or the colloquia of the Ecumenical Association of African Theologians. One could also mention a number of books, among them: John Mbiti's *New Testament Eschatology in an African Background* (London, 1971); and Charles Nyamiti's *The Scope of African Theology* (Kampala, 1973).

All are working for the elaboration of an African way of theologizing. In order to make their theology authentically African and authentically Christian, and in order to achieve the inculturation of their faith, they find their tools of analysis and conceptual categories in the Bible, in their African tradition, and in their culture.

It is also possible to mention other examples. Theologians as different as: M. Mothlari, *Essays on Black Theology* (Johannesburg, 1972); J. M. Éla, *Le crei de l'homme Africain* (Paris, 1980) — English translation: *African Cry* (Maryknoll, N.Y., 1987); F. Eboussi Boulaga, *Christianisme sans fétiche, révélation et domination* (Paris, 1981) — English translation: *Christianity without Fetishes* (Maryknoll, N.Y., 1986); Meinrad Hegba, *Libération d'Eglises sans tutella* (Paris, 1976).

All are concerned with the same major issue of African theology, the issue of liberation. Their approaches are both convergent and divergent; they are convergent when they use anthropological analysis; they are divergent because of the diversity of the living communities which give context to their way of theologizing. The more radical of these authors, probably because of the radicality of their personal experience (Eboussi Boulaga, for example, or the Kairos documents from South Africa), used a critical approach which is not typically Marxist, but which is rather anthropological and cultural. In approaching political, economic, social, and religious challenges, it contributes to the clear and radical exposure and dismantling of the anthropological pauperization system. It could be interesting to reexamine the chronology and the issues of the *Bibliography of African Theology*, published since 1984 by the *Bulletin of African Theologians*, whatever be their origin, their denomination, their linguistic or geographical position, in regard to their sources of inspiration, their tools of analysis, the main issues and orientations of their theologies.

The role of women is another issue in Africa. African anthropology considers the human being as bidimensional, both man and woman, male and female. This basic structure defines the human person as a complementarity of both dimensions—man, without woman, is not a person but simply a project. Nor is woman, without man, a person. Therefore, all political, social, economic, cultural, or religious institutions are established on the basis of that complementarity.

Unfortunately, this complementarity has been too often negatively interpreted for the woman. And that is probably because the complementarity concept consists in a distribution of roles and functions which is much more adequate than the famous sex-equality. In Africa, religion is certainly the domain where women, as a safeguard of life, play a unique role. In many African cults, the priestly function is properly a function of woman. In this field the sex-discrimination common to the Western Christian tradition is totally absent from the African tradition.

Here is the reason why in the African theology movement, the place of the woman is in the forefront. And it is so, first of all, within the churches. The African Women Christian Associations are achieving, in their programs, an ecclesiology of complementarity which is, in fact, the ecclesiology of the future. The charismatic action of Christian women, even in the traditionalist and conservative circles of the Roman Catholic church, is opening new ways of evangelizing, making room for the free action of the Holy Spirit. The role of the woman in theological research is as important as her central position in the society, where she has been considered, from time immemorial, as the keeper of life, culture, and traditions. And in the making of modern Africa, the woman has also been in the forefront of the struggle for the African man's liberation and promotion. Enriched by this experience, the African woman is to play a vital role in the African theological reflection. To prove it, let us consider the program of the first meeting of the African women theologians held in Yaoundé, Cameroon (3–9 August 1986). During that meeting the following topics were discussed: (1) the woman and the church; (2) the woman and the Bible; (3) the woman and theology; (4) the woman and Christology; (5) the woman and the struggle for liberation; and (6) the woman and spirituality.

There the African women theologians concluded their debates with the following recommendation: "The spiritual experience of our life shows that God addresses himself to any human person without discrimination. Isn't it a clear invitation to the church to give the woman her right place within the structures of the church?"

Meanwhile, African theology has already given the African woman her right place. This is a warrant of prosperity for the church and for Africa.

CONCLUSION: CHURCH, THEOLOGY, AND HUMAN PROMOTION

The African theology movement raises many questions. Let us conclude with only one question: Regarding the churches, is that movement marginalized, or is it part of the African churches' dynamism? The answer to that question, in Africa itself, is not so simple. And it seems that the same question is not simple anywhere in the Third World. In reality, the concrete experience of the African churches shows skepticism sometimes, sometimes full commitment, and even enthusiasm. The attitude of the churches is therefore very diversified. However we must recognize skepticism as being the attitude of some individuals. The general tendency is toward a global conscientization of the people in favor of human liberation and promotion in Africa. The solidarity of the churches with people who suffer, who are dominated and oppressed, is proclaimed all over Africa in such a way that it can serve as a model. The churches of South Africa, in this respect, are perfect models of ecumenical commitment and solidarity.

So the Kairos documents, in the history of the African theology movement, will stand as a monument for a new commitment within the church, a new ecclesiology, and a new relationship of the church with the secular world; with the same clear, firm, and determined voice, the church speaks in Uganda, in Ethiopia, in Zaire, in Burundi, in Sudan. The official statements of the Symposium of Episcopal Conferences of Africa and Madagascar, mentioned earlier, are an illustration of the commitment of the church. So are the declarations and interventions of the All Africa Conference of Churches.

Engaged in the struggle for liberation and human rights, the churches in Africa are also struggling for human promotion. This promotion today is called *development*. It is interesting to underline the fact that a document published by the Symposium of Episcopal Conferences of Africa and Madagascar (May 1985) is on: "The Church and Human Promotion Today in Africa." This document clearly states that evangelization and human promotion are one and the same task. And the African bishops conclude: "If in the past evangelization and human promotion have been considered as separate activities, we must now unify our pastoral program, in order to include, as a constitutive dimension of it, the task of human promotion within the evangelization process."

Is it necessary to mention here that African theology is also *evangelization?* It is, therefore, a mobilization for *liberation* and *human promotion* in Africa.

NOTE

1. On all these figures, see *Mundo Negro,* no. 275 (March–April 1985), pp. 98ff.

3

Latin American Report

INTRODUCTION

In recent years Latin America has become a center of theological debates. With the courage of the gospel, significant sectors of the churches have responded to the challenges coming from the economic poverty, political oppression, and cultural marginalization in Latin America. More and more the gospel is becoming an element of social mobilization for an integrating liberation of the various human dimensions. The preferential option for the poor is gaining ground in the thousands of basic Christian communities, in the biblical reflection groups, and among Christians participating in the process of change. There is a significant number of pastors who acknowledge and support a church of the people, thus contributing toward the emergence of a church with popular characteristics, a church which is truly the people of God. The Spirit has raised up prophetic figures of worldwide renown who confer legitimacy and credibility on the Christian message read from the perspective of the poor and against their situation of poverty. Because of this, there have been persecutions and martyrs in Latin America.

In this process, liberation theology—with its struggle against impoverishment of the Third World and against historical injustices—has been strengthened. The process of liberation conducted by the oppressed themselves is of interest not only to the churches. It also preoccupies all those persons who still maintain a minimum sense of humanity and compassion in the face of the suffering of the poor and of the innocent. It is for this reason that the theology of liberation has gained ground in the marketplace and has become the subject of conversations in the workplace and even in bars.

The two instructions of the Sacred Congregation for the Doctrine of the Faith about liberty and liberation (the first published on 4 September 1984 and the second on 22 March 1986) stirred discussion that continues to occupy the theological scene the world over. It is the first time in the history of Latin America that the voice of the periphery has been heard, discussed, and assessed by the center of Roman Catholic Christianity and by many other churches and religions. We can say that this liberative theology, which has its own versions in Africa, Asia, Latin America, and among the minority groups of the United States, is actually the most dynamic, open, ecumenical, and engaging in all the churches. It has immeasurable potential for evangelization as it helps people to face the questions which are central to the Christian message: the poor, their justice and liberation, the future of the victims of violence and oppression, and the true concept of God as the God of life.

In our report we want to situate the Latin American reflection within the wider context of society and of the various churches. We will also try to consider the various expressions that this reflection of faith assumes as it finds itself confronted by specific challenges meted to the Christian conscience. We live in a time of tensions and suffering. Theologians are pressured and are under the heavy surveillance of ecclesiastical authorities, as in the case of Gustavo Gutiérrez in Peru and Leonardo Boff in Brazil. The latter was called to Rome in 1984 to respond to an official interrogation about his ecclesiology, which he developed within the framework of liberation theology. However, all this is nothing compared with the suffering of the oppressed people who for about five hundred years have resisted domination because they know that God is on their side and, despite all difficulties, is fighting for their liberation.

I. CHALLENGES

A. Political Challenges

Four political challenges have marked Latin American life during recent years. They have not been the only ones, but their impact has been so strong that they have assumed prevalence.

In *the first place,* there has emerged a concern for the kind of democratic organization which the Latin American peoples want to assume for themselves. There was a period (the decade of the 1960s and the beginning of the 1970s) when the popular sectors associated the word *democracy* with an institutional order proper to the bourgeoisie. It was necessary to overcome that order, to break that model of liberalism and bourgeois domination. Unfortunately, in spite of the popular pressures that sought that transformation, the dominant classes succeeded in imposing the national security state, administered by the military, which brought repression, suffering, and death to the popular sectors. Human rights, personal and social, were violated. "Disappearances" and torture became daily occurrences, establishing terror, insecurity, and fear in the people. This situation still continues in countries like Chile, Paraguay, El Salvador, Guatemala, and Peru. Notwithstanding that, the power that the dictatorships of national security have been able to amass has undergone a process of deterioration, which determined their fall in Argentina, Brazil, Uruguay, Bolivia, Guatemala, etc. In other cases, such as Haiti, the dictatorial power was overthrown. These processes were the result of a tenacious resistance of the popular organizations, on the one hand, and the lack of administrative ability demonstrated by the military in power, on the other hand. Overwhelmed by the action of the popular movements, and not being able to control the situation anymore, the military returned to their barracks.

It is in this context that the question has surfaced: What democracy? If before this question was raised by the dominant classes, now it is being formulated by the popular sectors. The night of the dictatorships having passed, how do the people articulate a political order that will permit them better levels of life? Though the development of such an order seemed to be the intent when the military went back to their normal functions, no model for a new democratic organization has either been proposed or developed. For this reason, the bourgeois- and liberal-type of political order has returned to dominate. However, the popular sectors want to participate decisively in the history that pertains to them. This means that they have arrived at a new valuing of democracy, considered more and more as a space where they can combine various political projects. The dominant groups, who for the most part are experiencing a definite nostalgia for the national security state, do not sympathize with this requirement of the popular classes.

The popular sectors seek to create something new. In this sense, their action has a prophetic character, and their thought, which is open toward the future, underlines the positive sign of utopia. Compared with this, the project of the dominant classes, besides not being equal to the requirements of the people, possesses the prosaic character of a pragmatism without imagination or greatness. In these circumstances the challenge is: How to forge this new democracy with the participation of the majority? Also related to this is the question: How to construct popular unity which gives force to the movement of the people to assure the birth and the permanence of this new democracy?

In *the second place,* a dramatic challenge of recent years has been achieving peace in Central America in a way that the sovereignty of the peoples of this region would be respected. The popular program of these peoples emphasizes the need to formulate structural transformation which assures justice and liberty for all, thus ending the domination of the oligarchies supported by imperialism. The situation in Nicaragua, as well as the insurrectional struggle in El Salvador, Guatemala, and Honduras, expresses this fundamental reality. In the face of this popular determination the North American government has manifested the will to do all that is possible to block whatever would concretize these reforms. Therefore, it supports the counter-revolution, which attacks Nicaragua from Honduras and assaults that country in various ways. The North American government openly sustains the army of El Salvador in its antipopular and antidemocratic activities; it has contributed to the killing and repression of vast sectors of Guatemalan people; and finally, it has practically taken possession of Honduras, converting it into one big U.S. base.

The intent of the Nicaraguan people — to create a new society — has been deeply affected by the politics of the Reagan and Bush administrations. Since 1979, the Nicaraguans have been seeking to create a process of structural transformation (e.g., agrarian, urban, and industrial reform) as well as institutional change (e.g., the new constitution) in order to forge a more just and egalitarian society. It is a society which opens itself to the participation of the majority, who were practically excluded from the decision-making processes during the time of the Somoza dictatorship. That is, in Nicaragua today there is being offered a process which tends to give institutional weight and form to a republic of the poor. The experience inspires hope in the rest of Latin America, but the government of the United States is trying violently to block it.

All this signifies a profound distortion and grave deterioration for the Central American societies. It is a situation of open war, which tends to escalate. The peoples of the region, in the same way that the multitude in Nicaragua in March of 1983 cried out when Pope John Paul II visited their country, want peace. It is something very important for the life of these poor and suffering peoples. But despite this, the U.S. government maintains its imperialist attitude, creating a real source of disturbance, pain, and death in that region of Latin America. The result of this is dramatic: thousands of people dead, families shaken by pain and suffering, an arms race, and the danger that a situation similar to Vietnam is in the making in the region.

The Contadora group — composed of representatives of the governments of Colombia, Mexico, Panama, Venezuela, and supported by those of Argentina, Brazil, Peru, and Uruguay — was a force for peace, and it was systematically boycotted by the United States and its Central American allies. And the United States has ignored, attempted to subvert, or paid mere lip service to other genuine efforts toward peace.

The existence of this conflict in the hemisphere brings with it the perpetuation of militarism. This becomes evident when one considers the arms race (not only in Central America, but in all America) and the growth of military costs, which, outside of Argentina, have continued to increase in the rest of the countries. In this way the position of the armies is reinforced and the danger is that the ideology of national security, which has done so much damage in Latin America, will return and dominate.

In *the third place,* when one observes the historical process of the region during recent years, the growing challenge that the peoples of the "oppressed races" present in the political field has to be taken into consideration. Indians and blacks have been submitted to barbarous domination for centuries. Today their resistance is not a silent one anymore, but has been transformed into something organized, militant, with new projects for society. This can be observed in Guatemala, where the military dictators have submitted the native peoples to systematic massacres. It is happening in Peru, especially in the region of Ayacucho, where important indigenous sectors have entered into guerrilla action. This is equally so in Nicaragua, where the problems of the situation of the Miskito, Sumus, and Ramas still have not been satisfactorily resolved. This does not mean that each and every one of the claims of these groups is justified, but simply that they express a considerable political challenge, coming from the poorest, the most oppressed, those who have been left aside in Latin America.

In this context, we have to mention the serious fact of the invasion of Grenada by the U.S. government in October of 1983, which stifled a process of national liberation and of popular democracy. It was a shameful action, where the arrogance of a large nation against a small nation was manifested. It was also a clear expression of racism against the desire for liberation of one of the oppressed races.

In *the fourth place,* it is necessary to indicate the growing political participation of women, and especially of poor women in Latin America, as a new political fact whose consequence could be very great. This trend, which had already been perceived since the late 1970s, has grown in strength over recent years. Many times women demonstrate a valor in the political struggle which men do not always have, and a greater sensitivity in face of injustices and violations of human rights. Women are present in the struggle for liberation in El Salvador, in the defense for a free Nicaragua, in the claims of the landless in Brazil, in the militancy against the dictatorship of Pinochet in Chile, in the implementation of human rights in Argentina, etc. The presence of women in the political life of Latin America, besides enriching women's lives, implies challenges of considerable importance. Certainly, the Latin American political life has become less chauvinist and more open and inclusive.

B. Economic Challenges

If in Central America there is a situation of open armed conflict, if there is a guerrilla struggle in Colombia, Peru, and Chile, in the rest of Latin America a situation of social and economic war predominates which, in some cases, has reached devastating proportions. For example, as a result of five years of continued drought in the Northeast of Brazil, three million people have died. The lack of rain and its effects were the reason for the tragedy, but its true cause is in the structural conditions—monopolies of the land and water reserves—which go against the life of the people by denying them satisfaction of their basic needs.

It is true that it is not possible to generalize about Latin American economic life. The differences between the countries are very great: giant Brazil is next to small Uruguay, and the shadow of Mexico falls on the countries of Central America. Nevertheless, there is one prevalent fact which affects all the peoples of the region—mortgaging the future: the external debt which has risen far above the 1986 level of U.S. $400 billion. The seriousness of this can be seen in the tragedy of Mexico: deterioration of the public services, increase of hunger, insufficient housing and health facilities, etc.

The obligation to pay the interest on the debt in the context of a recessive situation in world economics has meant great sacrifices for the working masses. The requirements of the IMF have been clear in this sense: low salaries, cuts in proposed social programs, inflation followed by deflation (Bolivia, Uruguay), and unpopular monetary measures (plan "Austral" in Argentina and the "cruzado" in Brazil) have brought an increase in unemployment and in the poverty index. Over recent years one observes a diminution of the number of industrial workers in Latin America; for example, Argentina, which until the 1970s was one of the most industrially developing countries, has seen a dismantling of its industrial sector.

Transnational capital is what actually dominates the Latin American economy. It has profoundly penetrated almost all of the countries. It entered as a support to "joint ventures," but was rapidly able to consolidate its position. Closely associated with agrarian exports and industrial capital, transnational financial capital is what has benefited most during recent years. The majority of the people work for it.

The most developed branch of the industrial sector is military production. It makes up a considerable part of the exports of Brazil (sixth arms-exporting country in the world). It constitutes the most important part of the industrial production of Argentina. Chile also has followed the same road. This trend is not matched with other kinds of industrial production, except in Brazil, where the protectionist policy of "market reserve" for Brazilian computers has also permitted the growth of a national industry very much related to war production.

This situation has resulted in polarized social divisions: a small minority has the highest consumption and accumulation capacity, which because of its ostentation is an insult in the face of the poverty of the great majority who barely survive. The question today in Latin America is not economic development, but the survival of the large masses. The challenge of these last years is outlined by the need to shape an economic model which ensures the reproduction of life, the satisfaction of the basic needs of all, and participation in production and the benefits of production by all. It is a challenge to create an economy of justice for the poor. Capitalism does not offer space for that. The challenge is to exercise the imagination and creativity through the formulation of popular socialist alternatives which go beyond social democracy.

C. Challenges in the Area of Religion

A strong irruption of religiosity in the popular sector of Latin America is visible in the multiplication of religious movements and of Pentecostal churches, which expresses a rupture with dominant religion. This is also visible in the process of internal renewal in the Catholic church and in the traditional Protestant churches. In the Catholic church, with greater or lesser intensity, this phenomenon finds its realization in the growth of basic ecclesial communities among the urban and rural poor. The process is present in almost all of the countries, including Mexico, Ecuador, and Bolivia. It plays a key role in Central America and is considered a priority of the entire church, as in Brazil. The same process of popular communities is taking its first steps in the Protestant mainline churches. At the same time, in the former areas of black slavery, the Afro-American cults are being reborn. Also, indigenous cultures and religions are blooming in many countries.

The common feature in all this movement is its popular base, located in the rural areas affected by social and economic changes as well as in the periphery of the cities, swelled by the masses driven out of the rural areas.

One common element shared by the Pentecostal communities and the Catholic base communities is the central role played by the reading and use of the Bible. In this way, in the reading as well as in the interpretation and spreading of the word of God, there is a new actor or historical subject, the poor. The popular appropriation of the Bible may have a fundamentalist orientation, as among Pentecostal churches, or may lead to a creative and enriching dialogue between the life of the poor and the word of God. In both cases, priority is given to the reading, discussion, and celebration of the word of God, which are done collectively rather than privately or individually.

There exists, however, a strong difference in the direction of these churches and communities. Some emerge as alternate religions for the inarticulate and abandoned of the large cities. This seems to be the case of the Pentecostal movement, described by one intellectual as a "refuge of the masses." In this sense it can be seen as a form of rejection of the world of severe capitalist competition and the imposed marginalization of the great majority of the common people. It is, at the same time, a strategy of survival, as much social as psychological and religious. They are religious movements that arise as a consequence of social reflection, and they offer to their followers a welcoming community and an ethic which rejects the vices of a consumer society. They favor reconstruction, within the community, of a fraternal world, free from lies, from fraud, and from exploitation, and full of the intense experience of the God who saves. The Pentecostal movement, however, is for the masses not an organizing or mobilizing factor leading to the transformation of society. It accommodates itself, in fact, to the existing order and develops a tense expectation of the end of the world, as the judgment and punishment of God for the evil ones, and justice, joy, consolation, and happiness for the elect.

The basic ecclesial communities have been developed, in many areas, in close connection with the popular movement, being at times the matrix of this movement and especially of the neighborhood associations in the large cities and rural trade unions in the country.

In the sectors of the countries which have known the slavery of black people, does not the flowering of the Afro-American cults have the same sense? These cults have become more and more a real and autonomous religion, after having survived clandestinely in syncretism with Catholicism, sometimes as an important part of the so-called "popular Catholicism" manifested in the cult of the saints and in African traditions. Voodoo, rooted in the rural population of Haiti, and the Candomblé of Bahia, of a clearly urban nature, are perhaps the two most finished and dynamic expressions of the Afro-American religion. This is also expressed in the "Santeria" of Cuba, in the "Shango" of Trinidad-Tobago and Grenada, in the Afro-cults of Colombia, Venezuela, and the Guianas, in the "Batuque" of Puerto Alegre (Rio Grande do Sul, Brazil), or in the "Xango" of Recife (Pernambuco, Brazil). In Brazil there has come forth a new religion that is typically urban, of the black popular classes, mestizos, immigrants, and poor whites, that unites the Afro-elements with Eastern Catholic elements and, above all, with "kardecist" spiritism: Umbanda. "Macumba" of Rio de Janeiro can be considered a middle road between traditional "Candomblé" of Bahia and the white-oriented "Umbanda" of the south. The Afro-cults, besides having offered a response to social abandonment, and having expressed the long fight for physical and spiritual survival of the Afro-American population, allow the recuperation of ethnic identity and human dignity of a group historically marked by the stigma of slavery and socially tinged by racial discrimination. Culturally and politically the centers of the cults are what sustains the life of the black community.

In the English Caribbean and more particularly in Jamaica, the Rastafari movement offers a combination of religious movement with cultural renewal and socio-political messianism. Africa becomes again the mythic and utopic horizon of those who were torn away violently to be slaves in the Antilles.

Catholic blacks who had been organized in *cabildos* (townships) in Hispanic America, or in the brotherhoods of Our Lady of the Rosary of the Blacks, St. Benedict, and St. Efigenia in Portuguese America, today try to discover their proper space in the church. They denounce and try to overcome the old and new discriminations, demanding access to the ministries and to a black hierarchy, to their own proper liturgical expression, and to a theology which is not white or Western. Creole is taking the place of French in catechesis and in the Catholic liturgy of Haiti and in some sectors of Guadalupe. The black communities of Colón in Panama have revolutionized the liturgy and songs of the local Anglican church while the Baptist blacks of Bahia have begun to rethink their relation with African tradition.

The indigenous renewal, always in symbiosis with the religious renewal, can be expressed in diverse phenomena, as in (1) the recuperation of indigenous peoples' proper tradition and dignity within the Catholic church.

which happened in Riobamba in Ecuador, and in Chiapas in Mexico; (2) the constitution of a Protestant indigenous church, as found in the Methodist church among the Aymaras of Bolivia; or (3) the recovery of old rites and celebrations, as it occurs in Guatemala, in the Altiplano, and among groups which have lost their culture, like the Bororos in Brazil. The religious renewal is profoundly connected with the political, social, and labor union struggles of the Latin American rural world. Religion springs up as a factor of resistance, as a struggle for land, and as the recovery of the ethnic and cultural identity.

There is a strong religio-cultural aggression against the Latin American popular universe. For example, the actuations of the "Summer Linguistic Institute" of certain fundamentalist Protestants and of missionary groups within the Catholic and evangelical churches are disquieting for the indigenous churches. On the other hand, it is important to underline the positive attitude of Catholics, Lutherans, and Methodists working together with indigenous peoples. Outstanding in this sense is the action of CIMI (Conselho Indigenista Missionário) in Brazil, CENAMI (Centro Nacional de Missões Indigenas), and similar groups in Peru, Ecuador, and Panama.

The religious world is also crossed by currents which direct their efforts to the new social sectors created by the expansion of the network of the service economy, that is, the modern middle classes, which sustain the charismatic movements of the Protestant mainline and the Catholic churches. This movement has a transnational character, and its organizational matrices and ideologies are outside of Latin America, mostly in the United States and in Europe. Conservative sectors persist on the continent: for example, the actions of an organization like Opus Dei concern progressive people because of its alliance with the powerful and the support which it enjoys from important sectors of the Vatican, as well as the growing number of bishops who come out of this organization.

From the United States there have also arrived in Latin America the so-called electronic churches, which reach their public by TV programs. The phenomenon of these churches, whose expansion and consolidation are detailed by daily radio programs, is also important, as they penetrate with major force the nonliterate and semiliterate segments of the population, and take the place of the former influence of the religious press.

At least in Brazil one cannot ignore the phenomenon of the religious movements of Japanese origin. These movements expand among the populations of non-Japanese origins, offering above all a religion of interior peace, disconnected from any criticism of the social and political order. This movement is concomitant with the expansion of transnational Japanese capital.

Another challenge comes from the complex relation the churches have with the political and social entities in civil societies, and with the state. The national security regimes created a crisis in the traditional relationship of the state with the various churches. In Argentina the church collaborated with the regime, and the Catholic hierarchy did little in denouncing the violation of human rights. In Chile, under the Pinochet regime, the Pentecostal movement has supported and given legitimation to the dictatorship. The same happened with the regime of Rios Montt in Guatemala. On the other hand, Protestant and Catholic laity created commissions of justice and peace, both in Argentina and Uruguay. In other countries these commissions relied on the support of the hierarchy, like the Vicariate of Solidarity in Chile and in El Salvador, the Commission of Justice and Peace in Brazil, or, more directly, the resistance of the Catholic church in Haiti in the struggle against the Duvalier regime. The relation of the Catholic hierarchy with the Nicaraguan government has been tense, but at the same time, there was a deep involvement of Christians in the Sandinista revolution and in its consolidation.

The relation between faith and politics is one of the critical questions for the basic Christian communities in the continent. For certain regions, such as Central America, Chile, Colombia, and Peru, it presents new theoretical-practical challenges: (1) the problem of armed resistance in the struggle for life and liberty of the exploited and brutalized majorities, who are exploited and brutalized by private militias and bullies, as well as by the police and the army; and (2) the problem of the political use of violence and the Christian commitment to the search for a peace through justice. In many countries, as in El Salvador and Chile, the church has been called to participate in actions for peace and to look for a new political order. With growing frequency, this question of the relation between faith and politics is raised regarding the working together of Christians of different churches and with non-Christians, such as Marxists, in the consideration of a new society.

In Nicaragua, the involvement of a large number of Christians in the revolutionary process, before and after the triumph of July 1979, the presence of priests in the Sandinista government, the gradual distancing of the Catholic hierarchy in relation to the Nicaraguan process, the tension created by the pope's visit to the country, the repressive measures of the hierarchy against the lay ministers of the word, priests, and Christian communities in the popular sectors—all have brought much suffering. At the same time, there has been an enormous growth in prayer, reflection, and pastoral and theological discernment in the communities. Amidst the economic, military, political, and ideological aggression that the country suffers at the hands of the United States, Nicaragua has raised serious questions to the Latin American Christian conscience in terms of solidarity, of actions for peace, and of the right of the Nicaraguan people to rebuild their country in peace. Rome has been challenged evangelically because of its position, support, and alliances in the Central American conflict.

In Cuba, a process of reflection was undertaken regarding the positions of the state and the party as well as of the Cuban Episcopal Conference, culminating in February 1986 in the first pastoral assembly of the country since the 1959 revolution. The discussion of the role of religion and the churches in a socialist regime in Latin American societies and, particularly, in the Cuban society, received a great support with the publication of a book by Frei Betto, *Fidel and Religion,* whose Cuban edition exceeded more than a million copies and produced a strong popular impact.

Finally, we must point out the use of religion by the U.S. administration as an ideological tool in the struggle against liberation theology and against the popular Latin American movements inspired by religious faith. The U.S. administration has favored the emergence of a counter-insurgency religion with research centers (the Institute of Religion and Democracy), budgets, and publicity, supporting the diffusion of fundamentalist sects, and aimed at the religious manipulation of the popular sectors.

D. Challenges in the Cultural Arena

A fundamental theological challenge for Latin America is to elaborate a reflection which starts from a dialogue with the different indigenous cultures with their myths and their vision of the world. Even though it has become clear for us that evangelization is not a synonym for European or North American enterprise, liberation theology does not yet have the religious world and the culture of the Indians and blacks, who are the majority of the most poor and exploited, as its principal interlocutors.

The other theological challenge is the critical dialogue that faith and theology must have with the dominant culture — with the technical, scientific, and cultural sectors which are connected to the university, to research, to individual production, and to the dissemination of information in society, with its new language and its new presuppositions. The new questions related to genetic engineering, research on human beings, ecology, and nuclear armaments have not yet had repercussions among base communities and among liberation theologians and have not been the target of sufficient reflection. This has been due to the lack of theological tools.

One theological sector — that which is more closely linked to academic theology and to the middle-class church through its network of colleges and universities — insists that the central challenge before theology resides precisely in the emergence of a society with an urban-industrial, technological-scientific culture. In other words, the principal challenge comes from modernization, understood as the emancipation of reason, scientific progress, and industrial and technological expansion under the leadership of an international bourgeoisie, but always in alliance with the techno-bureaucracy of Latin American nations. According to this opinion, the only hope for overcoming poverty and misery resides in the economic advance of this stratum, rural and urban. It will be necessary to favor, through modernization of the economy, the growth of rural and industrial productivity and a greater offering of basic products. It will be also important to reform the injustices and mistakes through the action of the state and the application of the social teaching of the church.

For this theological sector, the theoretical response does not reside in liberation theology, but in the social teaching of the church. The historical actors or subjects of social changes are not the popular classes, but the educated middle classes.

It is true that we cannot conceal the challenges presented by the process of modernization, but this process has been difficult in Latin America, and we have to interpret it differently from the way it was interpreted in Europe. In Europe, as a result of the Industrial Revolution, a new directing or leading class came forth, the bourgeoisie class, with its ideology, liberalism. At the same time another class came forth, the working class, the proletariat, with its critical vision of the process, thanks to socialism and Marxism. Therefore, to respond to modernization means to answer not only the questions raised by liberalism and the bourgeois, but also and with equal force, the questions raised by the working class and Marxism.

In Latin America, modern capitalism necessitates a different interpretation along three aspects:

Historically, modernization did not produce a directing class and a free, independent nation, as in the European process. What happened was the passage from Iberian, to British, to North American domination. The rise of the middle class was an illusive process even in countries like Mexico, Argentina, and Brazil, which had an older industrialization and wider markets.

Economically, Latin American industrialization produced a "modernization" mainly in the rural areas. The class protagonist of the process, at the end of the nineteenth century and at the beginning of the twentieth, was the *fazendeiro* (large coffee plantation owner) in Brazil, in Colombia, and in several countries in Central America; also the large *hacendado* (hacienda owner), producer of wheat, cattle, and wool in Argentina and Uruguay. The exploited class included the farmer or the rural worker, as well as the poor Indians, whose lands were expropriated and subordinated to commercial farming for export.

Socially, the process led to the marginalization of the great masses not integrated in these "modern" segments of the economy in both the rural and urban areas.

Modernization in Latin America, therefore, puts the question of domination and capitalist exploitation as a national problem, as a problem of the working class, as a problem of the *campesinos* (farm workers), but also and above all, as a problem of the Indians and of the great marginalized masses in the countryside and in the cities.

Liberation theology, critical of capitalism in its imperialist dimension through the theory of dependence; sensitive to the abandonment and suffering of the great masses through its option for the poor; committed to the indigenous population through the pastoral organizations, and to the struggles of the rural areas through a theology of the land, has not sufficiently approached the working class and its social, political, and religious questions. It has still not adequately confronted the questions coming from the technological and scientific world and their practical applications to the countries of the Third World. These raise new questions beyond the ethical and theological responses which are being worked out in the First World.

The present challenge to the theology of liberation is to answer the questioning coming from the specific culture of the indigenous world, of the Afro-American, of the world of technology and of science, of the world of the worker, of the world of the poor and marginalized women and of the feminist movement in general. However, in the cultural arena, there is yet another challenge coming from the monopoly of the means of social communication, specifically of television. The practices of manipulation, the masking of information, the direct campaigns against the popular interests of the church sectors committed to the poorest are very common. The communication enterprises are almost all subjected to the interests of large businesses, and they are the visible part of the publicity machines of these businesses, in particular of the multinationals which finance, together with the state, the expenses of publicity.

All of the countries suffer from international control of the flux of journalistic information and are invaded by the cultural industry of the countries of advanced capitalism. The means of social communication become fundamental vehicles of the process of cultural and ideological domination by the United States.

On the other hand, a process of popular resistance and great creativity in the sector of cultural production is present in Latin America, for example in song and in music. This creativity reached the church of the poor and today it has its own hymnal, its own biblical production, its political and social writings, and its artists and designers, as well as its singers, musicians, and poets. The reencounter of popular religion with art is one of the most promising aspects of the new way of being church and of its cultural expression.

In the same way, there is an advance in the recovery of the historic memory of the poor and oppressed, of their traditions, of their resistance and struggles, as nourishment and guide for the actual struggle, as a source of hope and constancy in their sufferings and adversities. In this context we are facing a more committed reflection about the theme of the "religious expression" of the people, overcoming the false identification between popular religion and alienation, between Indian or black heritage and superstition. Unfortunately, in the beginning of liberation theology, pastoral agents and theologians led a doltish fight against the religious feelings and expressions of the people, which they termed "popular religiosity."

II. THE WORKING METHODOLOGIES IN THE THEOLOGICAL PRAXIS OF LATIN AMERICA

A. Theology in the Third World and from the Third World

There are as many theologies as there are organized practices of the churches. There is a praxis of the churches which prolongs the colonial and neocolonial past, because these churches unite themselves with the dominant sectors of society. The theology which accompanies the pastoral life of this type of church is normally conservative. It is oriented to neo-Scholasticism. There is another praxis of the modern church whose social base is formed by the progressive sectors and which is open to the project of social reform. Here the theology is also modern, in the mold of the metropolitan centers of Christian thought, of the critical and academic style. But this is also the church that, in the face of the misery of the great majority, takes seriously the preferential option for the poor. It possesses a popular praxis, considers the oppressed as the principal subject of liberation, and associates with them in a pastoral praxis. The theology which accompanies and illuminates this praxis will be a theology of liberation.

In Latin America there exists, not without tensions, these and other theological currents. By the fact that our continent is dependent and associated with central capitalism, we know that theology participates in this dependence and association. But we also realize that having a process of liberation, one which begins with the oppressed, permits the existence of an adequate theology of these processes. That theology comes under the name of liberation theology. We want to dwell lengthily on this theology because we judge it the most representative of Latin America. It shows not only that there are theologians *in* Latin America, in the Third World, but also, principally, that these are theologians *of* the Third World, who think upon the faith of the people starting from their oppressed situation in the Third World, in view of an integral liberation.

B. Deepening the Point of Departure

The Latin American theology of liberation has penetrated practically all of the ecclesial fabric. There exists a popular liberation theology elaborated by the participants in the base ecclesial communities and by the biblical reflection groups. It produces commentaries, celebrations, dramatizations, and norms for action, favoring an informal and popular language. In addition, there exists a theology of pastoral liberation normally done by pastors and pastoral agents. Its principal places of elaboration are the ecclesial assemblies and meetings of pastoral reflection. It uses a logic which is concrete, motivating, and prophetic. Finally, a professional liberation theology is in an advanced phase of elaboration, done by scientific and methodical theologians, whose work appears in courses and writings.

For all the forms of liberation theology there exists a fundamental motivation: a living commitment with the oppressed. Before formulating a liberation theology, it is necessary to have a previous commitment to the concrete liberation of the poor. The point of departure is not simply the reality of exploitation under which the oppressed suffer, but the praxis of Christians and of the poor in general, working for the transformation of the oppressive situation. The theologian finds himself or herself placed on this road. Starting from that commitment, he or she elaborates this theology. The oppressed do not constitute only a point of reference for liberating reflection; nor are they only its addressees. They are principally the subjects and actors of liberation. Their reflections are incorporated in the reflection of the theologian in such a way that the theology becomes a community production. They are not only an object of theological interpretation, but principally are interpreters of their own situation in the light of faith.

This praxis seeks to be efficacious. For this reason, a more critical analysis of the mechanisms producing oppression and of the strategies of liberation is necessary in the light of Christian faith. In recent years there has been a deepening with reference to the socio-analytical mediations. The empirical and functional explanations of poverty (poverty as vice in the first case, and as technical backwardness in the second) have been largely surpassed. On the other hand, the dialectic interpretation (poverty as oppression) of the Marxist tradition has largely been assumed by the principal tendencies of liberation theology, and has received some enriching elaborations, which it is necessary to underline.

In the first place, the concept of the poor has been widened. The socioeconomic aspect of the poor remains, but it possesses concrete faces and specific oppressions, as in the case of blacks (racial oppression), of Indians (ethnic-cultural oppression), and of women (sexual oppression). These specific oppressions need to be captured in their theoretical and practical differences. Beginning from the Christological reading of poverty, there exists a recovery of the social status of the "lumpen," who were excluded from Marxist analysis. These constitute the poorest of the poor, like the lepers, the *boiafrias* (daily hired farm hands in Brazil), the marginalized and prostituted women, the abandoned and exploited children, those who are physically and mentally deficient, the *favelados* (slum dwellers), the squatters, etc. All of them have to start the process of liberation beginning from their specific oppressions. The poor themselves give an interpretation of their misery. Critical analysis is not put aside but enriched. Thus the poor understand themselves as children of God, created in the image and likeness of God, but at the same time they are disfigured, humiliated, and offended by their oppressions. This concrete reference is included in the more formal and scientific considerations of social analysis.

In the second place, the resistance of the poor against oppression and their struggle for liberation have been better understood. The oppressed cannot be considered only from the oppressor's point of view. We have to pay attention to the way they protest and react against oppression. In recent years, particularly through the contribution of CEHILA, the memory of the struggles of the poor, of their martyrdom, of their advances have been recaptured. The poor are also social actors in spite of the regime of submission, and their dreams of liberty and of a different society continue nourishing the resistance and the commitment for social transformation.

In the third place, special attention has been given to the pedagogical process in the journey to liberation. It starts from the bottom, from popular praxis, from the valorization of the vital knowledge of the people, from their communitarian forms of acting, from the values of their religiosity. In this process there is an attempt to live a real democracy. The leaders are formed without breaking contact with the communities.

The elements of Marxist social analysis are never taken by themselves as instruments of already completed knowledge. They are used starting from the liberating process of the poor, and because they are at the service of the poor, there is more freedom in the analysis.

C. The Importance of the Bible in the Hermeneutic of Liberation

After discerning analytically and concretely, Christians come to judge in the light of the Christian message. In the last few years the people increasingly have been appropriating the Christian scriptures. The Bible constitutes the great code for reading the oppressions suffered and also the source of inspiration for liberation and life.

First, the Bible is read beginning from the praxis of the poor, organized in their communities and in action/reflection groups. Not only the parts or verses which more directly address oppression/liberation are read. The whole Bible is read from the viewpoint of the poor who discover there the history of an oppressed people who in the light of faith sought to resist all oppression and subjection, and struggled for a free and liberated life. Evidently, the Exodus, the prophets, Jesus, and the apocalypse have a privileged place, but not an exclusive one.

Secondly, the liberative reading of the Bible considers with attention the material and social conditions in which the text was written. In this way, there exists a coincidence between the poor and their oppressions as they are reported in the Bible and the inhuman situation of the poor today.

In the third place, people rediscover the power of commitment and of transformation which is present in all of the Bible. It is important to arrive at personal conversion and social liberation. This is not to instrumentalize the scriptures, but to respect their nature and enter into their dynamism which is open to prophecy and to God's Reign, which comes from the future in the direction of the present. Thus, we are dealing with an interpretation which is not content with an explanation of the text, but which strives also for its application. The Bible is a book of life and not only of interesting stories.

Finally, the biblical reading is communitarian. It is done within the journey of liberation in community meetings, in the context of reflection about life and celebration. This ecclesiality constitutes the hermeneutical atmosphere and favors union in the struggle more than divergence of opinions.

The importance of the Bible in the struggle for liberation made it necessary to have more systematic and complete texts of support for the people and for pastoral agents. Thus, a popular commentary on the Bible is being published in Brazil with the collaboration of some Hispano-Americans; this work includes commentaries on all the biblical books. The growing interest of popular agents to learn the biblical languages (Greek and Hebrew) in order to better understand the liberating message of God, is observed with satisfaction.

D. The Constructive Task of the Theology of Liberation

Besides the deepening of biblical study, the systematization of the theology of liberation has advanced significantly during recent years. Likewise, some significant orientations have been affirmed within the common trends: always beginning with the oppressed looking for their liberation.

In the first place, there has been a more complete recapturing of the content of the great theological tradition. Not only have the Christology and ecclesiology been consolidated, but also the themes of the God of life and of trinitarian communion (the Holy Trinity as the best community), the spirituality of commitment, of struggle and martyrdom, the anthropology of the new woman and man, and the importance of the Spirit in the communities.

Latin American history, told from the point of view of the victims (the Indians, blacks, and other oppressed), has helped to define more concretely the task of evangelization, to discover the memory of the oppressed people, and to bring to light the value of their historical struggles. It also has helped a rethinking of pastoral action with respect to other social classes, which are evangelized in light of the preferential option for the poor.

A new field has been opened when we study more systematically the relation between theology and economics. This has permitted the unmasking of the idols of the capitalist system; it has clarified how we can be against them and in favor of the poor, and how we can know the true God who is alive and the giver of life. Starting with the living God we have discovered the basis of the option for the poor. It is born out of the proper nature of God. By being alive and the giver of life, God opts for the poor threatened in their life and condemned to "die before their time."

Both men and women have opened themselves to understand better the feminine dimension of the personal and the social. Some women have begun to do theology starting from their condition as women, historically and socially subjected to the patriarchal system and to a chauvinist tradition. Coming from this situation, new themes have emerged proper to the specifically feminine.

Finally, the theology of liberation is becoming more and more ecumenical. It is ecumenical in its origins, practices, and objectives. Oppression and liberation are not denominational. Oppression affects everybody in a distinct manner, and liberation is for all, beginning with the oppressed. Many Christian denominations, in the liberation theology mold, enter into deep communion in order to join their forces in implementing a common mission: the service of liberation.

III. CONTENT AND ORIENTATIONS

1. The poor are the central concern of liberation theology. This is not something completely new. This theme belongs to the heart of the gospel message. What is really new is the emphasis and the perspective. People as "impoverished" and not only poor have been presented as privileged theological or pastoral actors. To consider the poor as impoverished means to go to the roots of their condition. Their poverty is the result of social injustice. We can neither understand them nor love them unless we use the tools of sociological and economic analysis. The poor have many faces. It is urgent to perceive that their face is the face of the woman, of the Indian, of the black, or of the underprivileged and abandoned child.

The itinerary followed by the communities has made evident the oppression of women. In a society dominated by the male, their salaries are lower. Black and Indian women suffer multiple oppressions. Pastoral engagement with women who are poor requires new themes, like the importance of the body. A theology done by women and from the perspective of women who are poor is now taking shape in Latin America.

The poor not only have the face of the Indian, the black, the mestizo, and the mulatto. They also have special voices. Their religions and cultures offer contributions relevant to the liberation of peoples. To those faces are added others, each one with its own distinctiveness. When we perceive these differences with great depth, we come to believe in the radicalism of the theology which comes from the poor. The face of the God who is life is made more transparent and precise.

2. God created life. The experience of faith in the God of life, who, as a free gift, generates life in abundance, runs through the ecclesial tradition. It is an old ecclesial tradition and a universal tradition at the same time, becoming alive in the midst of the poor. The poor are killed; socio-economic exploitation degrades them in their condition as human beings; but in spite of this, they still can proclaim: "God lives!" The paschal mystery permeates the cries and groans of the oppressed. Each martyr is as if he or she were the last, the one who puts an end to injustice. Entire peoples proclaim with prophetic voice that God is a God of life.

The God of life is God the Father. But also in this sense there is a significant progress. After having overcome all the obstacles, the category of "God the Father" still is very provisional: it is not totally absent of androcentric influences. To speak of God as the God of life is one step forward, since it qualifies the experience of God.

3. The God who promotes life is celebrated with life. During recent years the liturgical dimension of the communities has been consolidated. These communities pray and celebrate with intensity. They dedicate them-

selves to sing their pain, their progress, and their utopias, because the poor value their poetry and their symbols. They evangelize through liturgy and consider theology as their own work. These strengthen the poor in their faith in the God of life.

The liturgical celebrations are experiences of great importance for the pastoral agents and theologians. They convert us to prayer. They make us more skeptical about the power of rational discourse. At the same time they invite us to run the risk of the mystical and the symbolical. The God of life celebrated in the liturgies of the people strongly influences our theology.

4. This experience of the God of life is not limited to liturgical celebrations. It strengthens witness in the midst of the historical processes. The militancy within the popular movement and in the political organizations is one consequence that is almost inevitable. On the other hand, the participation of Christians in political life forces some people to distance themselves from the Christian communities, and that can create divisions and internal contradictions. As a result of this, recently there has emerged the need to develop a theological reflection to accompany the political militancy of the members of the Christian community. The content of this reflection constitutes a proposal for a liberating political ethic.

5. The struggle is not only in the political field, outside of the churches. As it has been pointed out in the introduction, we also have had to defend ourselves. Attacks against liberation theology mark its trajectory from the beginning. There have been attacks against it from both Protestantism and Catholicism. Nevertheless, these attacks have intensified especially during recent years. The objects of these attacks have been principally Gustavo Gutiérrez and Leonardo Boff. The penalty of silence placed on the latter was the culmination of this process. In these circumstances it was necessary to defend and to justify the rights of faith of the theology of liberation.

In the light of these circumstances it has been clear how connected liberation theology is to the church. It is not an elaboration of freethinkers, but of theologians and pastoral agents integrated in ecclesial life.

In the same way, the debate on liberation theology shows how deeply rooted in the people the theologians are—they share their way of doing theology. Thus the communities have reacted with great dynamism to the debates on liberation theology. They have prayed and celebrated. The theology of liberation became a subject discussed in the streets, and it made the headlines in the newspapers. Liberation theology reached the public. In the face of debates and criticisms new theological perspectives were formulated. After the publication of the Vatican's instructions on liberation theology, new challenges were placed before us.

The debate helped to clarify the new focus, the new methodology of doing theology. Liberation theology is neither completed nor finished. It is a new point of view, beginning with the liberating praxis of the poor.

6. This fundamental reference to the liberating praxis of the poor

requires taking into account not only the popular struggles, but also the religious expressions of the poor. This subject is not a novelty for Catholicism, but constitutes a new demand for Protestantism. The Protestant theologians today understand that they have to be open in their theological reflection to the religious forms through which the poor express themselves.

Catholicism as well as Protestantism are invited by the poor of Latin America to understand that "modernization" is not limited to the academic erudition of the dominant groups. It is urgent to perceive the dialectical character of this modernization: alongside academic enlightenment, very often in tension with it, the wisdom of the workers is developed, which is presented in popular forms. This means the opposite of modernization. This was not perceived by those who proposed a "theology of culture" at the Catholic episcopal conference in Puebla. According to that proposal the great challenge to evangelization of Latin America was the urban culture, where science and technology are emphasized. That is the modernization of the oppressor. Together with it, a culture of the oppressed has been taking form. It is on this territory that the seeds of liberation grow. Therefore, it is necessary to consider the popular traditions and values, which are a privileged instrument of expression in the religiosity of the people.

7. This liberating theological journey is ecumenical. A liberation theology which is not ecumenical is a countersign. It is not even possible to formulate it in an exclusive manner. Its inclusive character is a mark of its origin. This ecumenical mark, however, is not always visible. There are few Protestants in Latin America. They are a minority. In these circumstances, it is normal that the Catholics predominate. Notwithstanding, an ecumenical solidarity actually prevails, with both groups working together, shoulder to shoulder. In ecumenism we practice dialogue. It is the openness one to another, the encounter with the other. Protestants and Catholics are converted to what is different in the other. All are discovered in their differences. There is, therefore, a mutual enrichment in the ecumenical process.

However, ecumenism does not limit itself to relationships between Catholics and Protestants. It does not exhaust itself in an interconfessional relationship. It transcends that. The dialogue with the poor is essential. In this relation between distinct confessional traditions and the resistance of the poor people, the more creative ecumenical interaction has taken place. In this specific area great surprises emerge. On one hand, the people come closer together. Different confessional communities discover that they are journeying in the same direction. On the other hand, when we return to consider the confessional differences in the light of popular practice, we discover how close are the confessions. The poor teach us to perceive the similarities through the confessional differences.

8. Liberation theology has been criticized for not being universal, but limited to a determined geographic horizon. Nonetheless, the conscience of liberation theology has a universal dimension. Because it is formulated

from the perspective of the poor and oppressed, it is universal, since poverty and oppression are worldwide phenomena. It is the opposite of the theology which is generally elaborated in the dominant centers, a theology which has a perspective of power and authority. In this sense, Western theology tries to establish limits on the theologies of the Third World, forgetting that it itself is limited. It pretends to be universal, and for this, it is dominating. The worldwide character of theology does not depend on a geographic perspective, but on its social and cultural options.

9. Finally, CELAM (Episcopal Conference of Latin America) has launched a proposal of formulating a "theology of reconciliation" in the Latin American context. In the face of the social struggles which shake the Latin American reality, this theology intends to underline the reconciliation of the classes in spite of the conflicts between them. In this case the perspective of the poor and oppressed is abandoned. Generally, the supporters of social reconciliation understand it from above to below. For the poor, reconciliation would mean resignation. Reconciliation through Jesus is a process which passed through the cross. The poor already have theirs: they are "the scourged Christ of the Indies." Or as was said in Chile on the occasion when two young people were burned alive by the oppressive forces: "Jesus burned among the youth." The cross also should be accepted by the rich. That is to say, the rich should accept the need to change, to repent, to leave aside dominating and share what they have accumulated through injustice. The need for justice dominates in the reconciliation of the cross. If it is not thus, "reconciliation" signifies oppression and maintenance of the status quo.

IV. COMMONALITIES AND DIVERGENCES AMONG THIRD WORLD THEOLOGIANS

For Latin American theologians, the knowledge of their realities and the dialogue with the theologies of other continents, especially through EATWOT, have been enriching and really decisive. Latin American theologians have discovered other realities, have learned to nuance their own experience in a global context, and have been challenged on how to talk about God starting from other cultures.

Dialogue is a painful and difficult process. It is also a very long process, because time is necessary to perceive the truth of the other and to accept other experiences challenging ours. EATWOT will really become a place of dialogue and enrichment when there is mutual trust among its members.

A. Common Elements

These are some of the common elements coming from the international conferences and from other experiences like readings, travels, encounters, etc.

1. *Peripheral theologies:* Theologies of the Third World belong to the margins of the world, in relation to the traditional centers of science, power, and the exclusive privilege of interpreting the gospel of Jesus. Historically these theologies have developed and are growing in the wide geographical and human spaces of the countries colonized and oppressed for centuries. When these countries became independent and their people started a process of self-development, Christians also stated their right to think their faith in the context of their own cultural and religious traditions.

Third World theologies break their links with historical and cultural models of Western civilization, which is considered as one particular experience. Even though it is true that social and ecclesial leaders of the Third World are an integral part of the Western way of life, the majority of the people live their religious experience in the context of their own inspiration and wisdom.

There is a break between these theologies and the official Catholic and Protestant model of only one universal interpretation of the gospel. It is true that there is only one lord and one baptism, but the inspiration of a Western theology is considered as a theological component of a whole way of domination. The new countries and cultures are not a "no man's land." The Spirit of God had been active and spreading its gifts of wisdom and life well before the Western minorities arrived. Cultural theologies express human plenitude and the divine vocation to celebrate God's presence in every country and every culture.

2. *Methodology:* These theologies are coming from suffering and humiliation. They are a sign of rebellion and protest against white domination and against models of Western development. At the same time they express a new way of doing theology arising from painful experiences. They are signs of the vitality of the young churches of the Third World. For this reason, they are not a carbon copy of European theology. They accept and recognize the authentic tradition of Jesus of Nazareth kept alive in the different confessions, but at the same time they want to reread the event of the Jews in the light of their own scriptures and native religious experiences.

Theology in the Third World is related to the life of the poor. People are becoming the center of new religious experiences—people who are emerging from their silence, looking for a new historical identity, and struggling against all forms of domination.

Third World theologies are related to the life and death of people. They are not elaborated mainly in academia or ecclesial institutions. They are developed by Christian communities; they are nurtured by their own cultural and liturgical experiences; and they confront the new idols of death, who want to replace the living God of Jesus.

The dialectical confrontation with the old Western model of theology is helping to develop a new sense of universalism. Our world has become diverse and pluralistic through the new techniques of communication.

Today there is more unity and at the same time more respect for richness and diversity. The world is growing closer to the universalism of the *oikoumenē*, and religion and theology are integral parts of this new vision. But at the same time, there are new forces of division, hate, and degradation.

Third World theologies cannot accept anymore the old universalism coming from Western civilization, ancient and failing. A new universality is arising with the new "ecumenical" interaction of religions and humanisms, expressing the divine vocation of all peoples. These theologies from the very beginning have developed as an ecumenical enterprise. They do not accept artificial divisions imposed by old missionaries confederated with colonizers. They also want to be open to the new expressions of their own religious traditions. They want to incarnate and inculturate the message of the gospel and enter in dialogue, attempting a new focus of authentic syncretism and synthesis.

3. *Content:* It is more difficult to talk about similarities in content precisely because we are talking of contextual theologies. However, there has been some progress in past years. Christians and theologians in the Third World have found common elements in celebrating God and rediscovering Jesus. In general, this progress has made more relevant that content of theology which meets the aspirations and needs of the people. Christian communities are more equipped to discern the presence of the Spirit in every context and culture. Hopefully, these common elements will be appreciated more clearly in dialogues in the future.

B. Differences

The differences among theologies of the Third World come out of their particular cultural and religious experiences. They have to be accepted and respected. Mutual enrichment among these theologies has been one of the best results of EATWOT's dialogue.

There are other differences imposed by old missionaries or by present ecclesial hierarchies. There are still in the Third World "conservative" and even "progressive" theologies which accept passively the forces of domination and do not interpret the aspirations of the people.

Moreover, among Third World theologians there are also differences. Sometimes mistrust, lack of respect, and imposition have affected negatively the dialogue and understanding. Thank God, in EATWOT these problems are being resolved. Some of the legitimate differences are as follows:

1. *Indigenous development:* Latin America is part of the Western world and has more continuity with its cultural and social traditions. Africa and Asia do not belong to that world and have kept their cultural identities. This difference has impelled Latin American theologians to pay more attention to and to reflect theologically on the oppression of Indians and black people on this continent.

2. *Presence of Christians:* While in Asia Christians are a minority group,

and in Africa they are growing steadily, in Latin America Christianity is part of the racial and cultural reality of the continent. Latin American theologians admire the oral traditions of Africa, the Negro spirituals of the United States, and the wisdom of the scriptures of the great religions of Asia.

3. *Analysis:* In Latin America, especially in the first stage, there was much emphasis on the use of analytical tools for social analysis. These have helped to uncover the mechanisms of oppression, which have prevented true love of neighbor, as seen in the parable of the Good Samaritan. Latin American theologians have been enriched by the other continents insisting on the analysis of cultural, racial, and sexual discrimination.

4. *Appreciation of other theologies:* Among Latin American theologians, theologies from Korea and Sri Lanka are highly appreciated. They also value the efforts of African theology and admire with interest the wisdom of traditional religions of Africa and Asia.

Through these commonalities and divergences there is a growing concern to build together a Third World theology, relevant to the dialogue of the peoples. The common elements will lead to a new theology, in continuity with the best traditions of the churches, but open to new developments in the Third World.

CONCLUDING PROPOSALS

The Latin American group presents two proposals for the consideration of the general assembly of EATWOT: (1) To select, translate, and disseminate basic texts of theology from each continent for the benefit of all the continents and regions; and (2) To invite visiting professors from other continents to promote more dialogue and better understanding of other theologies.

4

Report from the U.S. Minorities

I. SOCIO-POLITICAL AND CULTURAL REALITIES

A. A Comment on the Histories and Cultures of U.S. Minorities

No context of EATWOT members is more complex and less understood than that of U.S. minorities. Although most of our historical and cultural roots stretch back to the continents of Asia, Africa, and Latin America, we also have roots that have become deeply a part of the United States, the most dominant and oppressive capitalist nation among First World nations.

Native Americans: The original people of the area of what is today called the United States are the Indians. Like so many people whom the white Europeans encountered, they were nearly exterminated, and those who managed to survive have been pushed off their land and placed on reservations. Today they are the most oppressed and ignored people of all U.S. minorities. To retain their land from greedy capitalists so as to preserve their cultures and histories, Indians are currently engaged in legal battles with those capitalists.

In the popular mind of North Americans and in the discourse on U.S. history and politics, the indigenous people of this land are often invisible. Indians are defined by their absence from the dominant discourse about the meaning of U.S. life and culture. They are also often absent from the discourse among U.S. minorities who are challenging the dominant white understanding of North America. But the absence of Native Americans in our discourse is itself a "striking presence." For, when we search for the deepest meaning of our freedom in the United States, we also know that it can only be found in relation to the freedom of its original people.

Afro-Americans: No people has provided a greater challenge to the public understanding of the United States as "the land of the free and the home of the brave" than its citizens of African descent. Unlike Europeans who came freely to the Americas, Africans came against their will on slave ships and were sold as property. It is difficult for those who do not have a slave legacy to know what it means for a people to be defined as property. To be property means not only that your worth is defined in terms of your monetary value in a slave market; it also means that you and your descendants are not persons; and, thus, family ties can be disregarded as well as other aspects of dignity that human beings take for granted in a civilized society.

African presence in North America began in 1619. After 244 years of slavery, the sixteenth president of the United States, Abraham Lincoln, issued the Emancipation Proclamation in 1863. Although legal slavery ended for many slaves at that time and for all slaves two years later, the ordeal of being black in a white racist society merely moved into another ordeal which is often called segregation and which Martin Luther King referred to as "another form of slavery dressed up in certain niceties of complexity."

Black resistance began when the Europeans first tried to enslave Africans and has continued to this day. The idea that blacks were passive and freely accepted their oppression is a myth promoted by Europeans so as to justify their evil deeds. African resistance to slavery took many forms. It was collective and individual, violent and nonviolent, religious and secular in orientation. During the nineteenth century, most fighters against slavery were called abolitionists, and in the twentieth century they are often referred to as civil rights activists. Although representing only 10 percent of the population, Afro-Americans' history and culture have challenged the dominant, white capitalist idea of the United States as the land of freedom and democracy.

Hispanic Americans: Hispanic Americans have always been a part of the United States, but they have never been recognized or treated as ordinary citizens, probably because they became a part of the United States not through migration, but by way of conquest. Generally speaking, the Hispanics can be characterized as a people who have been *twice conquered, twice colonized, and twice mestisized.* The first process started with the arrival of the first European illegal immigrant in 1492 — Christopher Columbus. The second one started in the 1830s when the United States, during its great expansionist movement, took over and made its own 50 percent of Mexico (from California to Texas) and all of Puerto Rico in 1897. Thus the Mexicans and Puerto Ricans discovered themselves to be foreigners in their own land.

Because of the initial contacts which gave birth to what we today call the Hispanic Americans of the United States, Mexicans and Puerto Ricans in the United States have never had a sense of migration, but more one of having been a colonized people who, regardless of the passage of time, want their original traditions, language, and lifestyles to survive and flourish in the United States.

During this colonial existence, the Hispanics have been exploited economically, denied educational opportunities, effectively distanced from participation in the political system, portrayed as irresponsible and inferior by all the media of communication, kept out of the structures of society, and ignored by their church. For the most part, all the institutions of the United States have kept the Hispanics out and have functioned more against the people than in favor of them. Yet, in spite of the multiple obstacles and threats to a collective existence as a people, Hispanics have not only survived but have struggled to overcome.

The struggles for betterment and against injustice have always been a part of the life of Hispanics in the United States; however they have certainly intensified since the experience of World War II. Returning war veterans discovered that they did not enjoy at home in the United States the principles they had fought for abroad. The fight was on. *Ya basta* (that's enough) became the battle cry of the new struggles within the United States to bring about justice and equality on the home front. Young men and women started to enroll in law schools to learn how to challenge the institutions of society. Movements started from the barrios to the universities, from farmworkers to government employees, from political parties to church institutions—no institution in the United States was left unchallenged.

In spite of the many efforts, few really visible gains were made. Some Hispanics were elected to public office; the church named a few Hispanic bishops; the news media put a few brown faces on the screen; some made it in the professions and in business. Yet the very success of a few gave the false impression and security that Hispanics had really made it in the world of the United States. As a group, those who have found success have pretty well closed their eyes and ears to the suffering of the greater number of their people who are still poor, illiterate, and exploited. Today there are fewer Hispanics in higher education than ten years ago.

Furthermore, there is a new factor: the new Hispanic immigration since the time of the Cuban exodus, which includes many persons from the Caribbean and Central America who have fled economic and political oppression. Generally speaking these people come more with a sense of immigration than of having been colonized.

By the year 2000, it is estimated that Hispanics will number some 30 to 35 million or 11 to 12 percent of the total population of the United States. Some people have labeled this the quiet *reconquista,* for the native life of the land will return to flower once again within its own native soil.

New Immigrants: In recent years, the United States has received many immigrants from all parts of the world, but especially from Asia. Whereas originally most of the immigrants came through New York City, today they are coming through Los Angeles. In the Los Angeles area, 104 languages are in active use. The main ones are English, Spanish, Korean, Vietnamese, Cantonese, and Armenian. What is happening in Los Angeles is happening in all the great cities of the United States. One TV station in Los Angeles already has programs in English, Spanish, Arabic, Farsi, Armenian, Vietnamese, Korean, Japanese, Cantonese, and Mandarin.

B. A Comment on the Political Realities

Today the United States is experiencing a moment of great political revivalism and fundamentalism. During the Vietnam War, the people of the United States experienced a great sense of shame and guilt. The people were not accustomed to this and did not like it. Today, it seems that the people of the United States are trying to compensate for this by extolling a new Americanism. New patriots are emerging as was evident in the very popular symbolic image of Rambo-Reagan. The popularity of Presidents Reagan and Bush is an unquestioned fact. Once again, the civic-missionary mentality is found throughout the country. This new patriotic-religious consciousness is being nourished by the new religious fundamentalism which is flourishing in the country. There seems to be a definite relation between the political and religious fundamentalist revivalism which is taking place.

U.S. minorities live in a nation in which a recent president was one of the most popular presidents in its history while also being one of the most racist. There is no doubt that Ronald Reagan was the enemy of the Third World. His policies in Central America — arming the contras and describing them as "freedom fighters" — clearly symbolized where he stood in relation to the poor who are struggling for liberation in Third World countries. President Reagan's refusal to support strong economic sanctions against the apartheid regime in South Africa was further evidence of his active aid to the enemies of freedom. But in spite of his actions against freedom in the Third World, Ronald Reagan was still one of the most popular presidents in U.S. history.

The enormous popularity of Ronald Reagan raises questions about the nature of the American political process and the people who support it. How could Reagan be so popular when he was the enemy of the poor throughout the world? The answer to this question is not difficult to find if one carefully examines the history of politics in the United States. Most racist presidents in the United States have been popular, because the psyche of white Americans has been shaped by their attempts to exterminate the original people of the continent and to exploit others who later came without European heritage. To be racist has always meant to be patriotic. Thus, the resurgence of patriotism associated with Ronald Reagan's presidency was directly related to his racist domestic and foreign policy decisions, and in these matters George Bush is following in his footsteps.

It is revealing to note that one of the most popular presidents in U.S. history was one of the most unpopular among black citizens. Each time Ronald Reagan was elected president by a large popular vote (1980 and 1984), more than 90 percent of the black voting population cast their ballots against him. Blacks knew what Third World people knew: Reagan was the enemy of the poor and a friend of rich capitalists. We discovered that firsthand during his eight years as governor of California. Black people's rejection of the policies of Ronald Reagan and George Bush has been widespread and deeply felt. When a black Republican ran for governor of Michigan against a white Democrat whom Reagan supported, the majority of the black population again voted against Reagan, contributing to the white candidate's defeat.

Blacks are beginning to realize that their political future is best served by forging links with their Third World brothers and sisters who are fighting for a humane distribution of the material resources of the earth. Support for liberation struggles in the Third World (especially in South Africa and Central America) is increasing in the black community. Jesse Jackson's presidential bid did more to place Third World issues in the consciousness of black Americans, and before the nation as a whole, than all the actions and words of all the white candidates combined.

Just as rich elites combine their political forces in order to keep the poor in a subordinate state, the poor of the world must find ways to combine their political efforts in order to liberate themselves from poverty. U.S. minorities in EATWOT hoped that this organization would become an instrument to that end. For the powerlessness which Third World people feel in relation to the United States is analogous to what we minorities also feel daily as second-class citizens in this nation. Some blacks feel so politically alienated that they deny their American citizenship. They say, with Malcolm X:

> No, I'm not an American. I'm one of the 22 million black people who are the victims of Americanism, one of the . . . victims of democracy, nothing but disguised hypocrisy. So, I'm not standing here speaking to you as an American, or a patriot, or a flag-saluter, or a flag waver— no, not I! I'm speaking as a victim of this American system. And I see America through the eyes of the victim. I don't see any American dream. I see an American nightmare!

Hispanics have yet to wield anything like the political clout the blacks have been able to bring about. For the most part, Hispanics have been uninvolved in the political process and despite great drives for voter registration, many of the qualified voters have not exercised their right to vote and therefore have not made use of their potential political power. Many come from countries where the vote has been useless and therefore they do not take the vote seriously. They simply want to earn a living and stay out of trouble.

If Hispanics could be united, they could well be a significant force in the determination of political life in the United States. However, this will probably not be the case. Before, Hispanics experienced unity in their Catholicism and in their segregated existence. Today, they are divided religiously and by the various degrees of assimilation that the people have achieved. Any basis for ultimate unity of the Hispanics is rapidly disappearing. Many are convinced that the well-financed apostolic efforts of fundamentalists are more aimed at political division than at religious experience. The potential is great but the question remains: Will it ever be activated?

C. A Comment on the Economic Realities

In the beginning of the 1980s it was predicted that that would be the decade when ordinary good products would disappear from the market, giving way to either luxury or mediocre items. This certainly took place in the 1980s and is taking place as we enter the 1990s, as more and more people find out that they can afford less while fewer and fewer people find out that they can afford almost infinitely more. While some earn astronomical salaries, others begin to find out what it means to live in poverty.

Contrary to popular opinion among people in the United States and in other countries, blacks are worse off economically today than they were during the 1960s. The civil rights movement did not increase the life chances of poor blacks. In fact, at an alarming rate that staggers the imagination, blacks are consuming drugs, filling prisons, joining the military for economic survival, and hanging out on the streets of U.S. cities, searching for purpose and meaning in a world that has no place for them. They represent a high percentage of the unemployed, uneducated, and homeless. Black children are having babies at a rapid rate and in situations that provide little hope of a humane future. In short, economically the black community, as is true of other minorities, is in bad shape.

The black community is so desperate economically that it is now possible to begin to speak of a socialist alternative in the churches and other community contexts and receive a positive response. Black communities know that capitalism is an economic system that supports the rich and exploits the poor. The development of a highly visible black middle class has angered many poor blacks. The latter realize that being black does not necessarily place one in solidarity with the exploited and marginated.

Poverty is increasing rapidly among the Hispanics of the United States. In 1973, according to an August 19, 1986 article in *U.S. News and World Report,* there were 2.4 million Hispanics living in poverty, and in 1983 there were 4.2 million. In 1986, the news media reported that there were 5.2 million Hispanics living in poverty. Nearly two out of every five Hispanic children under the age of eighteen live in poverty.

Hispanic women are far worse off than the average Hispanic. The poverty level of households headed by Hispanic women rose from 52.9 percent in 1983 to 53.4 percent in 1984, and seven out of every ten Hispanic children living in a female-headed household in 1984 were living below the poverty level.

The rate of increase of poverty among Hispanic families is the highest for any racial or ethnic group in the United States. Given the new immigration laws which will hit the Hispanic undocumented workers in the country (two to three million) in a brutal and harsh way, it is certain that the increase in poverty will be far greater than in previous years. Yet the leadership of the Hispanics seems to be ignoring this painful reality.

D. A Comment on Cultural Realities

No one has described the paradox of black identity in the United States with greater insight than W. E. B. DuBois in his classic statement of 1903:

> It is a peculiar sensation, this double consciousness, this sense of always looking at one's self through the eyes of others, of measuring one's soul by the tape of a world that looks on in amused contempt and pity. One ever feels this two-ness—an American, a Negro; two souls, two thoughts, two unreconciled strivings; two warring ideals in one dark body, whose dogged strength alone keeps it from being torn asunder.

The problem of identity acutely felt by blacks is an experience common to most U.S. minorities. Insofar as they live in a nation which they did not make or control, the two-ness which DuBois described is a part of their reality.

One side of most minorities' two-ness is an identity whose origin is found in the Third World. The great majority of minorities come from Africa, Asia, and Latin America. This is one aspect of our commonality with our brothers and sisters in the Third World. We are culturally Third World people.

The other side of our two-ness is that we are also citizens of the most powerful capitalist nation in the world. This is an important difference from our brothers and sisters of Africa, Asia, and Latin America. This difference creates a great paradox in our existence. Some minorities, in an effort to overcome their feelings of rejection and inferiority, will become "exaggerated Americans," becoming superpatriotic in their commitment to the values of capitalism. Other minorities affirm their Third World identity and express their solidarity with the poor of Asia, Africa, and Latin America.

Like the poor of the Third World, the masses of our people are poor. But, unlike the poor of Asia, Africa, and Latin America, we do not represent the majority on our continent. We are a small minority searching for our place in a society that has no place for us. Our uniqueness is precisely in our minority status, for we are often ignored or pushed aside in our own country; and because we are small in the midst of the strongest country in the world, we are equally ignored or not even thought about when the problems of poverty and exploitation in the Third World are being considered. Thus we are the permanently excluded other. Yet as such, we can be the vehicle for dialogue since we are at one and the same time citizens of the world fellowship of the poor and citizens of the strongest nation in the world—exclusively neither, yet fully part of both!

II. RELIGION AND THE CHURCHES

The significance of religion and the importance of the churches are deeply felt among minorities in the United States. For the original people of the continent, Christianity is not the most dominant religious expression. It is often known as the "white man's religion" which had little respect for the gods who had sustained the indigenous Americans before Europeans came to the continent.

For the blacks, too, their religion has been important in empowering them in their struggle for survival and resistance. Black religion has been characterized by two elements: its African heritage and its encounter with Christianity through the preaching of white missionaries. With these two elements, blacks developed a distinctive religion that is neither exclusively Christian (when Christianity is defined by European definitions) nor primarily African (when African is defined by the traditional religions of Africa). Black religion is a perspective on the Christian faith that has been developed out of black peoples' struggle to liberate themselves from the oppression of whites.

From this independent religious expression that had its origin in slavery, independent churches have been developed as well. The oldest black churches were founded in the late eighteenth century, and they played significant roles in the abolitionist and insurrectionist movements of the nineteenth century. Gabriel Prossor, Denmark Vessey, and Nat Turner were prominent revolutionists who used religion in their resistance movements.

Martin Luther King, Jr., and Malcolm X are twentieth-century examples of blacks using religion in the fight for freedom. Black theology must be understood in the context of black religion which gave birth to independent black churches. Without black religion and black churches committed to black liberation, there would be no black theology of liberation.

Hispanic religion, like black religion, can be defined by two elements— its native American heritage and its encounter with white missionaries. However, it differs from black religion in two ways: (1) the indigenous religions of Hispanics' native ancestors appear to have been quite different from traditional African religions; and (2) the missionaries to native Americans were marked by all the characteristics of the Iberian Catholicism of that period, which was quite different from the Catholicism or Protestantism of the rest of Europe.

The Hispanic religion of the masses is a direct contact with and celebration of God's presence without the intermediary of the institution or the sacraments of the church. The people, generally speaking, tolerate the clergy but do not consider them to be a part of their ordinary religious expression. The clergyperson always appears as a distant other and not as one of the people. Hence the clergy appear more as icons than ministers.

Like black religion, Hispanic religion seeks to express itself through good congregational music enriched by dynamic preaching. Unlike black religion, it is deeply rooted and dependent upon sacred rites and expressions which keep it in continuity with its ancient past. Furthermore, there is one major difference from black religion: Hispanics have never had their own men and women to serve as their ordinary pastors — religious expression and church attendance have not been one and the same thing, but have often taken place apart from each other. Even though over 30 percent of all U.S. Catholics are Hispanics, less than 2 percent of the total clergy are native-born Hispanics. Hispanics in the United States have virtually no churches, seminaries, colleges, or church institutions that they can truly call their own. The only exception is the Mexican American Cultural Center in San Antonio, Texas. Thus we cannot really speak of an Hispanic theology of liberation. Small, isolated efforts are taking place, but on the whole, it is not yet happening.

Whereas blackness has served as the ultimate bond of identity and unity for the blacks, popular *Catolicismo* (deep-rooted cultural Catholicism) has served as the ultimate bond of unity and identity for the Hispanics. Blackness has been to the Afro-Americans what *Catolicismo* has been for Hispanic Americans. Blacks have been able to affiliate with different churches while remaining black, but for Hispanics, affiliation with different groups which destroy their basic Catholic symbolic system has divided the people at the deepest level of their existence.

With the rapid expansion of churches which destroy the deep, Catholic symbolic system which has served as the ultimate ground of existence of the Hispanic, two very important and fundamental questions arise: Can Roman Catholicism, with its rigid insistence on an ordained male-only clergy which has traditionally excluded the Hispanics, respond today to the needs of Hispanic Catholics who want and have a right to a clergy of their own? Can Protestantism give up its fundamentally Nordic-European symbolic system and assume unto itself the mestizo-Catholic symbolic system of the Hispanic, so that it can save and liberate without destroying the very soul of Hispanic identity — and worst of all, destroy it in the name of Christian salvation?

Hispanic Catholics are awakening and demanding full participation in Roman Catholicism. Protestantism is actively recruiting Hispanics. What will be the basis for Hispanic identity and unity in the future?

The new immigrants who are arriving today in the United States are bringing their own native ministers with them and erecting ethnic churches. For the time being, these churches serve the needs of the people quite well.

How they will respond to the needs of future generations, only time will tell.

The United States is rapidly becoming a multiethnic country. The basic Nordic-Protestant ethos will no longer be the unifying base of U.S. culture. A new base will emerge and the minorities will face the choice of simply melting into the dominant culture or making their own significant contribution to the build-up of a new multiethnic society such as the world has never known. There is no blueprint for this, and the minorities seem to have no real effective power to bring about change. Yet, it is precisely out of this apparently impotent situation that we dare to dream and to risk creating something really new! This is the mission and unifying element of all the suffering and impoverished minorities of the United States—out of our nothing to help create something new.

III. DOING THEOLOGY OUT OF MINORITY (BLACK) WOMEN'S EXPERIENCE

By Jacquelyn Grant

A. Doing Theology on Black Women

Black women, wherever they are, often find themselves involved in various struggles simultaneously. This is true of all Third World women, who are often concerned not only with the great struggle for the socio-political, cultural, and religious liberation of their people as a whole. Many of them are now recognizing the additional burden they must bear as they fight the limitation and sometimes the blatant oppression placed upon them by virtue of their gender.

The same is true of Third World women living in a First World context. Ethnic minorities in the United States increasingly find themselves on two battlefronts. On the one hand, Asian-American, Native-American, Hispanic-American, and African-American women all struggle with their men for human dignity. On the other hand, they have begun to band together for solidarity as women to reject the historic attitude of machismo which has its origin in patriarchal society.

These comments are related to African-American women, sometimes known as Afro-American women, and most often referred to as black women in the United States.

Who is the black woman? The black woman is one who is often misunderstood and mislabeled. This happens in the white community, in other Third World communities, and even in the black (especially male) community. Let us briefly indicate how this occurs in these three instances.

1. In the white community, black people in general and black women in particular are perceived as having been created to be at the disposal of white people. Perhaps this is one reason why even in postslavery times,

black people and black women are largely located in service-oriented jobs. Proportionately, even today black women make up the majority of domestic servants in the United States. This is true partially because of the relationship between the white and the black, which is characterized by white superiority and black inferiority.

Because of this, we are cautious when we begin to address the question of black women. Black women find themselves in the position of having to affirm the need for the liberation of women from oppression, while at the same time making a distinction between the struggle of white North American women and black North American women. This is so because the lived reality of these two groups of women has been so radically different. In fact we can argue that they have lived in two different worlds.

One is the world of the slave master, the other is that of the slave; one world is marked by privilege, the other by underprivilege; in one world there is an experience of (at least relative) accessibility to the benefits of the system, in the other an experience of inaccessibility to those benefits. One is a white world, the other a black world.

These differences are related to the fact that while white women are victimized by gender oppression, they are active participants in other forms of oppression. Black women have stepped forth to say that integral to any significant understanding of human liberation is an analysis (or analyser) that addresses the various forms of oppression reflected in the lives of black women and others who are oppressed even by the oppressed.

2. Black women's lives are complex to say the least. This is reflected in the fact that they are often mislabeled in other Third World communities. In relation to other Third World communities, black women find themselves in a precarious position of being "in, but still out." This is so because many Third World women assess black women's situation on the mere fact that they live in the First World. Yes, black women are in, but they are still out. They live in the First World, but because they are not a part of mainstream North America, they are still essentially out. Perhaps it could be said that black women are First World people living under Third World conditions. However we feel it more accurate to say that they are Third World people living in a First World context.

Why make this claim? African-Americans were not brought to America for a better life. They were not among those ethnic peoples who emigrated to the new world for religious freedom or economic advancements. They were torn from their land. They were captured, beaten, bribed, tricked, threatened with death and torture, imprisoned and crowded on ships, even one named *Jesus;* they were brought to the new world and forced to live a life of slavery for the personal, political, and economic advancement of white people. Families were torn apart, cultures were threatened and often destroyed, religious ties were broken, and slaves were presented with an oppressive religion designed to keep them in their place. They were taught the catechism to ensure an understanding of this:

Who made you?
God made me.
Why did God make you?
To serve my earthly master.

Clearly, the situation of Afro-Americans in general and Afro-American women in particular requires more than lumping their experience together with that of the colonizers; it demands more than categorizing their experience and the colonizers' experience into one socio-political context—i.e., that of the First World.

3. Whereas black women freely participate in the struggle for liberation of black people in general, they nonetheless affirm the belief that a chain is only as strong as its weakest link; none of us is free until all of us are free. Where a community directs a disproportionately small amount of its resources to more than half of its people, liberation cannot happen for that community. Realizing this, black women are challenging black men to be faithful to their claim that liberation has its origin not in a patriarchal structure, but in the divine reality. While insisting that the black liberation movement recognize the contribution of women toward the struggle, they also insist that the broader struggle of black women be addressed.

Hence, who is the black woman? In the North American context, she is the one who is most likely to be underemployed and unemployed (especially the young or teenage black female); she is more likely to be on welfare and victimized by the welfare state; she is more likely to be the single head of a household, and to live below the poverty line; she is more likely to be victimized by violent crime including rape; she is more likely to be blamed for the "pathology of the black community" (blaming the victims).

B. Implications for Theology

Black women's situation of oppression results from the convergence of racism, sexism, and classism. The critical questions which black women theologians bring to the theological discussion table are: How is theology done out of a context which is multifaceted? How is it possible to do holistic theology so that one aspect of one's experience (communal or individual) is not negated or ignored in order to affirm another? On the other hand, how is it possible to do theology out of the contradictions of race, sex, and class without negating or minimizing the importance of any part?

Black women theologians are moving toward the development of a womanist perspective in theology. Womanist theology (or black feminist theology) takes the best of black liberation and feminist theology to formulate a perspective which is more holistic in scope and more adequate in addressing the needs of people whose oppression is multifaceted.

The preceding comments were written from black women's experience. The experience of other minority women in the United States would be similar in some respects and different in others.

PART II

COMMONALITIES

5

Commonalities: An Asian Perspective

Mary Rosario Battung

INTRODUCTION

The six major and interrelated commonalities that I will discuss below
are culled from the three continental reports. The passages I quote from
those reports are those that make the common realities more vivid and
graphic, not only for one region but for all the Third World.

I. THE REALITY OF POVERTY

In all three continents, poverty is all-encompassing. There are the enormous disparity and glaring unequal distribution of wealth and power in
Asia, and the widening gap between the rich and the poor has endemic
consequences that reverberate in the economic and political life of the
nations. In Africa there is the paradox that despite the huge natural wealth,
the continent is one of unequal chances and of misery. A small minority in
Latin America has the highest consumption and accumulation rate, which,
because of its ostentation, is an insult in the face of poverty of the great
majority who barely survive.

As regards Asia in particular, the massive and grinding poverty of large
numbers of people despite presumptuous claims of economic progress and
economic miracles attests to these basic socio-economic facts: the enormous
disparity and the glaringly unequal distribution of wealth and power, the
widening gap between the rich and the poor, and the endemic consequences
which this entails in the social, economic, and political life of Asian nations.

II. EXPERIENCE OF COLONIALISM AND NEOCOLONIALISM

The majority of the countries in these three regions have been colonized
by the Western countries, and, though these countries have gained their

independence, they are presently under a neocolonialist system. In these countries, neocolonialism walks under the guise of technical assistance and cooperation. The authors of the African Report describe Africans' experience, which can very well be true for the peoples of the other two continents as well:

> African unity is especially hindered by the situation whereby Africa lives in a permanent state of military, cultural, economic, political, and ideological occupation by the most antagonistic powers of the world. . . . All those in power in Africa are real hostages at the mercy of foreign powers through the mechanisms of military assistance. . . . New structures of oppression . . . make [the Africans] politically, economically, and culturally poorer and poorer and more and more dependent. We call this whole system: an anthropological pauperization system.

III. NEOCOLONIAL ECONOMY

Neocolonial policies abide in the economies of these Third World countries. In Asia, the imperialist powers, principally through the operation of transnational financial capital and multinational corporations, continue their structural and material control and manipulation of the economies. The result is severe debt crisis and dependence on the dictation of international financial institutions. The authors of the Latin American Report describe this as a mortgaged future wherein the payment of the large interest on the debt is a great burden on the working masses. The Africans see the world monetary system as a skillful machinery of exploitation, domination, and pauperization of the Third World countries.

These neocolonial policies in the three regions are manifested in their export-oriented production, exportation of labor and the migration of workers, and the economic underdevelopment that is at the same time social underdevelopment. These policies, supported by structural machineries, succeed in impoverishing the majority and enriching a small minority.

Given the variety of colonial experience, Asian countries at present are mostly neocolonial economies, structurally and materially controlled and manipulated by the economic superpowers. The result is "economic miracles," debt crisis, export-oriented production, unemployment, and migration of workers.

As a result of these factors, few can claim economic sovereignty and fewer still can sustain productive growth and economic stability without having to rely on the beneficence and "assistance" of outside and more powerful countries.

IV. POLITICAL REALITY

Because a small minority control the economy, it stands to reason that the majority, the impoverished masses, are excluded from any meaningful participation in the decision-making processes of society and in the political structures of the nations in these three regions.

Seemingly the countries are independent, but this presumed achievement of political independence is largely a farce. Imperialistic dictation from without propagates the national security state ideology and militarization which see to the continuance and entrenchment of political systems of repression within. Thus there is the subjugation of popular movements and organizations; military values, ideology, and patterns of behavior achieve a dominating influence on the political, social, economic, and external affairs of the governments.

The result of all this in Asia is that "democratic space" is narrow. Authoritarianism, political structures of oppression and dominance, the violation and restriction of basic human rights and civil liberties, foreign intervention, and the absence of authentic democratic political institutions through which popular will and sovereignty can be expressed—all these are the dominant political realities of the region. Further, militarization continues as a result to be entrenched not only as a mode of political rule but also as a way of life in the regions.

Beyond these very direct expressions of militarization, however, there is the process, mentioned above, whereby military values, ideology, and patterns of behavior continue to achieve a dominating influence on the external affairs of the Asian state. It is a process which has begun to seep not only into the political life but also into the structures of social, cultural, and educational life of the Asian countries. Violations of human rights, subjugation of popular movements and organizations, suppression of dissent and opposition, summary arrests, and even summary killings have become almost standard operating procedure in the political life of most Asian societies. The values of obedience, subservience, and "cooperation" which are predominant in the military ethos are equally becoming inculcated in the cultural and educational life of Asian societies.

These socio-economic and political realities have exacerbated and provided new ingredients to the traditional sources of social conflict, such as the suppression of minorities, the tension between religious groups, and the rivalries between ethnic and tribal loyalties within the countries of the region.

The continuance and entrenchment of political systems of repression, e.g., the national security state, are common, but the specific expressions of this may vary.

V. THE IDEOLOGICAL QUESTION

There is an ideological struggle in the countries of these three regions as represented by the socialist challenge.

As regards Asia, there are the intense ideological rivalries and the rivalries between the superpowers that have their peculiar flavor in the region and within each of the Asian countries. Witness the military bases, the Vietnam War, the "red scare," and the political divisions.

The challenge of the socialist models is present in the Asian region not only in theory but in the actual existence of socialist societies.

The ideological question represented by the socialist challenge is present in all of the Third World, but the peculiar political manifestation of this issue in the political division of countries such as Korea is peculiar to Asia.

VI. POPULAR MOVEMENTS

A very positive reality in the three regions is the presence of popular movements of social transformation and political change, movements which work for justice and liberty for all and which are concerned about democratic organization. This is the challenge presented by the oppressed people in the political field. They are no longer silent. They are organized and militant with a new project for society.

CONCLUSION

The Third World regions are experiencing a situation of great stress and unrest that is born out of the continuing and intensifying entrenchment of structures of repression and dominance on the one hand, and the rising movement and organization of popular struggles on the other. It is within this context of stress and contradiction that theological reflection must take place.

With specific reference to Asia we can say that amidst the persisting structures of economic poverty and dependence, uneven development within and among the various countries of the region, political repression and dominance, ideological conflict, and foreign incursion, there are popular movements of social transformation and political change that have grown in varying degrees and importance in different countries. These also constitute a major component of the socio-economic and political landscape of the region.

As to the religious landscape: the Asian religions have a common humanizing core of teachings concerning personal, moral, and social life. They all stress the value and need of unselfishness and detachment from material things. They teach compassion, concern for the other, sharing of possessions, love for the family, respect for the elders, care of nature, and right

conduct in personal and public life. These present occasions for self-purification and for serving human beings in their needs. This core of common
values can be the bases for integral human liberation and for cooperation
in building human communities in our pluralist societies of Asia. In working
for the common human concerns, base communities or action groups can
deal with issues as they arise in society.

The impact of the religio-cultural factors is notable in Asia. While the
basic motivations of the Asian religions and cultures are other-centered
and liberative, there are also harmful and enslaving aspects of these religions and cultures.

In the relationship of the sexes, the religions have had both liberative
and oppressive aspects.

Integral liberation demands an inner personal and group psychotherapy
that can help individuals and peoples to be free from inhibitions, fears, and
myths. The religions have been powerful critiques of injustice, inequality,
corruption, and authoritarianism.

In summary, the theological task in relation to Asia's politico-economic
reality has to do with the articulation of how and in what manner the
popular struggle for liberation and social transformation meets and coincides with the purpose of God. Such an articulation becomes a critical
"principle" by which the life of the church is assessed, including its "traditional" understanding of theology and spirituality. Such an articulation
would as well clarify critically the issue of who does theology and for what
purpose, and would redefine the meaning of Christian praxis and pastoral
action in the world.

In all these continents, theological reflection needs to be complemented
by an overall study and strategizing in relation to world capitalism, the
socialist countries, and the directions of the churches as a whole. The
continental approach being generally used may not bring out adequately
the global dimensions of the contemporary challenges to the peoples of the
Third World and to their doing theology today.

6

Commonalities: An African Perspective

Mercy Amba Oduyoye

Having read the paper on Africa's realities, I would like to make a few supplementary remarks before going on to the subject of commonalities. The paper does not contain illustrative material on the vastness and variety that is Africa from Cape to Cairo and on to Bojador. Southern Africa and most of English-speaking Africa are absent, yet even what we have hints at the complexities involved in the task of speaking about "the realities of Africa." West Africa differs from East and both differ from Southern. If we had had data on Central Mediterranean Africa and Madagascar, we would have presented you with Africa divided as it is by the Sahara, by colonial languages, and by apartheid. Varied as the scene is we can still speak of Africa. In spite of the difficulties of communications imposed by internal political arrangements of various countries, the linguistic barriers created by colonialism, and the logistic barrier of lack of adequate infrastructure for linking up our nations, we can speak as a continent. Africa's own development has been high-jacked by European expansionist policies leaving Africa to reassert its place in human civilization.

I would also have it recorded that there are several theologically trained women in English-speaking Africa whose struggle to be a part of the theological scene totally escapes EATWOT and the African Report. Several women from these countries are ordained ministers in the Western churches (i.e., they are Methodists, Presbyterians, Baptists, and Anglicans). After the United Nations decade on women, none can hide the existence and contribution of African women under the cloak of complementarity. There are real and deep unresolved issues in the extent, nature, and quality of women's participation in Africa's development and with regard to women's development per se. All EATWOT regions have made conscious efforts to include women in the analysis of the realities that inform and stimulate the theological enterprise.

The events in South Africa can be adequately interpreted only by South Africans; suffice it to say that in that arena, the very meaning of "humanity" is being defined. Racism with all its complex roots and manifestations is being exposed. The question is do we have *one humanity*? Let a South African speak.

INTRA-AFRICA

In spite of all this we are able to speak of what is common to African countries. Almost all African countries experience deep linguistic barriers. Some are indigenous while others have been imposed by colonization. Most official languages are foreign to the people who use them. The most trenchant and mischievous of these barriers is that between those who use French and those who use English. African writers like Ngugi Wa Thiongo (Kenya) and Wole Soyinka (Nigeria) have been suggesting that if Africa has to use "imposed" languages, then perhaps it is better to use Swahili, which was created on the African soil. The issue remains.

All of Africa is one in the experiences of neocolonial economies. The skillful machinery of exploitation set up by world monetary systems is like a rainbow that begins in the Mediterranean and ends where South Africa ends. All African countries are in the throes of social crises created by modern technology, modernization of traditional societal structures, and the multinational culture generated and promoted by the modern mass media. The crises created by certain legal structures, especially on the level of "personal law," have reached a distressing pitch where women's rights are concerned.

Having three main religions all vying for the soul of Africa has only added to the social crises. The most devastating to my mind is the type of Christianity being promoted by certain Western countries. It can be substantiated that the very people who own the wealth of the multinationals also sponsor this type of Christianity that orientates Africans toward buying into the capitalist system so that they may serve as its labor force and cannon fodder for its militarism. This religion is nothing short of the demonic. As theologians we are concerned with the impact of Christianity, for it claims 28 percent of Africa's population. We do Christian theology in a context that has 41 percent Moslems and 31 percent practitioners of Africa's own indigenous religions. We cannot ignore the Islamic revival that is spreading in Africa; neither can we close our eyes to the inseparability of Africa's religion from African culture and its impact on Christianity and Islam alike. Theology in Africa has to be dialogical. Christian theologians in Africa have to note that Africa's religion may not be expansionist but it does have a deep hold on the African soul. That it is not organized to proselytize does not mean that it can be ignored with impunity.

INTER–THIRD WORLD

Looking at the regions of EATWOT, one is struck by the similarities between Africa and Asia on the question of doing theology in a multireligious context. Religio-cultural realities are strongest where traditional religions and cultures have resisted the European attempt to Europeanize the whole world. Popular religious cults throughout the Third World are witnesses to the resistance to the hegemony of Western Christianity and Western culture. Even Latin America retains strong African and Native American religions. Brazil, Cuba, and Haiti provide us with lively examples.

We have common experiences as peoples facing socio-economic and political challenges. We EATWOT members have noted the role of foreign ideologies in our countries. We are aware of the economic dependency syndrome and the per capita income idea which only serves to mask the abject poverty in which the vast majority lives. This poverty is the most striking commonality of the Third World and a very crucial one. It raises the question of what humanity worships—the God of life or idol of gold. Economic success and high (or rather wasteful) standards of living are expressions of what the West believes to be truly human living. However, this style of life breeds racism, impoverishes other peoples' humanity, and sets up two humanities—those who live as if they own the earth and those who have to live as if they are owned by those usurpers of God's right.

In the face of these realities common to the Third World, we find a variety of theological responses, some of which are general and may be considered as commonalities, i.e., points at which Third World theologians may do joint work or at least collaborate to seek instruments for reaching further convergences. The living religions of Africa and Asia call for conscious incorporation of theologies other than the Christian into the factors that lead to theological statements, especially as regards Christology. This is very urgent because the inadequacy of traditional formulations of Christology becomes more evident as we study the religio-cultural realities of these two continents. African charismatic Christianity, folk religions, and the spirituality of Latin American base communities are all indications that theologies and Christologies other than the Euro-American are what enable people to cope with the unknowns and imponderables of human living. What the Asian Report calls the "humanizing core of teachings concerning personal, moral, and social life" is found not only in the "organized world religions" but also in Africa's religions and parts of the Latin American region, notably Brazil and among the minorities. The need for a relevant and energizing Christology must become an EATWOT concern.

Third World theologians are agreed that theology must be liberative and has to be a critique of "injustice, inequality, corruption, and authoritarianism." It must decry patriarchy and all that robs persons of their dignity as human beings. Working together on Christology with a strong consciousness of other religions, we may be able to contribute to purging the religio-cultural realities we experience of their antiliberation aspects, as well as contribute to the appreciation of cultures that European imperialism and colonialism maligned in order to destroy. It is true that Latin America serves as an example of how complex this Euro-Christian takeover can become. It is also true that modern technological culture invades our regions, but we are convinced by the "death refusal" stance of African culture that what is beautiful and liberative cannot be submerged forever.

A new hermeneutic for reading the Bible has surfaced in all EATWOT regions. Questions of the universality of the Bible and the nature of its authority rise out of our experience of other religions and emphasize the need for re-examining the "universality of Christ" and the Christian affirmation of the "uniqueness" of Christ. Theological responses from EATWOT regions and from Christian feminists underline the urgency of this need.

In undertaking this task, we begin at our common methodology of the-ologizing as people who feel in our bodies not just our own hearts but the pain of others. We theologize together and individually from our suffering and humiliation. We stand by our prior agreements to do theology and live our faith from the energy that flows from ecumenism and to which we pray our theology should make a contribution. Together we define poverty, in the comprehensive understanding of the phenomenon, as whatever robs human beings and groups of peoples of their humanity. All who are impov-erished because the culture they created has been trampled upon by others, all whose right to be human is challenged by socio-political, economic, and religious structures and demands that humiliate, all who have to struggle to have their humanity recognized and respected—all these *are poor*. The-ology done in the ambiance of EATWOT concerns itself with eradicating this "anthropological poverty."

We are agreed in the recognition of "commitment as the first act of theology" and that the doing of our theology is anchored in a method that involves us in action and reflection that issue in theological formulations that in turn empower us and others to further action and reflection. We are agreed on the necessity to read the signs of the times as Jesus recom-mended and to "reread" our ancestors as we go along, having learned the necessity to do this from Africa's religions as from others. We do recognize differences in our analysis and our methodology, but the convergences are striking and invigorating—hence the need for us to move to a stage of corporate theologizing across EATWOT regions.

We hold in common the need to retain our church base. Our churches differ considerably both as denominations and as regional expressions in their stance on the realities in which they find themselves. They differ in their involvement in theology and in the liberation process. They differ in their responses to the situations on which we agree. We belong to these churches. For some situations this is an asset, for others it is a challenge.

But we agree that the church of Christ is God's instrument for the liberation of the human spirit and for demonstrating the first fruits of God's Reign. On this commonality we root ourselves in our churches and pray that we, together and as individuals, become instruments of God's Reign on earth.

7

Commonalities: A Latin American Perspective

José Míguez Bonino

In 1976, at the founding meeting of EATWOT in Tanzania, it was already possible to discern commonalities and divergences among Third World theologies and to see the need for encounter and cross-fertilization. Three articles reporting on the birth of EATWOT illustrate very clearly how coincidences and points of disagreement were discerned at that time. Perhaps the most interesting thing is that the authors—coming from three different areas—fundamentally agree in their assessment.

James Cone[1] finds several elements "in common": the struggle for justice, a critique of Western theologies, the affirmation of liberation as the central core of the gospel, a rereading of the Bible in the light of the hermeneutical privilege of the poor, and the identification of theology as "a second act." When he speaks of differences, Cone comments: "Africans accented indigenization, Latins stressed class analysis, and Asians focussed on religious pluralism."

O. K. Bimwenyi[2] centers on the unity in the theological approach. There is, he says, a basic agreement: "it is time" for the Third World theologians to develop their own approach to theology; we have reached "the end of the illusion of the universal, all-inclusive discourse." Third World theologians must claim their right to do their work from within their own context; in fact, there is no other way of doing it; hence the falseness of the claim to universality of North Atlantic "academic" theology. To this context corresponds an epistemological shift: commitment as the indispensable organ of knowing. In commitment, there is "a militant reading of the Bible" together with an analysis of the situation. Rather than specifying differences, Bimwenyi poses a problem for further work: "Christianity and national religions." In other words, the relation of unity to plurality, of universality and locality.

Finally, D. S. Amalorpavadass[3] summarizes the commonalities at the start, calling attention to the "sense of belonging" together of Third World theologians. But this "sense" has some concrete, common aspects: reflection starting from reality and a committed praxis, the interdisciplinary and dialectical character of theology, and an awareness of the reality of evil. He relates commonality and difference when he speaks of the need for understanding the reality of the situations in order to minister to the totality of human life, but adds that there is a need to "address the socio-cultural in addition to the socio-economic and political" in clear reference to different emphases of the different groups. Amalorpavadass also raises the issue of worship and spirituality as a dimension that must be explored more vigorously.

I have begun with these memories of the beginnings because ten years later, the Mexico meeting is still basically dealing with the same issues, both in terms of commonalities and divergences. One may, in fact, wonder whether we have not fallen into a sort of "stereotyping" which, instead of deepening the reflection, blocks the road to a common work and provides an easy and superficial sense of self-identity by contrast to the different groups in EATWOT. One may further wonder whether that stereotyping does not become a tool for political struggle within EATWOT. If there is some truth in these suspicions, we should try to avoid this trap by reorganizing the consideration of commonalities and divergences.

I am not suggesting that the commonalities and divergences indicated in these articles are not real. It was very important to single them out at the beginning in order to explore them more deeply and to lay the ground for common work. But it is also true that in ten years of work at the continental and intercontinental levels, theological work has progressed; cross-fertilization has taken place; and, therefore, the initial characterizations need to be rethought. A careful reading of the reports presented to the Mexico meeting shows quite clearly that we can today find much more clearly our common ground and task and see differences in relation to such common endeavor. In fact, it is not a question of "inflating" commonalities and suppressing the awareness of divergences, but of realizing that commonalities and divergences are not fixed sets of issues, that divergences exist within our commonalities, and that there are uniting factors within our divergences. It is in this sense that I suggest an approach to the "common" among us. (Other articles will deal with the question of divergence.)

It could be said that the basic commonality is a common experience: that of being Third World. The expression, as we know, is ambiguous and debatable. The discussion about what "Third World" means, about its limits, and about who belongs, will continue. But there is scarcely any doubt that people clearly know whether or not they belong to the Third World. How different peoples "feel" that experience and how they account for it in analytical terms certainly differ. But it surely is a common "experience." Moreover, while the "commonality" of being Third World is more easily explained when we deal with the more "objective" or "macrostructural" dimensions (economic domination, dependence, exploitation), the "diversity" is much more visible in the more "subjective" dimensions (culture, religious experience). But the two aspects cannot be separated and any analysis or account of the "Third World experience" must try to see it as a whole. That is why we should strive to understand the divergences in our commonalities and vice versa.

I would suggest four ways of characterizing that common experience. This is not meant as a complete or satisfactory account; it offers only some "tracks" or "paths" for pursuing our common work.

(1) *The Third World experience is colonial and neocolonial.* In other words, the totality of our existence as peoples is marked by the North-South contradiction, which is the fundamental division and conflict-line in our world. We can analyze in common this aspect of our situation at least at three different levels:

(a) Our economies are dependent. The conditions of international trade, the world financial system, the exploitation of resources and labor by transnational corporations are certainly common factors in all our economies. The "foreign debt" is almost a universal symbol for the Third World economic condition.

(b) Our cultures are under external aggression. Beginning with colonial attempts to stamp out native cultures or to substitute Western culture for them through physical force and operating now with the psychological violence of "cultural invasion" (media/fashion/music/recreation/advertisement), our peoples have been subject to an aggression that combines the economic and social to induce in them a sense of inferiority, worthlessness, and alienation. For us, it is important to single out the "religious invasion" as part of that cultural axis of the Third World experience—from early missionary desecration of the aboriginal religion to the modern, sophisticated, lavishly financed, arrogant "evangelistic" operations centered mainly in the United States. We cannot leave out of consideration at this level the education of our own Third World intellectuals in theories that already incorporate the presuppositions of "the dominant."

(c) The challenge of modernity. Our societies find themselves in the difficult situation of having to establish relation in and with a world dominated by modern technology (with its own ideological presuppositions) at the same time that they try to recover and reestablish an identity which has been under attack for several centuries. The "modernity" toward which we are pushed is not the authentic movement toward the "new" of our own cultural and material reality but the "modernity" of the Northern world which is superimposed on our peoples, creating further anomie and alienation.

Naturally, there are questions as to the relation between these levels. Nobody will today deny their mutual relations and conditionings. Few would suggest reductionist theories (whether economic, cultural, or other). Such simplifications should be abandoned. But there are real problems to be pursued in order to understand better the exact nature and operation of such relations and conditionings; that understanding can help us to find a more adequate answer to the total problem. It is at this point that we could concentrate our work in this respect.

(2) *The Third World experience is the experience of the people's struggle for life against a system of death.* This is perhaps *the* fundamental commonality: "Third World," as it is used in EATWOT, means a new consciousness characterized by the growing common awareness of oppression and a commitment to struggle for liberation. This new consciousness is *irreversible*. The reports from the different areas show the variety of ways in which this consciousness is awakened and expressed and the resourcefulness of the people in finding the ways to carry on the struggle in the times and spaces that are available or that they can create. Any analysis of the Third World which does not take this fact into account will not be able to understand the Third World's reality or to discern its future. Again this struggle takes place at different levels:

(a) As the struggle for justice. This takes place at the international level in the different for a dealing with international economic relations and in the attempts to challenge and modify the conditions of dependence and to define a New International Economic Order (NIECO). At the national level this struggle takes the form of working for reappropriation and more just distribution (that is, against class exploitation and class system).

(b) As the recovery of the historical memory and identity of the people. The two aspects are integral to each other. Peoples seek to re-create (and not merely reproduce) their cultural identity (culture, language, religion, forms of social relation, styles of political organization, relation to the land and the environment). Such identity, however, is related to the struggle for liberation. Therefore it is particularly a recovery of the memory of the struggle for liberation in the history and the traditions of our peoples, an identification with the moments, the people, the events, the symbols of those "strong" memories of our past struggles, usually buried in histories written by the conquerors.

(c) As the enrichment of the analysis. Perhaps it is at this point that we have learned the most from each other. There is an effort to move beyond overly schematic analysis in order to *discern* the concrete face of the poor and oppressed as the different layers of analysis coalesce in the poor and exploited as woman, peasant, native or mestizo, black, marginalized person, child. People cannot be reduced to numbers or economic equations. It is not that theoretical analysis (whether economic, social, or cultural) is false or irrelevant. But the reality of the concrete people is more than the mere sum or combination of the different analytical grids. To understand it *imagination* is also required. To portray it and make this reality of the people operative in liberation, poetry, drama, symbol, and myth are as necessary as analysis and organization. We must explore this aspect in the concrete reality of our Third World people and find their singularity in different peoples, but we also must seek a deep unity.

(3) *The Third World experience is the concrete experience of the God of life who struggles against death.* Religion is neither alien nor unambiguous in relation to this reality and the struggle. We discover again and again the religious dimension and spirituality both as a force of domination and of liberation. We can express this religious experience of the people committed to liberation in different ways:

(a) It is the encounter with the God of life, not only in the Christian tradition but also in the wider religious experience of the people. They find the inspiration and the power of a God who wills and gives and restores life, who covenants with the people for life (and life means food, health, space and time, hope, and the overcoming of suffering from within, suffering imposed by injustice, suffering assumed as a price for liberation).

(b) Thus, we are already speaking of "a new spirituality" (not new in the sense that it has never existed but in the sense that it is being recovered in the midst of the struggle) which offers new models of holiness and "the heroic life" (saintliness) in the life of the people themselves: in solidarity, in "giving one's life for the brother and sister," in self-renunciation for the sake of the other.

(c) Ecumenism gains also a new meaning as the common experience of this God of life and solidarity in the effort for liberation, beyond confessional and even religious expressions.

The theological articulation of these experiences, particularly as they relate to the different religious expressions, remains one of our problems — partly because our experiences are very different; partly because these religious expressions are also different; and partly because of the lingering effects of certain dogmatic approaches of the missionary enterprise. But we also discover that, although these differences exist, we are *all* challenged by this question in particular ways. Some have long labored in this field, others are just beginning. This is another area where we should be able to deepen our common work.

(4) *The Third World experience has been for us — EATWOT — also a theological experience in common.* This has to do with issues of contents, of methodology, and of theological stance. Perhaps this has been the area where more has been done (as witness the books published from the various conferences and, in general, abundant literature on Third World theologies). I will therefore only make three brief comments:

(a) Aspects already mentioned by Cone, Bimwenyi, and Amalorpavadass, quoted at the beginning of this paper, have been deepened and reinforced. One of them is the importance of the Bible — or better, of Bible reading from within the concrete experience of life and struggle. To be sure, there is in Third World people's reading of the Bible no single hermeneutical model, but there is a common, underlying relation among life, reading, and commitment as the "locus" for reading the scriptures.

(b) A second aspect stressed from the beginning of EATWOT and slowly developed within the mutual support and encouragement of EATWOT is the affirmation of a "theological autonomy" in relation to the theologies of the Northern world. Autonomy does not mean here disregard or antagonism. It means, in the first place, awareness of the relativity of all theologies (their relation to their time, space, ideologies, peculiar experience) and therefore the rejection of claims to universal normativeness of any of them (our own included, of course). It also means that a theology establishes its own criteria of excellence in terms of its relation to the total tradition, to the people, to the religious experience, to the liberation struggle itself and does not submit a priori to the tests of excellence developed in the academic theologies of the West. Third World theologians are ready for open dialogue; however, they do not feel primarily accountable to Western academic theology (for the contribution of which they are grateful) but to their own context and the spiritual experience of the people in the struggle for liberation.

(c) Finally, we share the experience of being "suspect" theologies, under constant check, as "subversive" theologies. In many parts of the world such a situation is not confined to academic discussion: it has meant persecution, prison, torture, and death. It has also meant internal conflict within the churches and open or hidden ostracism and sanctions. Third World theologies have been targeted as enemies in the foreign policy of big powers and there have been efforts (sometimes partly successful) to enlist confessional bodies at the service of these policies. But there has also been committed and active solidarity on the part of many sister and brother theologians from the Western world and of some theological institutions and ecclesiastical authorities. Perhaps, just as we speak of an option for the poor, so must we speak of "an option for the Third World"; and perhaps we must come to see more clearly how the North-South line runs also vertically across North and South.

NOTES

1. J. Cone, "Ecumenical Association of Third World Theologians," *Ecumenical Trends* 14, no. 3 (Sept. 1985), pp. 119–22.

2. O. K. Bimwenyi, "The Origins of EATWOT," *Voices* 4, no. 2 (Dec. 1981), pp. 19–26.

3. D. S. Amalorpavadass, "New Comments: Ecumenical Association of Third World Theologians," *Indian Theological Studies* 14, no. 4 (Dec. 1977), pp. 403–21.

PART III

DIVERGENCES

8

Divergences: An Asian Perspective

Tissa Balasuriya

This paper deals with divergences between Asian theology, as being currently developed, and the corresponding theologies in Africa and Latin America.

CONTEXTS

These divergences are due mainly to the context in which theologizing is done. Although the poverty of the masses of the people is common to Africa, Latin America, and Asia, one key element that sets the Asian situation aside is its historical and socio-cultural background. The difference is in the large populations of some of the Asian countries and the consequent enormity of the problems of development and liberation. In Asia the religio-cultural traditions come down from ancient times and are experiencing a revival and modernization which give them a new vigor. Politically and socially, the ideologies of capitalism and Marxism are dominant influences in some Asian countries. The largest secular democracy as well as the largest country under a Marxist regime are in Asia.

Concerning theology in relation to poverty, there are more similarities than divergences among the theologies of Asia, Africa, and Latin America. The attitude toward Marxist analysis is of a critical nature, and other factors, such as sex, ethnicity, and religious communalism, are also important influences on society. Further, the influence of both popular religion and the more developed world religions brings in a dimension that is not adequately explained by Marxism.

It is mainly due to Asia's religio-cultural background that Asian theology contributes some special dimensions to Christian theology. Even concerning the struggle for social justice the Asians bring up the concept and approach of a "contemplative commitment" that is considered as one act. In it com-

113

mitment is a response to God and a source of empathetic understanding responding to the exigencies of reality; and contemplation is a union with God that leads to and is nurtured by commitment. This is an approach toward a spirituality of action that is holistic, unitive, and mystical. This spirituality takes place prior to the elaboration of theological concepts. It seeks God in the other, in the situation, and in creation. This is an influence of the meditational and contemplative traditions of the Asian religions Hinduism and Buddhism, including Zen, the mystical tradition of Islam, and the general Oriental temperament that seeks interiority and harmony. Spirituality in the other continents has also the dimension of contemplation—but Asians seem to emphasize this more and have also developed methodologies of personal liberation through reflection, meditation, a deeper consciousness of the transience of being, and escape from delusion concerning the nature of temporal reality. The Gnostic trends in the religions influence Asian Christian theologizing in this direction. In Hinduism and Buddhism ultimate liberation is in the fullest realization of the truth concerning one's existence. The path to *Moksha* and *Nirvana*, or release from the bondage of *Samsara* (this cycle of existence with its craving), is in the deep understanding of the true nature of existence and in liberation from craving.

The development of the theory and practice of *nonviolence* (*Ahimsa*) as a method of peaceful protest is a contribution from Asia. It is derived from the respect for life and the idea of offering oneself in self-sacrifice in order to create changes in public attitudes. This technique, evolved by Mahatma Gandhi, has been taken up by people's organizations. The practice of "people's power," which reached a climax in the "Edsa Revolution" of the Philippines in February 1986, is related to this tradition.

REVELATION AND THE SOURCES OF THEOLOGY

In the Asian context of religious pluralism there has been a radical questioning of the Christian theological view that God's revelation is limited to the Bible and (among Catholics) to Christian tradition. Many Asian theologians hold that God cannot be thus limited. God should be liberated from this limitation. The sacred texts of other religions can also be a source of God's revelation. They have contributed so much good to so many generations and hence cannot be without God's light and inspiration.

This raises a major issue concerning the nature of revelation, the sources of theology, and their interpretation. On the one hand, many Asian theologians hold that God has spoken to all the peoples of the world in diverse ways and continues to do so throughout history. On the other hand, they point out that the Bible and the other sacred texts need to be studied critically to exclude elements which cannot be from God. Thus an excessive ethnocentrism that views God as speaking to the whole of humanity only or primarily through one ethnic group, such as the Jews, seems to be a sort of exclusivism that smacks of "religionism" (a concept I developed in my *Planetary Theology*).

While the Old Testament of the Jews is accepted as unique and even nominative by many Christians in other continents, Asian theologians are now questioning this view. The Bible of the Jews is accepted and respected as one of the sacred books of the world. But not as so unique as to exclude the others.

Interreligious dialogue is considered a *source of theology*. Through it we can know better God's self-manifestation to humanity. It is one means of listening to God, contemplating the divine or the absolute, and participating in transformative action to realize the design of God for humanity.

There is also a critique of the concept of "Tradition," which Catholic theology especially emphasizes as a source of Christian theology. Asian theologians now question this perspective. The Christian tradition is only one spiritual and theological tradition and hence cannot be considered unique and exclusive. Further, both the Bible and tradition are subject to the criticism that they are male-dominated: written or retained in memory by males and interpreted by males. The history of the spiritual contributions of women is hardly recorded in either of these sources. This is applicable to the writings and traditions of other religions also.

Another aspect of the hermeneutic question is: Who are the *subjects of theology*? Asian EATWOT theologians accept that the poor are the ones who can best contribute to the development of Christian theology in the direction of the liberation of the poor. As Aloysius Pieris has pointed out, one of our problems is that the theologians are not poor and the poor are not theologians. The professional theologians can give a systematic and scientific formulation to the sensitivities and expressions of theology that come from the poor, the weak, and the oppressed. This is commonly accepted in the EATWOT community of theologians throughout the Third World. The significant difference is that in Asia 97 percent of the poor are not Christians, the Philippines being a notable exception. This means that if the poor are a source and subject for theologizing, Christian theology in Asia has to be helped in its development by these struggling poor who are not Christians. The minjung of Asia, the long-suffering and struggling masses for whom God cares, are not all disciples of Jesus. Insofar as they can be the agents of liberation and builders of society according to the values of the Kingdom, we have to ask ourselves: How do we theologize with them? How do they help and even lead us who are concerned with the evolution of a relevant Asian Christian theology?

This leads us to another consideration—the main agents of social change and human liberation in Asia (outside the Philippines) will be groups formed as people's movements without reference to the Christian faith as such. If religion is involved it will be within groups motivated by a plurality of religions. We may call such groups *basic human communities*. They will not be the basic Christian communities that are prominent in the Latin

American struggle for liberation. This means that Asian Christian theologians must think of a broader religious framework for their liberative action and thought. Thus in Asia the basic human community engaged in the struggle for justice, freedom, equality, peace, and truth is a theological community, though not an exclusively or expressly Christian one.

Asian Christian theology has worked out more systematically and practically the *dialogue* with other religions *at different levels*—that is, at the levels of study and research, of prayer and worship, of meditation and contemplation, of living together, and of struggling for common causes. This experience and sharing have enriched each religious group and have helped each to realize the value of unity in diversity without expecting uniformity. Thus we have theological reflections emerging from different experiences, such as in ashrams, meditation centers, research institutes, village encounters, and people's movements.

These in turn are leading to a growth of mutual understanding among the religions. Christian theology has been influenced to the extent of rethinking the goal of the Christian witness and *mission*. Influenced by the Asian (and African) reflections, the Vatican secretariat for other religions has now clearly stated that the aim of mission is to bear witness to Jesus, but the aim is not necessarily the conversion of others to the church. Action for justice and peace is an integral and constitutive dimension and adequate goal of mission. Proclamation of Jesus Christ can take place in the process without wanting to bring persons of other faiths into the church. The church has now come to express clearly that salvation can be realized in and through the pursuit of the good as proposed by other religions.

INTERRELIGIOUS DIALOGUE

The context and experience of interreligious dialogue are influencing Christian theology of Asia concerning its understanding of the basics of *dogmatic* or *systematic theology*. The nature of God, the absolute, and the transcendent is an issue that arises in the Asian context. The problems are varied. The Theravada Buddhist thinks of the absolute as unknowable or impersonal. The Hindu approach has a point of view that sees all reality pantheistically. Islam is so strictly monotheistic that it finds the teachings concerning the Trinity and the incarnation a rejection of or unacceptable compromise of monotheism. This plural environment makes Christians rethink their formulations concerning God and Jesus Christ. This is leading to a greater search for a clarification and purification of our concepts, as well as for a meaningfulness in theologizing concerning God. We see that the apodictic ways of expression derived from Hebrew, Greek, or Latin cultures are not the only ways in which the mystery of the divine can be articulated.

Asian Christian theology is further impelled by the plurality of philosophical schools in Asia to admit the possibility of other interpretations concerning the origin of the universe, the origin of human life, and life after death. Some Asian religions posit pantheistic propositions regarding the origin of the world. In this context the theory of *creation* may be relativized or debated.

More significant than that would be the questioning of the theological postulates concerning the origin of the human race, the state of original justice, and the fall of all humanity due to the sin of Adam and Eve. The teaching concerning *original sin* is seen as having had many undesirable effects on the Christian approach toward persons of other faiths. The traumatic experience of Christianity in Asia being allied to conquering colonial exploiters and of traditional theology legitimizing them leads to a questioning of the Western construct of Christian theology. This construct was built on the foundation of original sin and the need for a divine redeemer. Many of the elaborations concerning the state of original justice, the fall, the need for the sacrament of baptism, and the fate of unbaptized children are seen as theological developments built upon an interpretation of some texts of the scriptures in the background of given Western schools of philosophy.

An even more fundamental issue that arises in the Asian context is the nature and personality of *Jesus Christ*. The gospel story of the life and teaching of Jesus is acknowledged as an inspiring example of a noble life dedicated to the service of others unto death. But once again the theological elaborations concerning Jesus being divine and human with two natures in one person are less intelligible or presentable in the context of Hinduism, Buddhism, and Islam. This makes Asian Christian theologians inquire deeper into what in Christology is from Jesus himself or divine revelation and what is purely an ecclesiastical elaboration. A further question has to do with the relationship among personalities such as those of Jesus, the Buddha, and the Prophet Mohammed.

Many issues arise in this connection. Jesus, born in Bethlehem as the son of Mary, does not exhaust the Christ considered as the cosmic lord or second person of the Trinity: In that sense Christ cannot be limited to Jesus. How can we claim to know and interpret such a human-divine relationship? What is the nature of *redemption* by Jesus through his death? This in turn is linked to the presupposition concerning original sin. How was such redemption understood as limited exclusively to Christians—at least during many centuries? What is the content of *soteriology* in this context?

Asian theology today has an important aspect of seeking clarity concerning the dogmas which have been defined in the councils of the church, such as Chalcedon. In the context of religious and philosophical pluralism there seem to be trends toward a *dedogmatization* of theology insofar as some dogmas are based on assumptions that can be questioned or lead to consequences that are disastrous for many sections of humanity. The harmful effects of the Christian expansion into Asia were linked to such a the-

ologizing, and thus today there has to be a purification of Christian dogma
that was used for legitimizing that concept and practice of mission which
are no longer tenable and which even the church has changed.

Asian theology is evolving a dynamic understanding of interreligious
prayer, worship, meditation—a *communicatio in sacris* that is still unthought
of in traditional theology or Latin American liberation theology. What is
the meaning of the eucharist and of the sacrifice of the Mass if there are
evolutions in the theology concerning sin, redemption, Christology, and
missiology?

Latin American *ecclesiology* is evolving from a reflection on the church
of the poor and of service. Asian ecclesiology is going further due to the
rethinking of the churches as particular communions within a wider framework of several religious faiths and communities. This calls in question the
claims of uniqueness and exclusivity that the Christian church has attributed
to itself for fifteen or more centuries.

The Asian situation, while leading to much questioning of certain interpretations of dogma, lays great emphasis on being disciples of Jesus and
on the core of his teachings. The context of poverty and plurality of religions
demands greater practice of love of neighbor, sharing of incomes and
wealth, and respect for the views of others. Thus theology has to be developed in a more practical, committed, and contemplative manner to lead to
radical changes in people's lives, interrelations of faiths and ideologies, and
a sharing of the world's wealth among all.

The Chinese, Vietnamese, and North Korean experience of socialist
societies is another context in which theology is being rethought in a post-
colonial and postcapitalist phase. Chinese Christians call it postliberational
and postdenominational. They are developing a church life and thinking
that emphasize the need for local churches to be self-reliant in manage-
ment, in doctrine, and in development. This experience of a socialism that
is now more respectful of religions will in time lead to very valuable contributions to Christian theology. This situation is still specific to the Asian
context.

Asian Christian theology has also offered much thought concerning the
local church, the relative autonomy and identity of the local church, inculturation, openness to different ideologies, feminism, ethnicity, etc. These
trends are more prominent in Asia only because of the size of the Asian
populations and their plurality—for the other continents too have these
trends.

Asian theologians are more conscious of the global dimension of Asian
and human problems. Hence *planetary theology* is being worked out from
an Asian perspective, particularly in relation to caring for and sharing of
the earth's resources among the whole of humanity. This is particularly
important due to the increasing unification of the world, which is occurring
largely under the guidance of transnational corporations. The use of the

earth's land is especially important for Asian countries that have huge populations in relatively small land areas.

These are some distinct elements which the Asian theological effort is contributing today to the world churches. If they are taken seriously by Asians and the churches as a whole, there will be a flowering of theology in the direction of a more universal understanding of Jesus and of Christianity. The faith will then be more concerned with building the common home of humanity on this earth—based on the values of sharing and freedom that can ensure peace in a transformed world. Of course the contributions of all other continents will be essential in attaining this—almost utopian—goal.

9

Divergences: A Latin American Perspective

Sergio Torres

INTRODUCTION

The theme of the Oaxtepec conference, where we celebrated our EATWOT's tenth anniversary, can be seen as emblematic of an important step in EATWOT's short but rich history.

At the first conference, in Dar-es-Salaam (1976), we initiated a dialogue which was marked by historic, linguistic, and cultural difficulties. The main outcome was finding some common elements which justified the establishment of an association to continue that dialogue.

Afterwards, three more conferences were held to deepen the specific identity of African theology (Accra, Ghana—1977), the theology of Asia (Colombo, Sri Lanka—1979), and Latin American theology (São Paulo, Brazil—1980).

In 1981, in New Delhi, we attempted to make a synthesis of the common elements of Third World theologies. During the discussions it was realized that it was too early to talk about a synthesis and also that it was necessary to continue talking about a plurality of the Third World theologies.

For the Oaxtepec conference we chose the theme "Commonalities, Divergences, and Cross-fertilization among Third World Theologies." This theme expresses the actual situation in which we find ourselves at present. There are common elements in the economic, social, political, cultural, religious, ecclesial, and theological levels in all the continents. Due to historical and contextual differences, there are also differences in theological reflection. For this reason, EATWOT has become a privileged space for dialogue, enrichment, and cross-fertilization.

It is in this context of our previous discussions that we approach our differences. We believe that these differences help and enrich us mutually.

DIVERGENCES AMONG THIRD WORLD THEOLOGIES

Relation with and Dependency upon the West

After ten years of dialogue with our sisters and brothers from Asia and Africa, Latin American theologians are now more conscious that people from Latin America are the most Westernized in the Third World. It is true that the Latin American races and cultures were the outcome of an ethnic and racial mixture of Spanish and Portuguese people with the pre-Colombian indigenous peoples, but it is also true that this mixed race has been always dominated by the white minorities of the traditional classes and emerging bourgeoisie. New waves of people coming from Italy, Germany, and other countries made that supremacy stronger. Indigenous cultures and the descendants of the black slaves, who in some countries are the majority, have been invisible until now. This social, racial, and cultural situation has also affected the church and theologies. Bishops, priests, pastors, and theologians have come in large number from the white race and, therefore, from the Western culture. They have been indifferent to the reality of the black and the indigenous people.

This racial and cultural context has also made its mark on the theology of liberation. This theology has affirmed its Latin American indentity, becoming independent from European theology. However, only recently it has rediscovered its mestizo roots, and it has enriched its view about the poor — the starting point of this theology — incorporating the racial and ethnic components.

This social, cultural, ecclesial, and theological situation places us in a different position with respect to Asia, Africa, and the minorities of the United States. Within the last twenty-five years the Christian churches of Africa, Asia, and the Caribbean have changed the outlook of the Catholic and Protestant churches. The Third World is emerging with a new face and with different cultures which challenge the traditional white supremacy. For the Latin American theology of liberation this indeed is a true challenge.

Different Perception of the Latin American Role

Until now, the main contacts of the church leaders and theologians of Latin America have been mostly with Europe and North America. The contact with Asians and Africans is rather new. It began with the sessions of Vatican II and with the conferences of the World Council of Churches.

The contacts with black theologians in the United States and with theologians in Africa and Asia have helped the Latin American members of EATWOT to look at their role and at their theological contribution to common dialogue with a more humble spirit. We Latin Americans must

recognize that because of the Western influence, we had an arrogant attitude toward other theological trends in the Third World. Because we sys-
tematized our theological view earlier than did theologians in the other
Third World continents, we have given the impression of wanting to impose
our own theological patterns on others. Today we are aware that this reflection has to be placed in a wider context, where new questions and problems
arise. For instance, it is essential to keep in mind that the majority of the
oppressed people of the Third World are not Christians. And we have to
be aware also that universal liberation will not be achieved with the contribution of Christians alone, but especially with the contribution of the
main non-Christian religions. This makes our contribution somehow relative and places us in a more humble and modest position.

Christian Presence in Latin America and Asia

It is instructive to note the cultural and religious differences between
Asia and Latin America. In Latin America 90 percent of the population
have been baptized and there is a Christian presence which impregnates
history, art, culture, the "popular" piety, and the social and patriotic customs. The contrast with Asia is enormous. In Asia there is a Christian
minority of less than 3 percent of the entire population, and the prevailing
presence of the non-Christian religions — such as Islam, Buddhism, and
Hinduism — in the cultural and social life is obvious. These differences influence our ways of being Christian and our theologies.

Unity and Diversity

The Asian Report defines that continent in terms of its cultural richness
and its diversity — diversity on the geographic, demographic, economic,
political, linguistic, cultural, social, and religious levels. In Africa there is
also a great richness of historical, cultural, tribal, religious, and folkloric
traditions. In comparison, Latin America seems to be relatively uniform
and monotonous. There were two countries — Spain and Portugal, both
from the same Iberian Peninsula — that initiated the process of conquest
and colonization. They imposed a similar religion and similar traditions,
customs, and cultures; they also imposed their languages. This reality has
some advantage as it has helped maintain the basic unity of the continent.

Theological Issues

The Starting Point
Latin American theology was born among poor Christians, who were
struggling for their liberation, long before it was articulated by pastoral
agents (priests, religious, pastors) and by academic, professional theologians. This theology is a critical reflection by Christians who live in the mar-

ginalized areas and who are encouraged by their faith in Jesus Christ to involve themselves in the economic, political, and social liberation process of the continent.

The starting point is the faith experience of the impoverished and oppressed people who do not accept their state of injustice and oppression. They are always against the oppressive conditions of society, and they are struggling for a new world. The poor read the Bible and they discover that God has a liberating plan for humanity. They read the New Testament and they realize that Jesus Christ—God and human being—also had conflicts with the authorities, priests, and powerful people of his time.

Starting with these experiences of faith within the struggle for liberation, a concept of God as the God of life is articulated. In addition, a new relation with Jesus Christ emerges, as well as a view of a living church as a community among the poor.

According to what we know today, this starting point is similar to the experiences of Christians in other countries and continents. There is a similarity with the experience of faith of the blacks in the South of the United States, who fought and are still fighting to affirm their identity as free persons.

In Asia and in Africa, the starting point is also the experience of faith of the poor, but there are different emphases and nuances. In Africa the concept of "anthropological pauperization" has been developed. This concept is a criticism of all attempts to dehumanize and to deprive the people of that continent of basic dignity, their cultural identity, and their historical, tribal, and familiar roots. In Asia, traditional religions are working to liberate the person from the attraction of power and wealth, and they underline the liberating value of poverty.

The Use of Social Analysis

Latin American theology, struggling for a change in the situation of the oppressed, employs social analysis and transforming action. Like the Good Samaritan, it looks for the best way to help the "wounded along the road," that is, the millions of "wounded," marginalized, and impoverished of the continent. This theology denounces the injustices of the ruling system and proposes formulae for social changes and for transforming the old and unjust structures.

During the first period of Latin American theology, special emphasis was given to the analysis of social classes; social analysis was viewed as an instrument to understand and to transform society. Africa and Asia have emphasized cultural and religious analysis for understanding society. The contact with black theologians of the United States and the theologians of Asia and Africa has enriched the Christians and theologians of Latin America. It has been necessary to complete the economic analysis of classes with contributions of the cultural analysis and with the challenges coming from other religions and cultures.

Also, a great value has been given to the analysis of the struggle between blacks and whites. Moreover, the contributions of women theologians, who denounce machismo even in the progressive and "liberative" sectors, have been slowly assimilated. They propose a rereading of the Christian symbols, and that rereading helps them renounce the masculine interpretations done within the context of patriarchal culture. Asia has a "holistic" methodology which considers all aspects of reality, and Africa has emphasized anthropological and cultural analysis.

The Reading of the Bible

Social analysis helps us to know the dimensions and structural causes of poverty. But a discernment is necessary to detect the presence of sin and the presence of the liberating grace of Jesus Christ.

Reading the Bible can help us to achieve this discernment. In Latin America a liberative reading of the Bible has its roots in the practice of the poor working in the organization of basic ecclesial communities. It is not just reading passages that speak about oppression and liberation. The whole Bible is seen as a liberating project with a liberating message. Besides, this project has a historical and practical dimension. Personal conversion and social transformation are proposed in the Bible. The Reign of God is a utopian horizon, but it begins to be built here on earth.

In other continents, the Bible is also the basis of Christian theology. But there exist other realities and other challenges. In Asia traditional religions have their own sacred scriptures with an interpretation of life and of the world. Important questions arise about the concept of revelation, as well as about the interpretation of the historic Jesus within the saving plan of God.

In Africa there is a self-critical process going on; this process questions the way in which the West imposed Christianity on Africa without paying enough attention to the cultural roots of African identity. Africans want to read the Bible beginning with their own history.

The Dialogue with Other Religions and Popular Religiosity

Latin American theology has been deeply impressed by the spiritual and transcendent richness of the non-Christian religions of Asia and Africa. Efforts made by the theologians of those continents to express and to formulate the message of the Jewish-Christian tradition in the cultural and religious matrix of Buddhism, Islam, and Hinduism have begun to influence Latin American theology. In Latin America we do not have significant and organized non-Christian religions, except native and Afro-American religious interpretations. But in our continent there does exist popular religiosity, which is a "popular" appropriation of Christianity that is expressed through syncretist devotions and practices. This religiosity is a mixture of traditions, beliefs, and indigenous practices which never disappeared and which have reinterpreted Christian symbols, starting with their own practices. Moreover, in many areas there exist Afro-American cults and practices that keep up the traditions of black culture and that also reinterpret the symbols imposed by the white Christian minorities.

In order to appraise those expressions of popular religiosity, there is a critical process being developed among us, especially among Catholic theologians, but also among the Protestants. It is necessary to interpret these practices in a correct way, to respect that "popular" appropriation, and to find ways to transform them into liberating religious practices.

Liberating Spirituality

In its beginnings, Latin American theological reflection appeared as a motivating force of social action. Its detractors said that it was not a true theology, but only a sociological analysis or an ideology.

The truth is that those criticisms were false and without foundation. Christian identity has always encompassed the basic experience of Christians actively involved in the process of liberation. But perhaps it is also true that some theological articles and books from Latin America insisted mainly on the strategy to overcome the different forms of oppression.

Today, after a decade of persecution and martyrdom of the poor and their organizations, a committed spirituality has developed. This spirituality recognizes and celebrates God as the God of life, who supports the poor in their struggle against idolatrous forces of death.

This type of spirituality should enrich us with the different ways of spirituality of the minority groups of the United States and with the experiences of Asia and Africa. In Asia there are still large geographic and social spaces which are impregnated with the sense of the sacred and where there is no dichotomy between spirituality and the secular. African traditions in the villages are saturated with the presence of the ancestors and with the spirit of the extended family.

We are not looking only for *fides quaerens intellectum* in the Third World, but we are witnesses of new ways of contemplation, prayer, and spirituality.

New Ways of Ecumenism

In Latin America, a majority of persons are culturally Catholic. Protestantism, divided into many denominations, only recently has been structured on a national and continental level.

Ecumenism is taking form on a basic level in people's struggle against the violation of human rights and in the defense of those who are persecuted by dictatorships and dominant classes, which are supported by imperialism.

Authentic religious pluralism does not exist yet; neither is there a true respect for indigenous religious expressions and for the Afro-American cults. We hope to achieve this pluralism and respect, following the example of Africa and Asia.

Asia's reality, with a minority of Christians in the midst of non-Christian masses, is an invitation to a new ecumenism that would transcend the denominational barriers and gather all those who are looking for an integral liberation.

CONCLUSION

As a final word, I want to say that instead of talking about differences, we should talk about the particular richness each brings to complement the others.

The Oaxtepec conference was a wonderful opportunity to get to know one another better and deepen our dialogue.

There are differences, but they do not separate us; on the contrary, they help us come closer and they enrich us.

PART IV

CROSS-FERTILIZATION

10

Cross-fertilization: A Statement
from the U.S. Minorities

James H. Cone

It is not easy to speak with restraint and civility in a context in which your history and culture have been marginalized and thus not considered with the same respect and recognition as other histories and cultures. This is the situation of U.S. minorities within the United States and also within EATWOT. Our hurts and pains in our struggles for justice have always been treated as secondary to the activities of whites in the United States and also as secondary to the activities of EATWOT in Asia, Africa, and Latin America.

We have frequently and vigorously struggled against our second-class status in both contexts, running the risk of alienating ourselves and the people we seek to represent from the land of our birth and from the organization which defines the central meaning of our own theological vision. But we come from a history and culture in which to preach the gospel has always meant telling the truth, as clearly and as forcefully as the Spirit of God empowers one to say it. That is why black theology is so often regarded as offensive and is frequently ignored in the country of its origin and even by some liberation theologians in EATWOT. But despite the burden we might have in doing theology, our burden is nothing when compared with the exploitation and suffering of our people. Our people are exploited because they are not considered fully human, and our situation in the United States sets us apart, marginalizes us.

We, the U.S. minorities, have more in common with the Third World peoples of Africa, Asia, and Latin America than we do with the ruling classes and races in the United States. For we must not forget that the great majority of U.S. minorities come from Africa, Asia, and Latin America. We are your brothers and sisters and feel hurt when you reject us. We are culturally, politically, and economically Third World people living in the First World. Being Third World in the First World creates a hyphenated identity: we are African-Americans, Hispanic-Americans, Asian-Americans, and Native-Americans. No one has described the paradox of black identity in the United States with greater insight than W. E. B. DuBois in this classic statement of 1903:

> It is a peculiar sensation, this double consciousness, this sense of always looking at one's self through the eyes of others, of measuring one's soul by the tape of a world that looks on in amused contempt and pity. One ever feels this two-ness—an American, a Negro; two souls, two thoughts, two unreconciled strivings; two warring ideals in one dark body, whose dogged strength alone keeps it from being torn asunder.

The problem of identity acutely felt by blacks is not unique to them but is deeply felt by most U.S. minorities.

Our theologies have been created out of our struggle to define who we are rather than accept the definition of our oppressors. In the black community, our struggle began when we were first stolen from Africa, placed on slave ships, and sold as slaves in North America in 1619. The struggle continues today, and black theology is nothing but an attempt to make sense out of God in a society that has defined black as nothing.

Our double consciousness is intensified because we are often rejected not only by our white oppressors in the United States, but also by our brothers and sisters in the Third World. This is the pain and suffering we have felt so deeply in EATWOT. This is the reason why we are silent when we should often speak out. But when we do speak out with a force and anger that are motivated by our deep hurt, we are often accused of overstatement and of being loud and unreasonable. Well, Malcolm X taught us that what is reasonable to the oppressor isn't reasonable to the oppressed; what is logical to the oppressor isn't logical to the oppressed. Therefore, said Malcolm, we must devise new rules, a new logic created by those who are at the bottom, who are marginalized, if we are going to get some results in our struggle for liberation.

Malcolm's insight is as appropriate for EATWOT as it was when he first made it in the context of black-white relations in the United States during the 1960s. Malcolm told blacks: "Don't play the game by their rules, let them know that we got new rules defined by the struggle for justice." When Malcolm was called an extremist, his reply was: "Yes, I am an extremist. Black people in the United States are in extremely bad condition. You show me a black who is not an extremist, and I will show you one who is in need of psychiatric examination."

In contrast to Martin Luther King, Jr., who spoke of America as a dream, Malcolm saw it as a nightmare:

No, I am not an American. I'm one of the 22 million black people who are the victims of Americanism, one of the . . . victims of democracy, nothing but disguised hypocrisy. So I am not standing here speaking to you as an American, or a patriot, or a flag-saluter, or a flag waver—no, not I! I am speaking as a victim of this American system. And I see America through the eyes of the victim. I don't see any American dream. I see an American nightmare.

These words express the feelings of the masses of blacks in the United States and also many other minorities. That is why we find it difficult to understand why we are often marginalized in EATWOT. We are one of you and feel the way you do about the United States. That was why more than 95 percent of blacks voted against Reagan for president in 1980 and 1984.

But we cannot have genuine dialogue in EATWOT until we learn how to treat each other as equals with love and respect, until everybody's experience is valued as much as others. When this happens, we will be able to explore our commonalities and divergences with creativity, learning from each other. We, the U.S. minorities, know that we have a lot to learn from our Third World brothers and sisters, and we hope that you have something to learn from us.

11

Cross-fertilization: An Asian Perspective

Sun Ai Park

I would like to make a few remarks from an Asian woman's perspective. These remarks take into consideration the various reports and analyses presented throughout this book.

One striking factor has to do with the different terms and concepts used to discuss the commonality among the starting points of doing theology. The Africans used the term "anthropological poverty"; the Latin Americans, "the struggle of the poor for liberation"; and the Asians, "the suffering and struggling people as the subject of theology."

As a woman doing theology, I would like to echo the African expression. Although the Latin American inclusion of women and indigenous people in the category of the poor must be noted as a step toward a more holistic approach to the making of a new heaven and new earth, the term "anthropological poverty" is in many ways more useful for me, for it does more to expose Western colonialism, which has brought political, economic, and cultural fragility to Asia and to Asian women in particular. The term thus helps describe not only the situation of Asia in general but particularly that of Asian women.

Women in Asia have been made voiceless, with no identity of their own in male-dominated societies. Therefore, they do not have a way of expressing themselves politically, economically, or religiously. If one views women's domination not within the context of Western civilization but within the context of patriarchy, then the cultural structures of women's oppression can be generalized. But the domination of women is not done in only one manner. It is done in different combinations of economic, political, cultural, and religious categories. Therefore, Asian women's oppressions are characterized as double, triple, or quadruple.

Concerning spirituality, I wish to emphasize the feminine dimension of spirituality in contrast to the masculine dimension. This distinction comes

132

from women's particular life experience of giving, nurturing, sustaining life, and being relational, serving in the home and other human communities.

If androcentric patriarchal culture has brought violence—victimization, domination-subjugation, rape of both women's bodies and nature, and the destruction of God's world; if it has brought violence in the form of capitalism, militarism, and the nuclear weapons race—then feminine culture must bring love, equality, justice and peace, care for others and for all; it must therefore be people-oriented rather than authority-centered, life-giving rather than death-dealing.

In envisioning the new heaven and new earth, Latin American theologians often speak of a classless society; women are emphasizing that feminine elements must be included in this vision, for if those elements are excluded from any society, then the result will be not only a sexist society, but also a classist and racist society. All human relationships start from man-woman relationships at home; it is there that unequal relations between persons and peoples are nourished; it is there that the desire to control and dominate others is formed; that desire must be seen as the original sin.

If we really want the church to be the community of Jesus Christ, a community that lives in love as one body seeking the Reign of God with others, then the practice of classism, sexism, and racism in the church cannot be permitted. These irrational sources of suffering must be redressed, for the Lord's table symbolizes fellowship of all God's people and the sharing of food among all.

In Christian rituals and doctrines we find rich sources from which we can derive economic, political, and cultural ideologies which will lead all persons and peoples of the world to the new heaven and the new earth.

12

Cross-fertilization: A Latin American Perspective

Elsa Tamez

INTRODUCTION

When I started the preparation of this presentation, I faced two small problems. First, to some extent the subject of cross-fertilization has already been addressed in the dialogues and essays on commonalities and divergences. Second, as a representative of Latin America, I have been surprised to hear the criticisms of Latin American theology and Latin American theologians. It seems to me that these criticisms are not sufficiently grounded in reality.

"Cross-fertilization" between a woman and a man implies mutual fulfillment. In the same way, I think that we need a context of common understanding and friendship if our process of mutual knowledge and enrichment is to advance.

EXAMPLES OF CROSS-FERTILIZATION

As a woman, I have been thinking of two examples of "cross-fertilization" that can help us in the work of EATWOT. One is the example of the earth, which must be fertile if the seed it receives is to produce fruit. It is necessary to prepare and take care of the earth, to water it, wait for the sun to warm it, and finally, at the proper time, plant the seed.

The other, more obvious, example is the fertile union of a man and a woman. This also demands preparation — care for the body of the man and of the woman in order to be able to produce good fruit; care in seeking the right time for conception.

These images illustrate and illuminate by themselves our dialogue within EATWOT. They also help answer the questions which I am asking myself

134

at this time. Why should we meet, unite? Why do we need to get to know each other?

I think that in EATWOT we are really concerned about dialogue and cross-fertilization, in spite of the difficulties among us. I do not feel this concern when dialoging with people of the First World. I think that some of them consider our theologies as a fad—something exotic. I believe that this does not happen when Third World people get together.

I myself try to respond to the questions that I am asking. We are meeting, interchanging opinions and ideas, because we want to be able to understand and know each other better. We have already made progress in this regard through our analysis of our commonalities and divergences.

Why do we meet? I believe it is in order to bear fruit, to enrich our understanding, to be more helpful to our people.

OUR EXPERIENCE IN LATIN AMERICA

I want to continue using the image of the earth. In Latin America our land, our countries, have been attacked by the forces of death. We have had this experience from the early stages of colonial times. This painful experience is the same in all our countries, and I think it is a unifying force for all the countries of the Third World. On the international level, we have suffered exploitation and genocide. There is a common enemy, the international centers of economic power and the transnationals. On the national level we also are under the power of the forces of exploitation. Very often our national leaders do not take care of the poor and do not pay attention to the needs of those most marginalized: women, blacks, and Indians.

The earth of Latin America is dry and thirsting for justice. The earth is waiting for the miracle of fertility of which the Prophet Isaiah speaks in chapter 35:6–7. In this passage the prophet speaks about the utopia of the desert as a source of living waters:

Then shall the lame man leap like a deer, and the tongue of the dumb shout aloud; for water springs up in the wilderness, and torrents flow in dry land. The mirage becomes a pool, the thirsty land bubbling springs; instead of reeds and rushes, grass shall grow in the rough land where wolves now lurk [Isaiah 35:6–7].

The earth of our continent, waiting for justice and fulfillment, has already been fertilized by the blood of the thousands and thousands of people who have been killed throughout its history and especially in the last twenty years. This earth has also been fertilized by the people who have died from starvation, and people continue to die of malnutrition. We know that they are not dying because of a scarcity of resources, but because these resources are unjustly distributed.

This same earth has also been fertilized by the blood of martyrs, people who are dying because they are protesting against all forms of oppression. They are the victims of repression in their struggle for justice. In 1985 there were 1,650 people killed in El Salvador, and we have similar figures in Guatemala. This blood has fertilized our earth. It is ready to receive the seed and to produce the fruits, fruits of justice and hope.

THE UNITY OF THE THIRD WORLD

Unfortunately, after a time of solidarity among countries of the Third World in the 1960s and the 1970s, we find ourselves separated from each other. The countries of the Third World constitute the majority of the world's population, but we are not united.

We need solidarity: solidarity among Latin America, Africa, Asia, and the minority groups of the United States. We, in Latin America, want to offer our solidarity to all who struggle around the world. But we also need the support of our brothers and sisters. I would like to see more solidarity from the minority groups of the United States, especially with the struggle of the people of Central America.

The gap between the First World and the Third World is widening. The people of the Third World are poorer than ever before. Very often we talk in our day about the option for the poor. We have to remind ourselves that we are the poor. We have to be conscious of our common situations and to struggle together for development and liberation.

From the theological point of view, we have learned again that the Reign of God is built among the poor. Our task and our unity are helping in the building of this Reign.

WHAT WE HAVE LEARNED IN LATIN AMERICA

I think that within EATWOT there are people who do not know the Latin American context well. Our theology has been known through some books, but that theology is rooted in the experience and the sufferings of thousands and millions of people.

It is necessary to have dialogue and interaction. I want to sketch what we in Latin America have learned from the other continents and the other theologies. We have learned a great deal and we are grateful to all our brothers and sisters who have shared with us their own experience and suffering. We have been enriched by the experience of Africa and Asia. We have also known the complexity of the situation of the minority groups in the United States—Native Americans, blacks, Hispanics, and Asian Americans. To know all these realities has made an impact on our theology and has presented us with enormous challenges. I would like to spell out some of them.

a. We are used to living in a continent where the majority of the people consider themselves to be Christians. Our theology has the tendency to absolutize Christianity. Ecumenism for us means dialogue only between Protestants and Catholics.

When we listen to the experience of other continents, especially of Asia, we rediscover the meaning of revelation and we listen very carefully to the question of Asians about the exact role of Jesus Christ and the Holy Spirit in the context of the non-Christian scriptures.

In Latin America we have also begun to reread the content of revelation in the context of the indigenous religions with their myths and symbols. We have been enriched by the insights of Asia and Africa, and we are very grateful for this.

b. Christianity in Latin America came with the conquerors, both Spaniards and Portuguese. This continent has been baptized but not evangelized. In the present time all the churches are trying to deepen the content of faith among their constituencies. We are working on the evangelization of our culture in the midst of social conflicts and poverty. There are many challenges coming from this work, and we are very attentive to the experience of other continents.

c. There is another concern among ourselves. We have been forced to deal with the problem of idolatry. This old reality of idolatry, as it is described in the Bible and in the history of Israel, has become a new reality for us.

The capitalist system and the national security governments are asking the people to make a "religious" commitment to them. The principles of order, national security, free market, etc., appear as idols competing with the true God, the God of Jesus Christ. We are facing a confrontation, a battle between the idols and the true God. When we come to know the religions of the other continents with their anthropological, cosmic, and religious dimensions, we are enriched and pushed to deepen our search for Christian identity.

d. I also want to mention our work regarding evangelization and culture. We have been impressed by the centrality of the reality of culture and history in African theology. In Latin America there are several cultural realities. Unfortunately the culture of the white, urban middle class is the most visible in the international forums. However, the majority of the population of the continent is mestizo. There are many countries where the majority is indigenous, and there are other countries where there is a high percentage of blacks.

For us in Latin America the dialogue going on in the context of EATWOT has been fruitful and enriching. However, this does not mean that we started this process of self-criticism and evaluation only recently. In Latin America, we have been doing it over the past twenty-four years. We have to realize that a socio-ethnic system coming from the past centuries cannot be changed in a short period of time. The churches and theologies belong to their times and reflect their own social realities. It will take time for us to introduce some changes in our evangelization tasks and in our theology.

e. Finally, I want to mention the essential role of women in the process of cross-fertilization of theology. This role is visible in the three continents, where women are getting more possibilities and are exerting their special influence and particular opinions. I believe that we have to congratulate ourselves, because women in EATWOT are offering concrete openings for the promotion of women.

CONCLUSION

I have tried to answer my own questions. Why are we here together? Why do we want to be united? I hope that my presentation has been clear enough. I have tried to be sincere and honest. I know that the dialogue among different cultures is very difficult and could be discouraging. However, I am confident that the ten years of life of EATWOT have been significant for all of us. I hope that this general assembly at Oaxtepec will confirm our determination to be together, to be united, and be full of hope for the future.

13

Cross-fertilization in EATWOT

Patrick Kalilombe

In an association like EATWOT both the idea and practice of cross-fertilization are central to the objective of mutual enrichment. I understand cross-fertilization to mean the process whereby our intraregional and interregional differences become challenges for growth and the deepening of our commonalities. Our shared experiences as Third World communities and groups unite us in a general way. We have come to a common understanding of a new way of doing theology from our situation of marginalization and poverty. But the contexts in which we live and struggle, however much they may resemble one another, are different in their specificities: they are variant versions of similar concerns. In order to collaborate effectively, we need three things: first, to understand better the specific ways in which each one's concrete situation adds new dimensions to our common concerns; second, to discover how and where the differences enlarge each one's vision and challenge its limitations; and third, to find out how these challenges are a call to a more enlightened collaboration and mutual reinforcement.

We need therefore to look again more carefully at the list of our commonalities and our divergences. We can then combine them in such a way that they become a call to mutual enrichment as we continue to reflect on our understanding and to organize our strategies for committed action.

I would like to mention a few examples of areas in which such a cross-fertilization could be organized. And I select these examples from the many cases which are implied in the reports from the various continents.

One instance is the question of "non-Christian religions." Although all our regions recognize the importance of the questions raised by the presence of living, non-Christian religions among which we Christians live and struggle, Asia's special context is a particularly challenging one. There, Christianity is in a numerical minority, lost in the midst of ancient religious traditions which are still the determining ideological basis of the life and attitudes of the majority. As the Asian Report suggests, it is a fundamental challenge for our Christian theology when 97 percent of the people are non-Christians, and the majority of them are precisely the "poor" and marginalized who, according to the claims of our Third World theologies, are the subjects of theology. What does that mean for our understanding of theology itself? What does it suggest in the way of relations with people of other faiths, in the way of conceiving and practicing solidarity with *all* those who are struggling for liberation? Latin America, with its overwhelming Christian majority, will also need to listen more carefully to the special challenges posed by this fact. Africa particularly is encouraged to take more seriously the presence of Islam and traditional religions in its midst.

There is also the question of poverty. We all agree that Third World theologies take poverty and oppression as central themes. And yet the meaning of poverty and the identity of the poor are not the same in our regions. In EATWOT we are often tempted to think that we all know who the poor are, and know in the same way. This is dangerous and misleading. The understanding of "poverty" primarily from the socio-economic and political point of view should be enriched by the question of "poverty" as liberation from the slavery of materialism. And what the African Report calls "anthropological poverty" underlines some aspects and depths of "poverty" which are not equally present elsewhere.

Neocolonialism is another example. All the regions of EATWOT are conscious of its negative effects. And yet neocolonialism adapts itself to the different contexts so that it takes different shapes and uses different strategies in Africa, in Latin America, and in the countries of Asia.

We could add other examples, like the women's issues, evangelization, culture, or indeed the question of methodology in Third World theologizing. EATWOT has as one of its main objectives to help the different parts of the Third World to overcome their isolation and mutual ignorance. As long as they are divided and kept apart, the marginalized countries in the Southern Hemisphere, and indeed all oppressed groups, cannot organize themselves effectively for liberative action. That is why cross-fertilization is crucial.

PART V

EVALUATIONS

14

Women's Evaluation of EATWOT

Women have been asked to present a critique of EATWOT. For this purpose, we met at the end of our intercontinental conference, previous to the general assembly, and discussed the request. The following are our conclusions.

POSITIVE ASPECTS

One of the more evident developments of our association is the increasing number of women members. In 1976, when the association was founded in Dar-es-Salaam, there was only one woman present; now there are thirty-seven women members. This increase is very important because it shows the sensibility, concern, and maturity of an association whose constituency makes theology from a liberating perspective and recognizes sexual discrimination as a serious obstacle to liberation.

We think that the presence of women has been accepted not just to fill the quota asked by the association's constitution. We hope the majority of the members want the promotion of women not because of their feminine gender, but because they trust their theological expertise.

We want to mention especially our former executive secretary, Sister Virginia Fabella. She is a living and clear example of the administrative and theological abilities of women. She has played a key role in opening in this new space for women. She has helped to lessen the fear of men to trust women, and she has helped to increase the self-confidence of women. All of us are most grateful to Virginia.

Another concrete development of the association has been the organization of a women's commission to deal exclusively with the theme "Women and Theology." We consider this a real concern about the marginalization of women. So far, this commission has been working on gathering women together, discerning their theological values and inputs, and organizing them at the national, continental, and recently at the intercontinental level.

WOMEN AS THEOLOGICAL ACTORS

If we look at the theological community, where the presence of women is finally becoming visible, and at the ecclesial community, the starting point of theological reflection, we realize immediately that women represent the majority of the churches' constituency. This fact raises a critical issue: those who are the majority have been absent from leadership positions and decisions. They have been silenced in the theological reflection and in the ecclesial discourse. After having been consumers of theology and assuming the burden of the ecclesial organization through their anonymous and little recognized work, women are beginning to emerge slowly as theological actors, and they have begun to do and to write theology.

With this emergence, churches gain new vitality, and theological reflection receives a new light. Marginalization of women does not affect only women; it damages the whole society as well, diminishing its capacities; it affects the whole church, because women's flexibility, richness, and vitality are not present. Finally, it reduces and impoverishes theological reflection, depriving it of new and enriching views, taking away from it a good deal of possibilities and creativity, since women bring to theology important contributions.

By doing theology, women discover their own methodology. This methodology is a way of feeling faith experience and sharing it in community. It is a way of organizing and systematizing insights into God's revelation, which comes out spontaneously in the life of the people and in particular in the lives of women. It is a way of expressing a vision of the world that emerges from the vital processes, where women are deeply immersed. It is a unique way of articulating theological discourse—it looks toward integrating scientific sternness and sensibility, fidelity to the sources (scripture and tradition) and openness to new challenges. It stresses creativity emerging from life itself, helpless and threatened in all three continents.

The Final Document of the Intercontinental Women's Conference, which took place in Oaxtepec prior to the general assembly, intends to reflect the discoveries of women in their way of doing theology.

In this fascinating task, however, there are many difficulties. When women want to respond to a theological vocation, very often it means assuming a difficult and heavy burden. Churches still have a long way to go to recognize the capacity and the leadership abilities of women.

In the academic world, the number of women trained is less than the number of men, either because of the lack of interest and investment of the churches, or due to the familial or institutional responsibilities of women, who cannot dedicate enough time to study and obtain a theological degree.

In relation to higher education in institutes and theological faculties, despite some progress in the opening of new spaces for women, they still hold fewer teaching positions than men. Besides all this, the theological task means a double effort for women. In our society—as it is organized—to dedicate themselves to theology does not exempt women from assuming responsibilities of home duties and child care, tasks that very often are not shared by their spouses.

Therefore, we believe that the effort of EATWOT to incorporate more women in the association is very important. The evaluation and critique of its organization and activities asked of us by the steering committee are new evidence of the sincerity and consistency of this effort. We are ready to respond to that position with an honest and loving critique.

A CRITIQUE OF EATWOT

We want to examine several aspects. In relation to the aims of EATWOT, and looking at the constitution approved in New Delhi in 1981, we believe that more emphasis must be given to the promotion of dialogue between theology and the diverse cultures and religions in our countries. In the general assembly this issue was raised several times, and that is a clear indication of its relevancy.

We strongly support the call for more communication and interchange of theological opinions, through various publications, books, and journals. We know that the problem of language is a real obstacle, but we think that no effort should be spared to overcome it. It will be necessary to have more translations of the work done in our continents.

If we talk about membership, we recognize real advances, as was mentioned above, but there are continents, Latin America for example, where the proportion set by EATWOT has not yet been realized. It is true that there still is a lack of women adequately trained and with enough theological expertise to participate in this association. But this reality, instead of discouraging us, should alert us to discover the potential theological vocation of women and to support those who are already working in their formation, backing them financially and morally.

As regards the commission entitled "History of the Church," we want to point out the small presence of women. Given the importance of this commission, we would like to see this gap be filled as soon as possible.

We are pleased, in general, with our relationship with male theologians. However, we would like to stress the permanent need of an effort to have women present and participating at all moments and levels of decision making, writing of documents, printing of publications, etc. It is our deep desire that no woman member of EATWOT would ever feel discriminated against or left behind by our male peers.

Finally, we are concerned about the lack of communication within our association, not only about women's issues, but in general. We need more efficiency regarding this point.

RECOMMENDATIONS

Building upon the foregoing evaluation, we want to present some recommendations to be considered by EATWOT.

1. That the "Commission on Feminine Theology" should be continued. This commission should continue because it has performed a priceless service to the struggle of women in the field of theology in all three continents. After an adequate evaluation, the commission could set new objectives for the future.

2. We recommend new efforts to include more women in the commission entitled "History of the Church." It is very important to have a significant presence of women to help to read history from their perspective and to rectify the absence of women in the written history of the church.

3. That the recommendations of the Intercontinental Women's Conference be taken into consideration and that its Final Document be distributed and discussed as much as possible in our continents.

4. That all EATWOT members responsible for publications request the collaboration of women in EATWOT books, magazines, etc., to be sure that women's theological work will always be heard.

5. We ask the male theologians of our association to include the women's perspective in their work. In this way, we hope that some day theology will be more global and inclusive.

15

EATWOT and Third World Theologies: An Evaluation of the Past and Present

Frank Chikane

1. INTRODUCTION

The Oaxtepec, Mexico, EATWOT conference was held over just seven days, from December 7–14, 1986. But by the end of the conference it seemed we had been together for a much longer period of time. This was inevitable because we had to deal with the "Commonalities and Divergences of Third World Theologies," the theme of the conference.

When I went to this conference, which was the first EATWOT meeting I attended, I expected a glorious, high-powered, and extensive theological discourse which was going to look systematically through the commonalities and divergences of Third World theologies as they relate to the particular struggles for liberation in the various regions of the Third World. I expected us to share with the people from Nicaragua, El Salvador, the Philippines, and many other areas in the Third World which have been turned into battle grounds of death in the name of the preservation of the economic interests and the national securities of First World countries.

I believe that many other participants had the same expectation. But right from the start of the conference we found ourselves in a "combustion chamber," a term I also used in describing our 1983 Black Theology Conference in South Africa.[1] Throughout the week I observed so many similarities between this conference and most of our conferences and seminars at home. This looked like just another "synoptic gospel" of South Africa — this time according to EATWOT! It looked like it was just the work of another evangelist writing about the same events in a more global context.

1.1. South Africa, Microcosm of the Third World Theological Debate

As we went through the conference it became clearer than ever before that apartheid South Africa is a microcosm of the cosmic dimensions of the various forms of oppression, namely those of class, race, sex, religion, culture, etc. All are present in South Africa. Our country is both a First World and Third World country. It is a highly industrialized, developing country. It has a unique form of colonization: an internal form of colonization where whites, who make up less than 20 percent of the population, oppress and exploit blacks, who make up the vast majority of the population and who have no vote. This brings in the situation of *racism*, which is more comparable to that experienced by the black North Americans and manifests itself at different levels and different forms throughout the world. It is for this reason that there has been a close affinity between South African black theology and that of black North Americans.

This form of neocolonialism, with whites acting as the racist and privileged local elite at the service of the interests of international capitalism, has occasioned economic oppression and exploitation. For this reason it has become inevitable for some of those who are engaged in theological reflection on our dynamics of conflict and power in South Africa to employ Marxist tools of analysis and to take the question of class struggles more seriously. The *class-race* interplay in the analysis of our form of oppression in South Africa is of vital importance, and this makes it one of the elements which fueled the fires in the "combustion chamber."

The South African population consists of about 33 million people, of which about 73.8 percent is African, about 8.5 percent is classified as "colored," about 2.7 percent is "Asian," and about 15 percent is "white" (1984 South African government statistics). The feature of South Africa therefore is mainly African, sharing common concerns with the rest of the African continent. African *culture* and African traditional *religions* therefore are important elements in the development of theology in South Africa. We also have a small presence of Muslims (1.7 percent) and Hindus (1.8 percent) which South African theologians have not taken seriously. The struggle waged by the United Democratic Front (UDF) brought this feature of South Africa into the open when Christians, Muslims, and Hindus prayed and struggled together against the apartheid regime. The work of the South African chapter of the World Conference on Religion and Peace (WCRP), which was formed in 1984, is beginning to make this necessary dialogue possible. Involvement in struggle with the UDF and the WCRP therefore has helped some of us out of our Christian arrogance to a humble submission to the mission of God in the world.

The contradictions within the liberation movement and within the South African black theology movement of protesting vehemently—and even violently—against racial, cultural, and politico-economic oppression, while continuing to oppress and exploit *women*, emerged more during the first part of the 1980s, causing serious embarrassment to the "revolutionaries" of the day.

Instead of disillusioning me, the "combustion chamber" at Oaxtepec therefore helped me to reflect more seriously and critically on the nature of the problem we are dealing with at home. On the other hand, our praxis at home made me appreciate better what Virginia Fabella described as "a gamut of human attitudes and emotions" that ranged from "resentment, anger, and sadness to excitement, gratitude, and eagerness to continue the task and to face the challenge with openness and hope."[2]

1.2. The "Combustion Chamber" within EATWOT

The chain of theological debate and dialogue which has resulted in this combustion within the chambers of EATWOT started as early as 1973 in Geneva at the World Council of Churches,[3] well before the formation of EATWOT. This was followed by the Detroit meeting in 1975 on "Theology in the Americas."[4] Since the formation of EATWOT at Dar-es-Salaam in 1976 there have been three major continental conferences (Accra, 1977; Wennappuwa, 1979; São Paulo, 1980) and one general assembly (New Delhi, 1981), in each of which this heavy dialogue between Third World theologies occurred.

Since I was asked to reflect critically on this debate or dialogue as a "newcomer" in EATWOT, I took the trouble of going through as much EATWOT published and unpublished material as I could lay my hands on. What struck me most in the course of this painstaking reading was the progress which had already been made in addressing the commonalities and differences of Third World theologies, and how enriching this painful exercise had been to most EATWOT participants. In the course of this paper I will try to show the amount of ground which has already been covered in this regard, which to me is one of the major success stories of EATWOT. For this reason, I do not regret the time spent in Oaxtepec, Mexico.

Further, as I read the EATWOT documents I was struck by the number of times this painful process was repeated since Dar-es-Salaam. In fact I believe that those in the Americas who started this exercise as early as 1973 must be suffering from an overdose of this debate. In this sense some should have enough reasons to feel frustrated and disappointed by the Oaxtepec EATWOT exercise on this theme. I think this unnecessary repetition and the apparent lack of awareness of the progress made[5] can be blamed on the process of EATWOT itself. Although in most final statements of EATWOT conferences and in almost all the evaluation papers there have been a consistent reference to the commonalities and divergences and even suggestions of how to address the divergences, the conference process of EATWOT was not planned to effectively consolidate the material produced.

If this paralysis in EATWOT has to be dealt with, and if we have to save EATWOT for the important mission it has to fulfill, we will need to scientifically program this "combustion chamber" to produce the required results without unnecessary violent explosions, so that through this baptism of fire the genuineness of our faith, tested by this fire, may redound to praise and glory and honor at the revelation of Jesus Christ (1 Peter 1:7).

1.3. What Is the Problem?

I have already identified some of the problem areas while looking at South Africa as a microcosm of the cosmic problem that is facing EATWOT. The problem as I see it is twofold. Firstly, all the Third World continents (Africa, Asia, and Latin America) and the minorities in North America developed their theologies almost independently,[6] all assuming that theirs was the most authentic theology, *the all in all theology*. This of course is the inevitable danger of all contextual theologies, which remain ghetto theologies if they have no ecumenical dialogue with other contextual theologies. For any contextual theology to be authentic and not to be limited by its own situation it needs always to be alive to this danger. Failure to do so leads to the arrogance of assuming that one's theology is a "universal" theology, for which Western theology has been castigated. I shall return to this universalist tendency later.

The second problem is that the various Third World theologies, influenced by their concerns, lay more emphasis on some form of oppression or another, even to the exclusion of all the other forms of oppression. Thus, although all Third World theologies are based on the need for some concept of liberation, the Latin American liberation theologians have laid more emphasis on socio-economic and political oppression, using Marxist tools of analysis to uncover this form of oppression. This they have done, almost to the exclusion of all the other forms of oppression (e.g., those involving race, gender, culture, or religion). The North American and South African black theologians, on the other hand, have tended to emphasize racial oppression almost to the exclusion of class oppression, while both African and Asian theologians have dealt more with the religio-cultural forms of oppression with varying emphasis (Africans talk more about Africanization and "indigenization," while Asians focus on "contextualization" rather than "indigenization"). Above all, Asian theologians are engaged in a dialogue with the other great religions of Asia. Both Asians and Africans therefore run the risk of being so preoccupied with religio-cultural issues that the socio-economic and political issues could be completely neglected. Once all this has been said we still need to explain why all these Third World theologians were completely blind to the question of the oppression of women. Why is it that the very oppressed, who were themselves lamenting bitterly about their oppression, were not alive to this form of oppression?

At New Delhi (1981), at the first assembly of EATWOT, there was an attempt to synthesize these different elements with the hope of presenting Third World theology as one, but the participants realized that in fact this attempt was premature.[7] Evaluating the work of EATWOT five years after New Delhi, I believe that we have almost come to maturity in the sense that the weaknesses and strong points of all these traditions (Latin American liberation theology, black theology, African theology, and Asian theology) have been effectively analyzed and suggestions have been made as to how the limitations could be overcome. What I think has not been done is tackling these weaknesses in our theologies. In this essay I am going to try to make a critical appraisal of this discourse and analysis. I shall then conclude by presenting a possible synthesis of these Third World theologies.

2. A CRITIQUE OF THE UNIVERSALIST TENDENCY IN THIRD WORLD THEOLOGIES

From the first contact Third World theologies made with each other, the tendency of trying to "absolutize" and to assume "universality" of one form of theology in relation to all the others, was evident. Allan Boesak, for instance, criticizes James Cone for claiming "God *solely* from the black experience...." Cone's mistake, he says, "is that he has taken black theology out of the framework of liberation theology, thereby making his own situation (being black in America) and his own movement (liberation from white racism) the ultimate criteria for *all* theology."[8] James Cone has of course since moved a great deal from this "absolutistic claim" raised by Boesak.[9] In fact, almost every article he has written and published in EATWOT literature contradicts this position.[10] But what is clear is that there was initially an attempt to reduce all forms of oppression to that of racism. The same can be said about African and Asian theologians. In speaking of what he calls the "inculturationist," Aloysius Pieris expresses this view crisply.[11] But from reading EATWOT documents—particularly articles and papers by Engelbert Mveng, James Cone, Herbert O. Edwards, Aloysius Pieris, and by the minority groups in North America (Hispanics, etc.) and black and native Latin Americans—and from following the discussions at Oaxtepec, one senses the common feeling of suspicion that the Latin American theologians wanted to impose their form of liberation theology on the others.

From Virginia Fabella's comments in the preface to *Irruption of the Third World: Challenge to Theology* (Orbis, 1983), a book which she edited with Sergio Torres, it is very clear that there has been an attempt to project Latin American liberation theology as identical with Third World theology (p. xvii). Aloysius Pieris equates this "imperialist" tendency of Latin American liberation theology with that of Christianity. He says that "one regrets ... that the only Third World theology presently being given substance is circumscribed by the exclusively Latin and Christian context of its origin."[12] To avoid being misunderstood as being on the attack against the Latin Americans, he says that "this remark is not leveled against the Latin American model but against the ... attitudes it has evoked in the Africo-Asian churches, in that some 'liberationists' want to duplicate a Latin, Christian model in their non-Latin and non-Christian environments, thus driving the 'inculturationists' to a defensive extreme."[13]

For this reason, both Asians and Africans suspect the Latin American theology of liberation as "the next 'universal' theology to dominate the Third World."[14] J. Deotis Roberts, criticizing this "universalist" tendency, cautions against making the mistake of "transporting or transplanting from Latin America another form of theology without transforming it" to make it useful to specific Third World situations.[15]

The most scathing attack comes from Engelbert Mveng,[16] who says that the New Delhi conference (1981) helped to dispel all the historical mis-understandings, making it clear that EATWOT is not an "institutionali-zation of the Latin American theology of liberation"; it is not organized as a "hegemony" under the leadership of the Latin Americans. He says that this kind of hegemony would run the risk of returning to the old colonial tendencies of "intellectual, cultural, sociological, economic, and religious imperialism." This could relate to what he calls "new types of paternalism" and the declaration of the methodology of the Latin American system of analysis "as universal."

Gregory Baum, in his article entitled "The Christian Left at Detroit," expresses the reaction of one North American against the leadership offered by the Latin Americans. Writing about the relation between Chi-canos and Latin American theologians at the Detroit conference, he states:

> Of importance was also the Chicanos' reaction to the leadership offered by the Latin American theologians. These latter theologians appeared as sons of successful people, well-educated and well-spoken, possessing an articulate intelligence associated with university life. We are different, the Chicanos said; we are more simple people; we are still closer to the level on which we were held by the oppressor. If we permit you to be our leaders, they said to the Latins, we shall be in a situation in which we have been so long, unable to find our own words to express our situation and incapable of devising modes of action that correspond to our present needs and our past experience. Even the confident, holistic economic analysis proposed by the Latin Americans posed problems for the Chicanos. The analysis may be correct in principle, they said, but if we receive from you the key for understanding our own subjugation before we reach the maturity to argue with you from a basis of equal confidence, we will not move toward a liberated form of self-possession. Our struggle is our own. Other people can help us by being in solidarity with us, but the lead-ership direction of the movement must come from ourselves, however tentative these may be at the beginning.[17]

One could continue with this emotionally charged aspect of the critique of Latin American liberation theology which appears in almost every pub-lication of EATWOT[18] and even in publications that appeared prior to the founding of EATWOT. But why this heavy attack on the Latin Americans? To me there are at least two reasons for it. One is the assumption that the Marxist tools of analysis were dogmatically applicable to every situation in the world with no need of taking the differences of these situations into consideration. There is here some element of what some South African *black* theologians have called "internationalism," an attitude which does not take seriously the concrete conditions of a particular situation. This form of negative internationalism Pieris calls "occidentalism."[19] I shall deal with this question of using Marxist tools of analysis in the next section. The second reason is that liberation theology became so popular that those who propagated it thought of it as the classical form of Third World theology. But it is encouraging that through this confrontation some of the key Latin American theologians, like Gustavo Gutiérrez and Sergio Torres,[20] have come to accept that their form of liberation theology cannot be taken as the Third World theology under which all the other Third World theologies are to be submerged. In fact, Cone says that black theologians' encounter with Gutiérrez has been entirely different from those with any other Latin American theologian from as early as 1975.[21] I shall deal with this readiness to learn from others when I evaluate the progress made in the last ten years of EATWOT.

3. THE USE OF MARXIST TOOLS OF ANALYSIS IN THIRD WORLD THEOLOGY

One of the most controversial issues within EATWOT has been the use of Marxist tools of analysis in doing theology in the Third World. By the time the dialogue started between the various Third World theologians, the Latin Americans were almost the only ones who employed these tools in doing theology; the use of such tools led them to see some form of socialist future as the closest to their vision of the Kingdom of God. In this section I shall look at the use of these tools as indispensable for the analysis of socio-economic and political forms of oppression, and then discuss their limitations. Thereafter I shall try to develop a "corrective" to make them relevant to the different situations in the Third World.

3.1. *Marxist Tools of Analysis are Indispensable in Understanding Socio-economic-political Forms of Oppression and Exploitation*

Marx developed his tools of analysis of the politico-economic system of his time at the height of the industrial revolution and the growth of the capitalist means of production and distribution. Whatever one's opinion is about Marx, the fact of the matter is that his tools of analysis — especially of the capitalist mode of production, of the tension between those who own means of production and have control over the redistribution of the product and those who have only their labor to sell, and of the surplus value and profit—cannot be ignored. Even very hostile social scientists do refer to Marx at one stage or another. It looks like there is no adequate scientific method of understanding the forces at play in colonial and neocolonial situations, in questions of poverty, exploitation, and economic oppression, without drawing on Marx's tools of analysis. A classic example for me is the problem of South Africa, a problem which is popularly known as apartheid. Usually the system of apartheid is described as a crude form of racism; the international community (the U.N.) has described it as a "crime against humanity," while the international Christian community has declared it a "heresy." Because of this crude form of racism, South African black theologians, like their counterparts in the United States, became preoccupied with the question of racism to the complete exclusion of class oppression. The risk here is that one could remove racial oppression without dealing with economic exploitation, if that were possible. This could result in some being just co-opted into the existing status quo without any radical and total reconstruction of society right from its material and economic base.

It is for this reason that some South African black theologians, like Buti Tlhagale, are beginning to employ historical materialism to deal with the South African situation. In his article "Towards a Black Theology of Labor," Buti Tlhagale says:

We cannot continue for long in this speculative vein without raising the question of relevance for our situation. This broad Marxist cum Christian perspective has a bearing on the South African scene. It is against this background that we should like to examine the material conditions of the black laboring class and consider whether Blacks, through their work, realize themselves, construct their world and appropriate the products of their labor, whether through their activity they really become co-creators with God.[22]

He concludes his paper by saying:

This is the perspective upheld by Black Theology. In consciously intensifying their class struggle, workers are actively presenting themselves as co-creators. . . . Co-ownership of industries, the right to participate in the policy-making machinery and eventually the right to have a say in the labor laws and all the laws affecting the lives of workers, will not be given, but are to be appropriated through a class struggle. As the struggle rages, the image of God becomes closer and more convincing and the workers' partnership with God as the result of the Covenant becomes more meaningful. This Black Theology praxis authenticates Christian claims.

The quality of life for the Black majority is likely to be enhanced in a planned economic system. Entrenched privileges of the capitalist system preclude any radical changes. Again the Christian ethos of charity advocates a (radical) system of sharing and paternalism is not recognized as a value.[23]

For Tlhagale "a socialist system would harbor at its core the belief that man is by nature corporate, that his labor is social/communal, that capital is the result of this social labor—that justice demands an unconditional acceptance that all are equal before God."[24]

Takatso Mofokeng, another South African black theologian, in discussing the methodology of black theology says that "Black Theology does a three-dimensional analysis in which the Marxist tool of social analysis is used."[25] These dimensions consist of, first, the analysis of the material situation of the struggling community today; second, the analysis of the material situation of Palestine during the time of Jesus and his praxis as witnessed by the scriptures; and, third, a comparison of these situations to see whether both are at the "same level of engagement and radicality in this identical struggle that develops dialectically from low to high point. . . . The community then makes the necessary adjustment in its struggle to be with him [Jesus]" as they all go further into a high point of radicality.[26]

One could continue to discuss Simon Maimela, Lebamang Sebidi, and others. The reality is that during the first part of the 1980s a lot of progress was made within the "combustion chamber" in South Africa. From the end of the 1970s to the first part of the 1980s there was a historical shift in the political praxis in South Africa, making the 1984 Black Theology Conference accept that "what happens in the black struggle affects the process of theologizing about this struggle. Our present historical praxis therefore must affect Black Theology itself."[27] It is this reading of the South African situation which forces South African theologians to search for more effective tools of analysis.

Black theologians in the United States, like James Cone and Cornel West, have also started on this road of looking for relevant and critical tools of analysis to deal with their complex situation in the United States. James Cone, for instance, says that "if we define our struggle for freedom only within the alternatives posed by capitalism, then we have allowed our future humanity to be determined by what people have created and not by God." "Why not think that the 'not yet' is possible?" he asks. "Why not think of a completely new society . . . ?" "Perhaps," he suggests, "what we need today is to return to the 'good old-time religion' of our grandparents and combine with it Marxist critique of society." So that, "together—black religion and Marxist philosophy may show us the way to build a completely new society."[28] Maybe one could also find similar movements within Asian theology.

All in all, one sees an acceptance within EATWOT in general of the need to use Marxist tools of analysis to deal with the socio-economic and political realities of the Third World. In general it is understood that these tools are necessary if Third World theologies are to be relevant and bold enough to face the reality of class oppression. This attitude is found in almost all EATWOT evaluation papers and statements. Once all this has been said, all the theologians add a "but." The Asians, the Africans, the minorities in the United States, and the native and black Latin Americans raise some inadequacies of the Marxist tools for dealing with religio-cultural realities. And here they point at the weaknesses of Latin American liberation theology in its failure even to touch on these issues, accusing them of making both the native (Indian) and black Latin Americans almost invisible in their theology. This is the subject of the next section.

3.2. The Inadequacies of Marxist Analysis in Dealing with Religio-cultural Realities in the Third World

The inadequacies of the Marxist tools of analysis were already raised by a number of South African black theologians like Takatso Mofokeng, Jerry Mosala, and Bonganjalo Goba during some of our theological discourses at home, before I came to EATWOT. Mofokeng in particular had already suggested that maybe Amilcar Cabral of Guinea could help us in developing a corrective to the Marxist tools of analysis to make them more relevant to the African situation. Within EATWOT, I think Aloysius Pieris of Sri Lanka has presented the most extensive and elaborate critique of the Marxist tools of social analysis,[29] while Cornel West's comments at the São Paulo (1979) EATWOT conference are also very useful.[30] I propose here a brief outline of the inadequacies of Marx's tools of analysis without attempting to discuss the details.

First, we need to accept that *Marx was a person of his own time,* reflecting on a particular praxis to develop his theory. He was a nineteenth-century European (black theologians would add "white"), living during a time when Europe and the West were less informed than now about the complex structure and history of non-Christian cultures. We should not forget that at one stage missionaries believed that the people of the other worlds they were called to evangelize had no religion, and if they had, it was considered inferior. For this reason, Marxist analysis in its dogmatic form could not capture the seriousness of religio-cultural realities outside the dominant cultural reality of Europe.

The second point, which flows from the first, has to do with Marx's attitude to religion. He developed his theory during a time in Europe which was influenced by intellectual movements like the *Enlightenment, the scientific revolution, and rationalism,* which led to the secularization of the West today. The philosophical rejection of religion was characteristic of this period. During this time theologians like Strauss, Schleiermacher, and Harnack struggled to develop the historico-critical method of biblical research, which was a manifestation of the thought processes of the time. It is therefore natural that Marx's dialectical materialism sets religion against revolution.

But there is another reason why Marx called religion "an opiate of the people." We must remember that Marx said this during a period of transition from what Jürgen Habermass calls primitive and traditional societies to early modern society.[31] Habermass says that in primitive and traditional societies, myths, religion, and metaphysics served as legitimators of institutional frameworks, but with the development of early modern society, traditional forms of power legitimation were questioned. This process is taken to its logical conclusion in modern capitalist society where technocratic ideology replaces religion in legitimizing power structures. Although we may differ with Habermass's theory of religion (and this is no place to debate with him), which reduces religion simply to a legitimization of unjust relations and uneven power distribution, his description of this transition does help to understand Marx. The fact is that at that stage, religion did play a legitimizing role of the systems (social, political, etc.) of that time and still has the potential to do so today. But reducing religion to this function as a consequential by-product, or expression, of oppression and exploitation, or linking it up with the "economic infrastructure of capitalism," as Canaan Banana would say,[32] is underestimating the reality of religious expression, especially in Africa and Asia.

Canaan Banana engages Marx in a dramatic discourse about his dictum regarding religion. Both dogmatic Marxists and Western conservatives have treated it as the heart of Marxism and communism, as if this were the most important and the only gospel Marx preached all his life. For this reason Marx's important contribution in developing effective tools of analysis of society is reduced to his attitude to religion. But let us go back to Banana's discourse with Marx on this issue.[33] He says that Marx condemned religion as a whole, from a socio-economic point of view, linking it with the economic infrastructure of capitalism. To Marx, "morality, religion, metaphysics and other ideologies . . . no longer retain . . . their appearance of autonomous existence."[34] But Banana suggests that one could argue with Marx regarding the permanence of that dependence. Banana asks about Marx: Did he say that religion would be a mere ideological appendix of capitalism, and the ideological opium used to suffocate the conscience of the masses, and nothing else? Did he not recognize that the ideological stand of the workers could acquire a certain autonomy from the domination of the capitalist masters against them? Would he not also see that religion, although much dependent on the support given by the owners of the means of production, could also acquire an independent consciousness and strike against the oppressors? This, he says, would be the liberation of religion, morality, and theology (one would add "and the church"), much the same as the socio-economic revolution against capitalism liberates the workers.

Banana says that all that Marx said was that there was a clear relationship between a form of Christianity and a given mode of production. Therefore, in the same way that workers are allowed to acquire a different type of awareness and consciousness which makes them revolt against the system of production, so should religion be considered capable of revolting against an oppressive economic base when the adherents of that religion acquire a revolutionary and liberating form of consciousness. This Banana calls a *revolutionary Christianity*.

3.3. A Corrective

From the above analysis it is clear that Marx developed his theory of social analysis from within a European context, within a European dominant culture, that his theory could not capture the seriousness of the other cultures outside the European capitalist culture, that religion within his context would not have appeared otherwise than a reactionary phenomenon which was counter-revolutionary. For this reason the Marxist tools of analysis are not adequate to deal with the religio-cultural realities of Africa and Asia. Ignoring the concrete realities of these regions in doing theology and in engaging in a struggle for liberation is tantamount to subverting the very revolutionary intention.

To achieve the goal of the vision of the Kingdom of God; to effect a radical change of society to approximate this vision; to work for the "not yet" that is ahead, we need comprehensive and rigorous theoretical tools of analysis that are informed by a given praxis. A radical, revolutionary approach to culture and religion should, therefore, start from the concrete reality that there are such things as culture and religion; that both are ambivalent phenomena; that they have both a reactionary and a revolutionary potential. What we need to do as theologians is to discover this revolutionary potential of both culture and religion in the course of the struggle for the *basileia* or the new order. We should, through our analysis, release or unleash this potential for radical change. So, instead of condemning religion as counter-revolutionary and ignoring it, and at the worst fighting it, we need to enhance the liberative force in religion. There are models already in the offing. Nicaragua, for instance, is a classic example of this revolutionary Christianity which is consistent with the radical concept of the Kingdom of God.

There is therefore a need for a new understanding of the religio-cultural reality as part and parcel of the socio-economic and political reality of our context of struggle; and that being so, it is clear that we need to use both the religio-cultural tools of analysis and the Marxist tools of analysis. Maybe we need a corrective of Marx's theory by expounding it in such a way that the religio-cultural elements are integrated within this theory.

I believe that the only people who can develop this new, comprehensive theory of social analysis to deal with our complex religio-cultural and economic reality are Third World theologians who are committed to a radical change of society based on their faith. But this theory cannot be developed in abstract terms within a theoretical vacuum. It has to be developed in the course of the struggle for a radical change in society so that its authenticity can be tested by this praxis of struggle.

4. A CRITIQUE OF THE EXCLUSIVE RACE AND RELIGIO-CULTURAL MODELS OF ANALYSIS

My critique of the Marxist tools of analysis, which has been a critique of the Latin American theology of liberation, started from an acceptance that these tools are of vital importance for the analysis of socio-economic and political oppression. All EATWOT literature indicates grudgingly this acceptance, which is usually followed by a "but." As Cornel West would say, "Some form of Marxist analysis is indispensable to understand the international economic order, capitalist societies, and the perpetuation and preservation of gross inequalities and injustices in those societies."[35] In agreement with Cornel West, I have shown nevertheless that "the Achilles heel of Marxist theory is found in the issues of culture, self-identity, ethnic and racial communities, and existential security."[36] This has been a clear indictment of the Latin American liberation theologians.

We should now turn to the race and religio-cultural models of analysis. If these models are used exclusively without employing Marxist tools, is there no risk, as well, of leaving other forms of oppression? Is there no socio-economic and political oppression in Asia and Africa? Of course there is at different levels. Going through EATWOT literature and listening to the debates of the Oaxtepec conference one cannot fail to observe the reluctance on the part of some African and Asian theologians to confront the economic realities of their situation. One reads of some willingness on the part of both North American and South African black theologians to incorporate Marxist analysis into their theological reflection to supplement the race model they have been using, but one sees very little, if any, of that willingness in the rest of Africa and Asia. In South Africa, we have learned that although we are now involved in a national democratic liberation struggle where all participate irrespective of their class position (simply because they are oppressed en bloc), we must be conscious of the various class positions of blacks, and that there are classes of blacks which participate in the exploitation of those who are made more vulnerable by the very system we are fighting.

James Cone, who, I think, is one of those theologians in EATWOT who has confronted this question of commonalities and differences head-on (maybe because he was representing the marginalized group within EATWOT, as he expressed at Oaxtepec), has dealt quite effectively with North American black theologians' differences with African theology; this shows clearly the problem of the exclusive use of the religio-cultural approach in doing theology. He says that North American black theologians' dialogue with Africans began as early as 1971. In his evaluation of the New Delhi conference,[37] he says that while the North Americans placed more emphasis on socio-political liberation, Africans stressed cultural liberation. He says that in each of the meetings between the groups, Africans "shied away from the term 'liberation' because they say that the gospel is not political. It is not an ideology of the oppressed."[38] Some, he says, have even said that the gospel is concerned about all—the rich and the poor alike. In their emphasis on "Africanization" and "indigenization" they locate the problem at the point of culture, not politics. The following statement by Cone summarizes his critique very well:

> Like our African brothers and sisters, we believe that there is a spiritual ingredient in the gospel that transcends the material conditions of human life. What we reject is the tendency among some African theologians to reduce the gospel and theology to a spirituality that has not been carved out of the real-life sufferings of the poor who are engaged in political liberation. When the sufferings of the poor are individualized, privatized, it becomes possible to identify their sufferings with God without challenging the existing socio-political structures responsible for their suffering.[39]

This attribute of cause falls squarely within Marx's critique of religion. Religion here becomes an opium of the people, the "sigh of the oppressed creature, the heart of the heartless world, the soul of the soulless condition."[40] This would be a religion which is just a vehicle to meet the needs of the people and to pacify emotion, imagination, and fears. It is not a means for going down to the root cause of this experience of suffering. If this is the case then Marx would be right to say that these religious reflexes would "finally vanish when the practical relations of everyday life offer to man none but perfectly intelligible and reasonable relations with regard to his fellowmen and to nature."[41] Cone says therefore that in this approach of African theology "a suffering God and Jesus' cross become mere intellectual, theological concepts totally unrelated to the daily life of the poor."[42]

Bonganjalo Goba[43] expresses the tension between African theologians who use the ethnographic method (which emphasizes the African traditional religions and values) and those who use the socio-economic and political approach (focusing on the contemporary socio-political and economic issues from the perspective of blacks). Manas Buthelezi[44] confronts the ethnographic approach with what he calls the anthropological approach.[45]

Engelbert Mveng also talks of a methodological approach which he says is more anthropological, although for him this methodology is advanced as an alternative to the Marxist approach of social analysis. In his regional coordinator's report to the Oaxtepec EATWOT assembly (1986) he started by showing that although the past five centuries of African history of colonization imposed on Africa a phenomenon of alienation caused by Western capitalism, which could suggest that Marxist analysis would be key to this situation, it is necessary to see that the problem in Africa is not merely capitalistic alienation—it is also a problem of historical annihilation and genocide. In Africa, he says, "the situations are still rare where the praxis of historical nationalism" causes real social class struggles. Our struggle is a struggle for life, and when classes exist, it is the struggle of all classes."[46]

When going through this argument of Engelbert Mveng, one cannot but suspect that there is an attempt to obscure the class realities of the African continent. The fact of the matter is that the postcolonial powers have been replaced, in many independent African countries, by a small, local capitalist elite which is representing and safeguarding the interests of the international capitalist monopolies. These are, in fact, the gatekeepers of the international monopolists who do so at the expense of the poor and hungry masses of Africa. Mveng does accept that there is a problem of capital, of class struggle, of the exploitation of one human being by another. "But," he says, "for us Africans, the world's institutionalized poverty has other roots as well, and it is perhaps these roots that are more serious, more important, more relevant to the present moment: slavery, colonialism, neo-colonization, racism, apartheid and the universal derision that has always accompanied the civilized world's discourse upon and encounter with Africa—and still accompanies it today."[47]

Let us briefly look at Asian theology which, I must admit, I have not been exposed to sufficiently because of a lack of dialogue between South African and Asian theologians. The Asian scene is characterized by a unique presence of the great and ancient religions of the world. Because of this reality there is a strong emphasis on dialogue with these religions in the course of a development of the theology of liberation. It is this input of Asian theologians that has reawakened other Third World theologians to the need to enter in humility into a continuing dialogue with the different cultures and religions in Asia. After a rigorous analysis of the religio-cultural reality of Asia, Aloysius Pieris concludes that "a 'liberation' theopraxis in Asia which uses only the Marxist tools of *social* analysis will remain un-Asian and ineffective until it integrates the psychological tools of *introspection* which our sages have discovered."[48] But Pieris does not criticize just the "liberationist" thought system; he equally criticizes the "inculturationist" system. He says that "inculturationists" use what he calls the "Christ for religion theology," where there is no link between religion and material and structural poverty; where there is no link with the liberation struggles of the peoples. He says that the Afro-Asian "indigenizers" and the "ethnocentricists" have a narrow focus on religion and culture with no attention to the colossal scandal of institutionalized misery that poses a challenge to every religion.[49] In general, the advocates of the inculturation approach fail to see the class culture they have identified with.

J. C. Duraisingh and K. C. Abraham, in their evaluation of the New Delhi EATWOT conference (1981) from an Asian perspective, say, "We in Asia are prone to the danger of romanticizing the ancient religions and accepting them uncritically," while knowing that they have been used to exploit the masses and to "protect the vested interests of the high and mighty." These religions, they say, have been used to silence the masses and to make them "accept passively their suffering, resorting to other-worldly flights from reality."[50] One could say that like some African theologians, some Asian theologians are avoiding the use of the Marxist tools of analysis in order to side-step a head-on confrontation with the reality of class divisions in their societies.

I would like to propose that if we would like to remove the speck in our sisters' and brothers' eyes in Latin America (making the native and black Latin Americans invisible in their theology of liberation because of the inadequacy of the Marxist tools of analysis to deal with the religio-cultural forms of oppression), then we need to remove first the log in our eyes (ignoring and even becoming part and parcel of the local capitalist oppression of our people because of the inadequacy of the religio-cultural tools of social analysis to deal with socio-economic and political oppression and realities of our situation). The reverse should also hold.

5. THE IRRUPTION WITHIN AN IRRUPTION

The final statement of the National Feminist Theology Conference (1984) in South Africa says:

> Whereas women form the majority of the oppressed, we note with regret that Black Theology has not taken women seriously, but has seen theology as a male domain. We the participants of this conference feel that there is no way that Black Theology will be a meaningful liberating force if it does not allow women to participate as equals. Any struggle which does not take the oppression of women seriously cannot be an authentic revolutionary force.[51]

One year earlier black theologians in South Africa had already been confronted by this lack of sensitivity—they, who are oppressed themselves, had ignored their own sisters and were also responsible for their oppression. In that 1983 Black Theology Conference[52] the participants said that "blame has to be borne by the Black Theology project itself in this country since its inception." They acknowledged that "the true measure of liberation in any society is the extent to which women are liberated. For this reason Black Theology cannot be a theology of liberation unless feminist theology is a fundamental part—autonomously organized—of a broad movement of a Black Theology of liberation." They concluded by saying that the question of the composition of that conference in terms of the dominance of a male, academic, priestly group revealed for them the "class basis" on which they have so far attempted to do black theology.

It is interesting to me that by the time this irruption of women started in an organized form to challenge those who claimed to be doing a theology of liberation, the same process had already started within EATWOT. Virginia Fabella says that the attitude of these liberation theologians toward women spurred an explosive debate in New Delhi (1981).[53] Amba Oduyoye described this as "the irruption within the irruption."[54] She says that "EATWOT had come face to face with the fact that the community of women and men, even in the church and among 'liberation theologians,' is not as liberating as it could be. That 'irruption' could only have come from a woman."

Amba Oduyoye here exposes a reality that still intrigues me. It is a reality which raises the most perplexing question for Third World theologians of liberation. The question is, why didn't all these great Third World theologians capture the pain of their sisters who were suffering side by side with them? Why is an oppressed person (a man) capable of oppressing another oppressed person (a woman), or capable of being blind to the fact that he or she is also oppressing other people? To be more specific, why did the Latin American brothers and sisters—even with their rigorous tools of social analysis, with their elaborate and well-developed theology of liberation—remain blind to the oppression and presence of both native (Indian) and black Latin Americans? Are some of these progressive theologians not participating in the oppression of these marginalized people or otherwise benefiting directly or indirectly out of this structural oppression of these people? Why did they not pick up the oppression of women in their midst with their tools of analysis? Is there something wrong with these tools? One could ask the same questions about black theologians which Cornel West and others have already asked. The Africans and Asians in fact are almost the worst in the area of oppression of women. Why did they not capture this elaborate social oppression of the majority of the people (women) in their midst?

Let us take this prosecution of the oppressed for oppressing others a little bit further. While many women talk about a threefold oppression, especially in the Third World—i.e., oppression as women (sex), as workers (class), and as people of "color" (race)—women in South Africa take this issue further by arguing that the "oppression of women is multifold." They add in this list, for instance, the oppression of "one another as women both as individuals and as a group."[55] In elaborating on this issue, they say:

There is no sisterhood between black and white women on the basis of our womanhood. White women, whilst experiencing oppression as women, form part of the ruling class and therefore exploit and oppress black women. For them to participate more fully in the struggle of women in the South African situation, they must commit class suicide and reject the artificial barriers of race [that separate us] if any alliance is to be forged with them.

The other issue raised during discussions in these conferences is the middle-class woman's role in this struggle. Even if these women are black, they still exploit other black women. The critique therefore of the feminist theology movement is that it is led mainly by middle-class and white women who "enjoy" their freedom by simply transferring their "old" roles to other women of "lower" classes. They exert themselves in society and prove that women are equal to men, but at the expense of other women.

This irruption within an irruption in the Third World is a sufficient indication that the structures of oppression have become so complex that all of us need to be humble enough to realize that we are liable to be part of the oppressor classes in this world. Maybe we need to take more seriously the old-time religion which holds that there is a cosmic war between the forces of evil and those of justice (good), that as humanity becomes more sophisticated sin could just elude us, as I believe it has already eluded the church universal. For instance, while wars are systematically planned and encouraged in the Third World to secure the influence of powerful nations and to secure both their economic and "national" security interests, the church is completely absorbed by the actual misery, violence, suffering, and death in the Third World. This is what I have called a preoccupation with a secondary "sin" while being eluded by the primary "sin." You just have to listen to exposures of U.S. intelligence operations to see how serious this situation is.

Women have also said that their liberation cannot be delayed until the liberation of all the poor and the oppressed. History has proved that a revolution is no guarantee of the liberation of women. The liberation of women therefore cannot be "relegated to insignificance on the post-liberation agenda."[56] In the final statement of the 1984 National Feminist Theology Conference, women asserted:

> While recognizing that we are participating in a broader struggle for the liberation of our people, the women's struggle must not be subordinated to the broader struggle (against national oppression and exploitation). The two battles must be fought side by side so that when liberation has been achieved it will not have been at the expense of women.[57]

Once all this has been said, we still need to go back into the EATWOT "combustion chamber." What is the nature of the dialogue among Third World women? In their second draft of the final document of the Intercontinental Women's Conference (Oaxtepec, Mexico, December 1-5 1986) we can see signs of the "combustion chamber" of EATWOT we have already discussed. In that final draft they say that they have perceived a common perspective in the three continents—that the women's struggle is deeply connected with the efforts of all the poor and the oppressed who are struggling for liberation in all aspects of life. But, they say, this liberation process "happens differently in the three continents. In Latin America women organize themselves around survival strategies. In Africa, the rebirth of women goes hand in hand with the struggle to overthrow the oppressive elements in traditional African cultures and religion and the evils of colonialism. In Asia, the struggle is centered in discovering the pride of being women, in building womanhood and humane communities and in fighting against political, economic and sexual injustice."[58]

The divergences therefore are due to "religious and cultural differences among the continents, and within various regions in each continent and in the way the different churches assimilate these new experiences."[59]

In this same draft they express the fact that their task of doing theology encompasses a common goal of bringing a new dimension to the struggle for justice as women, and it involves the rebuilding of the Reign of God. These are dimensions which are not theirs; these dimensions are given to them both by the voice of the people who are clamoring for justice and by God who inspired and convoked them. They conclude by saying that humanity as a whole, not only women, stands to benefit from the whole endeavor.

6. A SYNTHESIS

What have Third World theologians really been trying to do which led them into these intricacies of social analysis? It is their methodology of developing theology from their praxis, the ecclesiastical praxis, that forced them to face these complexities. We are concerned here with God's history of redemption. Carlos Abesamis says that "doing theological reflection is above all 'describing' the present moment in the history of redemption (= deliverance and coming into possession of salvific blessings = salvation, which, by the way, is total salvation)."[60] To him, the Christian faith is first and foremost about this history of redemption, a history of salvific actions, of salvific events which evolve into a hope for the final salvific action/event which has been already inaugurated in the works, death, and resurrection of Jesus of Nazareth. This action/event will be completed at the Parousia.[61] Allan Boesak agrees here with Abesamis when he says that "Black Theology knows that the biblical message of God's liberation has historical as well as eschatological dimensions."[62] This message of God's liberation does not only rest upon the historical event; it also points to the future.

Abesamis says that the second aspect of this gospel is that it teaches also about a way of life, an ethic, the ethic of Jesus. For Abesamis, therefore, theological reflection is "reflecting on contemporary human life situations within the context of salvation history and in the light of the ethic of Jesus."[63] This then constitutes what Boesak calls "total liberation,"[64] which Buthelezi calls the "wholeness of life."[65] According to Boesak, black theology focuses on "the dependency of the oppressed and their liberation from this dependency on several levels: psychological, cultural, political, economic and theological."[66] He thus concludes that "the ethic of this theology must be an ethic of liberation."[67]

To understand the history of redemption and the ethic thereof, we need to make an analysis of our concrete situations where this history is unfolding. This necessitates a process of social analysis as part and parcel of this process of theologizing. The great achievement of EATWOT is that it has, during a dialogue which lasted a decade, exposed Third World theologians to realities of others which have had an impact on all, and it has made all of us more conscious of forms of oppression in our areas which we had not taken seriously, and to which we were completely blind in the past. EATWOT dialogue has also exposed the weak and strong elements of our tools of analysis which we employed for our own situations.

I believe that given the amount of work done in the last decade, and the ground covered, all should have been sensitized enough to realize that:

1. No single Third World theology can be regarded as the whole truth, "a universal truth" on its own to the extent that all others could be subsumed or submerged within it.

2. A Third World theology must include the particularizations of all the emerging Third World theologies and should never be reduced to any one of them—as Cone has repeatedly said.[68] He argues that a genuine Third World theology cannot be exclusively Latin American or African or Asian or black American. It must instead be all of them and much more. He says that EATWOT theology must be "somewhat similar to all of the theologies represented in EATWOT and also quite different from them. It will be a genuinely new theology, derived from our common struggle together, transcending our narrow viewpoints in order to embrace a higher truth embedded in the histories and cultures of the poor throughout the world."[69]

3. Although our situations are different, the various forms of oppression (social, economic, political, and those based on class, race, sex, religion, culture) are present in different degrees in all of them and therefore cannot be ignored. We all need to be alive to them and criticize them rigorously and engage in concrete activities and programs to root them out. The related theological development will be advanced during this process as part and parcel of these struggles.

4. To achieve this level of consciousness and sensitivity we need to use all effective tools of analysis for all these forms of oppression. The tools of Third World liberation theologies must, therefore, include both the religio-cultural and socio-economic and political perspective. We must use both the religio-cultural and the Marxist tools of analysis. In fact, I have earlier suggested an integrated approach—integrating these two models of social analysis into a comprehensive system of social analysis which is capable of capturing any level or any form of oppression in our societies and in the world at large.

The Delhi conference made it a priority of the five years between 1981 and 1986 to develop "a synthesis between the two major trends in Third

World theologies: the socio-economic and the religio-cultural, both of which are essential for integral liberation."[70] I believe we have reluctantly reached two syntheses, but because of fear of the unknown some are keeping their heads above this reality. EATWOT must plan its program in such a way that we face this eventuality head-on and move into the "unknown" beyond the bounds of our traditions. We need to be prophetic!

NOTES

1. See I. S. Mosala and B. Tlhagale, eds., *The Unquestionable Right To Be Free: Essays in Black Theology* (Johannesburg: Scotaville Publishers, 1986), p. xviii.

2. See V. Fabella and S. Torres, eds., *Irruption of the Third World: Challenge to Theology* (Maryknoll, N.Y.: Orbis Books, 1983), pp. xi–xii.

3. See J. Cone, "From Geneva to São Paulo," in S. Torres and J. Eagleson, eds., *The Challenge of Basic Christian Communities* (Maryknoll, N.Y.: Orbis Books, 1981), p. 266. For the account of the dialogue see *Risk* 9, no. 2 (1973).

4. See Cone, "From Geneva to São Paulo," pp. 267–70. For a full account of this conference see S. Torres and J. Eagleson, eds., *Theology in the Americas* (Maryknoll, N.Y.: Orbis Books, 1976).

5. J. Cone seems to be aware of this progress (see "From Geneva to São Paulo") although he seems to be clouded by his frustration over the slow pace of some of the Latin Americans.

6. As regards the relationship between black theology in the United States and that which developed in South Africa, see Mokgethi Matlhabi's paper in *The Unquestionable Right To Be Free*.

7. See the final statement of the Delhi conference in Fabella and Torres, *Irruption of the Third World*, p. 192.

8. See his "Coming Out of the Wilderness," in V. Fabella and S. Torres, eds., *The Emergent Gospel: Theology from the Underside of History* (Maryknoll, N.Y.: Orbis Books, 1978), pp. 87–88, and J. Cone, *A Black Theology of Liberation* (Philadelphia: Lippincott, 1970), pp. 23, 76.

9. See Cone's *For My People: Black Theology and the Black Church* (Johannesburg: Scotaville Publishers; Maryknoll, N.Y.: Orbis Books, 1985).

10. See also his article in *EATWOT Visits China: Some Theological Implications* (2–13 May 1986), the joint report by the six members of an EATWOT delegation edited by V. Fabella and published by EATWOT, Manila, 1986. Here he says explicitly that "no continent or country has a monopoly on God's truth," p. 29.

11. See his "Towards an Asian Theology of Liberation: Some Religio-cultural Guidelines," in V. Fabella, ed., *Asia's Struggle for Full Humanity* (Maryknoll, N.Y.: Orbis Books, 1980), and his "The Place of Non-Christian Religions and Cultures in the Evolution of Third World Theology," in Fabella and Torres, *Irruption of the Third World*.

12. See his article in Fabella and Torres, *Irruption of the Third World*, p. 114.

13. Ibid.

14. See Fabella and Torres, *Irruption of the Third World,*, p. xv.

15. See Torres and Eagleson, *Theology in the Americas*, p. 389.

16. See his "Evaluation of the New Delhi EATWOT Conference," in Fabella and Torres, *Irruption of the Third World*, pp. 217–21.

17. In Torres and Eagleson, *Theology in the Americas,* pp. 413–14.

18. For another of these critiques see, e.g., Herbert O. Edwards's article entitled "Black Theology and Liberation Theology," in ibid., pp. 177–91.

19. See A. Pieris's "The Place of Non-Christian Religions and Cultures," in Fabella and Torres, *Irruption of the Third World,* p. 119.

20. See J. Cone, "From Geneva to São Paulo."

21. Ibid.

22. See pp. 25 and 26 of the conference report of the 1983 Black Theology Conference; the report was entitled *Black Theology Revisited;* the conference was organized by the Institute for Contextual Theology, Johannesburg. The paper has since been published (under the title "Towards a Black Theology of Labor") in Charles Villa-Vicencio and John W. De Gruchy, eds., *Resistance and Hope: South African Essays in Honour of Beyers Naudé* (Grand Rapids, Mich.: Wm. B. Eerdmans, 1985), pp. 126–34.

23. *Black Theology Revisited,* p. 31.

24. Ibid.

25. See his article entitled "The Evolution of the Black Struggle," in Mosala and Tlhagale, *The Unquestionable Right To Be Free,* p. 125.

26. Ibid., p. 126.

27. See my preface to Mosala and Tlhagale, *The Unquestionable Right To Be Free,* p. xviii.

28. J. Cone, *My Soul Looks Back* (Maryknoll, N.Y.: Orbis Books, 1986), pp. 123–38. See also Cone's *For My People.*

29. See two of his articles: (1) "Towards an Asian Theology of Liberation"; and (2) "The Place of Non-Christian Religions and Cultures in the Evolution of Third World Theology," p. 119.

30. See Torres and Eagleson, *The Challenge of Basic Christian Communities,* pp. 255–57.

31. See his "Technology and Science and 'Ideology'," in *Towards a Rational Society: Student Protest, Science and Politics* (London: Heinemann, 1972).

32. See his chapter on "Christian Faith and Socialist Revolution," in *The Theology of Promise: The Dynamics of Self-Reliance* (Harare: College Press, Ltd., 1982), pp. 106–34.

33. Ibid.

34. Karl Marx, *The German Ideology.*

35. See his article in Torres and Eagleson, *The Challenge of Basic Christian Communities,* pp. 255–57.

36. Ibid., p. 256.

37. See his article in Fabella and Torres, *Irruption of the Third World,* pp. 235–43.

38. Ibid., p. 242.

39. Ibid.

40. For Marx's well-known statement, see "Introduction to a Critique of Hegel's Philosophy of Right."

41. Karl Marx, *Capital.*

42. Fabella and Torres, *Irruption of the Third World,* p. 242.

43. Ibid., pp. 19–29.

44. See his article in Fabella and Torres, *The Emergent Gospel,* pp. 56–57. See

also K. Appiah-Kubi and S. Torres, eds., *African Theology en Route* (Maryknoll, N.Y.: Orbis Books, 1979).

45. See his article in Fabella and Torres, *The Emergent Gospel,* pp. 56–57.

46. See R. P. Mveng's regional coordinator's report to the Oaxtepec, EATWOT conference (1986), p. 27.

47. See his article in Fabella and Torres, *Irruption of the Third World,* pp. 217–21.

48. See his article in Fabella, *Asia's Struggle for Full Humanity,* p. 88.

49. Ibid., pp. 113–39.

50. See Fabella and Torres, *Irruption of the Third World,* p. 212.

51. *Women's Struggle in South Africa,* Feminist Theology Conference report (August 31–September 2, 1984) (Johannesburg: Institute of Contextual Theology).

52. *Black Theology Revisited,* conference report (August 16–19, 1983) (Johannesburg: Institute for Contextual Theology), pp. 60, 63.

53. See her Preface in Fabella and Torres, *Irruption of the Third World,* pp. xvi–xvii.

54. See her essay in Fabella and Torres, *Irruption of the Third World,* pp. 247–55.

55. *Women's Struggle in South Africa,* p. 38.

56. *Black Theology and the Black Struggle,* a conference report (September 10–14, 1984) (Johannesburg: Institute for Contextual Theology), p. 141.

57. *Women's Struggle in South Africa,* p. 38.

58. See the second draft of the final document of the Intercontinental Women's Conference (Oaxtepec, Mexico, December 1–5, 1986).

59. Ibid.

60. In Fabella and Torres, *The Emergent Gospel,* p. 113.

61. Ibid., pp. 113–14.

62. Ibid., p. 89.

63. Ibid., p. 123.

64. Ibid., p. 88.

65. Ibid., p. 73.

66. Ibid., p. 88.

67. Ibid., p. 88.

68. See *EATWOT Visits China.*

69. Ibid., p. 30.

70. See the final statement of the Delhi conference, in Fabella and Torres, *Irruption of the Third World,* p. 205.

16

A Latin American Evaluation of Oaxtepec

Pablo Richard

A POSITIVE ENCOUNTER

A conference with the participation of fifty-six male and female theologians—from Asia, Africa, Latin America, and the Caribbean, and including minorities of the United States—is an extraordinary event in itself and a symbol of the future. Today everything is manipulated by the superpowers. The poor and underdeveloped countries of the world get together only when they are convened by these centers of power. Our conference in Oaxtepec, with all its limitations and mistakes, was the expression of a new universality, not based on the axis of Washington-Paris-Moscow-Tokyo, but one emerging from the unity of all the countries of the Third World.

The preparatory work for the conference—continental reports, the efforts of working commissions, the friendly dialogue, the interchange of information, and the mutual enrichment—constitutes a new and important ecclesial and theological praxis. Starting from this praxis, little by little we are building the theology of the future—the theology of the Third World.

LATIN AMERICAN THEOLOGY CHALLENGED BY AFRICA AND ASIA

Latin American theology is positively questioned and challenged by men and women theologians from other continents. African theologians are helping us to deepen our work in the cultural dimension of life, with its ethnic and racial roots, and to rediscover the structural importance of culture in the reality of our people. Africans have challenged us to integrate Afro-American peoples and realities of our continent into our ecclesial and theological movement. We have been pressed to pursue an internal dialogue between Africa and Latin America, a vital dialogue within our own continent to discover and enrich our roots and our identity.

Asian theologians, on the other hand, are helping us to discover the spiritual value of traditional religions. They have helped us to go beyond the ecclesiocentric view, to open ourselves to the autochthonous, indigenous religions, and to pierce more deeply into "popular religiosity." Once again, dialogue with Asia takes us into a dialogue within Latin America.

TOWARD AN INDIGENOUS THEOLOGY

The most important result of the theological dialogue between Africa, Asia, and Latin America is the process of indigenization of Christianity and the church itself. As it is known, Christianity, starting in the sixteenth century, expanded throughout the Third World from the colonial centers. The missions coincided with colonial enterprise; even though Christian mission was not identified completely with this process, it was deeply marked and influenced by it.

When we, Latin Americans, use the African and Asian perspective to read our own history, we discover more easily our colonial heritage and the destructive effects of colonialism.

We are especially indebted to Asia because the Asians have shown us their resistance to colonial domination by European Christianity. If we want to indigenize Christianity in Latin America, in order to root it more deeply in our own reality, the Christianity of Asia is a powerful and necessary example. The small groups of Christians in Asia are a powerful point of reference and help us to rediscover our own identity and to deepen our ethnic and cultural roots.

Therefore, we are convinced that only a profound and fruitful dialogue between Africa, Asia, and Latin America can help Christianity to escape from a definite and fatal identification with Western colonialism. A colonial Western Christianity, identified with European or North American centers of power, has no future among the poor of the Third World.

BUILDING THE FUTURE OF THE CHURCH

At Oaxtepec, we had a clear understanding that the majority of the population living in the Third World is threatened by poverty and death. Between 1900 and 2000, the world population will increase over six billion people, and this overwhelming increase will happen primarily in the Third World. Most of the inhabitants of the world are concentrated in the Third World. Today there are more Christians of color than white Christians, and very soon there will be more Catholics in Latin America than in the rest of the world. The future of Christianity is clearly in the Third World, and it has to develop its fundamental work there.

However, this majority of humankind is sunk in poverty, misery, and death. This fact was unanimously recognized by the theologians who met in Oaxtepec. When we look around in our continents, the first thing we see is poverty and death. A clear consequence of this observation is that Christianity will survive in the future only if it is able to articulate the Christian faith within the material life of the poor of the world. The relation of the gospel with integral liberation of men and women is a test for the survival of the Christian identity. The church has no future if it is not linked with the life of the vast majorities living in the Third World. The dialogue in EATWOT has developed a clear consciousness of the significance of liberation, at all levels, for the survival of Chrisitan faith in the world.

TOWARDS A NEW ECUMENISM

We recognize that ecumenical dialogue among Christians is an essential aspect of our task. At the same time we have to admit that this kind of Christian ecumenism is stagnant and in captivity of the developed Western world. There is no progress in traditional ecumenism, and we are lacking new visions and horizons. Every step for Christian unity has been taken, but the desired unity does not come. Sometimes we are tempted to realize that this lack of unity is a Western feature of Christianity almost impossible to overcome. For this reason we are attracted by the new possibilities of ecumenism.

In the Third World a new horizon is emerging and becoming more and more visible: the dialogue with non-Christian religions. We ask ourselves: Will this dialogue and coming together be more urgent and enriching than the endless and petty discussions among Christians? Do not these petty discussions pertain more to a Western pathology than to the authentic evangelical tradition?

The Third World is poor but deeply religious. The great religions of the world, especially those with written traditions, belong to the Third World. Christianity also was born in a Third World country of the Roman Empire, expanded throughout Europe, and later spread abroad in the Third World through the colonialist expansion of the more powerful Western countries. Today, as was said before, we are recuperating the Third World status of Christianity. The outstanding richness of the Third World is in its culture and religion (even though secularized people from the First World do not like this). The fact is that we are economically poor but culturally and religiously rich. We have a great reserve of the world's culture, and this culture is enriched by religion.

However, if we want to arrive at a self-realization, all the poor have to work united in this effort. The dialogue of Christianity with non-Christian religions is essential. The theological context of this new ecumenism will be human life itself, liberation of human life from poverty and death, and the encounter with God within liberation and the enrichment of life.

We believe that this new dialogue will be difficult, but fruitful and enriching; it will be less complex than the Western inter-Christian dialogue. This dialogue among Christians, Jews, Moslems, Buddhists, etc. has already begun. It is a fact, though incipient. This dialogue focuses on the basic liberation of human life: on economic, political, cultural, spiritual, and religious liberation.

When we look at this new ecumenism, we become more optimistic. Then we turn back to our Latin American reality and we discern our task. We must stress the dialogue between Christianity and indigenous religions and black culture, in a continent that is sociologically and culturally Christian, but has been spiritually colonized. We feel the call to work for human liberation and to discover the common God of life.

17

Reflections on the Second General Assembly of EATWOT

Kelly Delaine Brown

As a black woman trying to understand the meaning of God's liberating activity for the poor, and as one who had read most of EATWOT's publications, I had high expectations for Oaxtepec.[1] I looked forward to being challenged by the different contexts of oppression represented by EATWOT's members. I knew that the socio-cultural situations of Africa, Asia, and Latin America might reveal some aspects of God's meaning that the socio-cultural situation of black women did not. Therefore, I eagerly anticipated an exchange that might broaden my knowledge concerning the significance of God's revelation in human history.

During my week at Oaxtepec my expectations were fulfilled. Therefore, in this paper I will share some of my experiences as a first-time participant in EATWOT's discussions and some of the issues which challenged my own theological perspective.

During the week I encountered passionate dialogue as each delegation expressed the nature of the oppression found within its own country. As I expected, the dialogue challenged all of us, as members of EATWOT, to broaden our analysis of the oppressive systems within our own contexts. However, there were puzzling aspects of the dialogue.

The heated exchange which often occurred between black Americans and Latin Americans initially surprised me. It seemed strange that black Americans and Latin Americans would have so much tension and distance between them since we are so close to each other geographically and have more opportunity to get to know each other. However, the history of differences provided clues to the hostility between the two groups.[2]

The Latin American theologians have been consistently accused of ignoring the problem of racism within their own context. Who other than their black American neighbors are a better reminder to them of this shortcoming? Not only have black American theologians verbally reminded Latin Americans of their silence about, and thus perpetuation of, racism, but black Americans' mere existence, which symbolizes a history of racist oppression in the United States, also acts as a constant reminder. Thus, it is no wonder that a non-black delegation from a continent with a sizable black population and concomitant race problem would be uncomfortable with its black American neighbors.

On the other hand, black American theologians have been consistently accused of not having a socio-economic analysis, and hence not having a critique of capitalism. There have been no better reminders of this shortcoming than the Latin American theologians. They have not only verbally reminded black American theologians that a lack of economic analysis serves to ignore class issues present within the black community and to perpetuate capitalist oppression across the Third World; but their mere presence, which symbolizes a history of capitalistic class oppression within Latin America, also acts as a constant reminder. So again, it is no wonder that black American theologians would be most uncomfortable with their Latin American neighbors.

In addition, I was also initially puzzled by the dialogue between black American women and the other women of EATWOT. A week prior to the second general assembly, women from Asia, Africa, and Latin America met in order to share experiences and to express their mutual concern for the elimination of gender oppression. Black American women were not invited to be a part of this week-long meeting. Black American women's exclusion from the meeting was an outgrowth of EATWOT's long struggle to understand the role of First World minorities in a Third World organization. Consequently, the EATWOT women of the Third World accepted an organizational procedure which resulted in the marginalization and oppression of some of their sisters in the struggle.

During the meeting of the general assembly, an overture was made to the U.S. black women. However, it was made as a step toward meeting with white feminist theologians of the First World. The women of Asia, Africa, and Latin America had already accepted an invitation to dialogue with white North American feminists. They reasoned, however, that it would be beneficial to meet with black American women first, since it was we who had the most experience of and interaction with the white feminists. At this point in the dialogue I began to wonder if the women from Asia, Africa, and Latin America were more interested in those who have contributed to their oppression than in getting to know their sisters in oppression.

If Third World women are going to move toward a world community where gender oppression is eliminated, we must first be careful not to adopt, for whatever reasons, the kinds of structures which might keep us separated from each other. Second, if God truly came to "the least of these," there can be no greater representative of the least of these today than the poor, Third World women whom we as EATWOT women claim to represent. Therefore, if we are truly committed to the struggles of our sisters, we must forge links with each other whether we are Third World women living in Third World countries or Third World women trapped in the First World. It is only together that we will be able to free our societies from the evils of race, class, and gender oppression that keep our sisters in bondage. Sojourner Truth put it best when she said:

> "If the first woman God ever made was strong enough to turn the world upside down all alone, these women together ought to be able to turn it back, and get it right side up again."[3]

It is *together* that Third World women will be able to turn the world right side up again. Fortunately, by week's end, EATWOT women from the Third and First Worlds were united in their desire to get to know more about each other.

In general, the dialogue at Oaxtepec made me realize that as members of EATWOT, male and female, we must recognize that the oppressive structures which we are forced to live under will thrive if they keep us divided. Their job is done when those of us who are oppressed are not able to come together and speak as one voice against systems of oppression. In essence, division is a demon of oppression. Therefore, following the lead of Jesus, we must name and call out all the demons that keep us in bondage. Jesus called forth the Gerasene demoniac so that the man inhabited by it could be set free from his "bonds and fetters" and become once again a part of his community (Luke 8:26ff.). In similar fashion, EATWOT must name and call forth its demons of divisiveness, so that we can be set free from the bondage that keeps us from talking to and learning from each other and becoming a part of a liberated community.

On the other hand, in spite of tense moments which occurred during the dialogue, there were still much fruitful exchange and theological challenge. The issues I found most compelling were raised by the Asian theologians: the religio-cultural issue, and the Christological issue.

The Asian theologians reminded us that their continent is the home of all the great world religions. Moreover, confessed Christians are a very small percentage of the Asian population. In addition, each religion brings with it a particular culture. Consequently, the challenge for persons on the Asian continent is to maintain their particular religious belief while respecting the religion and culture of others. More specifically, the challenge for the Christian theologian is to do theology in such a way that it shows a deep and sincere respect for the other religions and cultures.

Related to being part of a religiously and culturally pluralistic society is the problem of Christology. An Asian theology of liberation must speak of Jesus' divinity in such a way that it does not preclude or impede other equally valid incarnations of God in human history.

To this point, Tissa Balasuriya of Sri Lanka suggested that instead of focusing on Jesus as the only example of the Christ, the only incarnation of divinity, Christians need to begin to concentrate on seeing the Christ present within all people. In this respect, Jesus should be viewed as only one example of the divine/human encounter.

After hearing the Asian Report I asked myself: What do the religio-cultural situation of Asia and the related Christological problem mean for poor, black women and the development of a black feminist theology? First, given the fact that the Asian continent contains at least 58 percent of the world's population, to do theology and ignore the situation of Asia is to show blatant disregard for the majority of the world's oppressed. Such a theology could not be a Christian theology; for, although it might have significance for a particular situation, there would be no universal significance. Therefore, even if our own particular context is one in which the majority of persons are Christians, as is the situation with black Americans, we must struggle to do theology in a way that speaks to and respects the other religions and cultures of the world.

Second, the representatives from the Asian continent reminded me that oppression has respect for neither persons, nor cultures, nor religions. The systems which oppress do not ask questions about a person's ethnic background or confession of faith. In this regard, neither should our theologies of liberation. Although they emerge from our own context of oppression, they must link us to other contexts. If it is true that one is not free until we are all free, then such a freedom can be achieved only if our liberation theologies become just as inclusive of people from various cultures as systems of oppression are. This means that a true liberation theology in the context of black women cannot be developed apart from a dialogue with others around the world who are oppressed. EATWOT has provided the opportunities for such a dialogue. It is my hope that it will continue to do so.

Finally, the Christological concern raised by the Asian context caused me to reflect further upon the Christ's significance in black women's lives. For black Christians, male and female, there is rarely a distinction made between Jesus and God. Jesus is understood as God; that is why black churchpeople sing:

> He's King of Kings, and Lord of Lords,
> Jesus Christ, the first and the last.
> No man works like him.

This understanding of Jesus as God, as the Christ, allowed black slaves to know that what their masters said about God was not true. God did not ordain and support their slavery. Instead, God's revelation in Jesus showed that God was there to sustain them in their sufferings and to free them from their bondage. Because black Christians have known Jesus, through scripture and in their own lives, they have known that God is for them and not against them.

Thus, people's confession of Jesus as the Christ is an affirmation of God's commitment to the poor and oppressed. It is a confession born, not out of the tradition of Nicea and Chalcedon, but out of the history of slavery. Therefore, such a confession is not an effort to show that because Jesus is the divine/human encounter he is unique; instead it is an affirmation that God is a liberator, not an enslaver.

On the other hand, this confession of Jesus as Christ has had an oppressive aspect within the black community. Specifically, it has contributed to black women's marginal status within the black church. For instance, black women are often told that the reason they cannot be ordained is because Jesus, the church's model for the ordained ministry, was male, not female. In addition, similar to Asians, when confessing Jesus as the Christ—that is, linking Christ so firmly to the historical Jesus—we must ask if such a confession will ever allow black women to see themselves in Christ and Christ in themselves. Can Christ or God be conceived of as anything but male? The urgency of this problem was made clear to me when a black woman asked me not to refer to God as she. "It just does not sound right," the black woman said.

While the confession of Jesus as the Christ has had liberating significance for black Christians, it has also contributed to the oppression of black women. So, like Asian theologians, black women must seek ways in which to speak of Jesus as the Christ (given the liberating history of that confession) which do not impede perceiving Christ in others, particularly in black women.

To this end, a black feminist theology of liberation must make at least a twofold affirmation. First, it must affirm that for black Christians Jesus is the Christ; it is he who is the ultimate witness to God's revelation in human history. Yet, given the oppression which can be the result of such a claim, a black feminist theology must also affirm that Jesus is not the only example of Christ or incarnation of God in the world. Instead, Jesus should act as a guide for allowing black Christians to see other manifestations and incarnations of God present within different contexts of oppression.

In summary, when looking back over my week at Oaxtepec, it is best characterized as a continual challenge from different social, political, and cultural situations of oppression. EATWOT members were challenged to find ways of listening to and sharing with each other, as well as ways of developing theologies which have liberating significance for the poor and oppressed outside of our own context. Moreover, as I look to EATWOT's future and my continued participation in it as a black American woman, it is my hope that EATWOT will offer a glimpse of God's Reign, not just because it represents a community of people committed to the poor and powerless, but because it represents a community liberated from its own demons of oppression. Just as our theology should not fall short of its commitment to God's liberating Reign, neither should the organization under which we come to dialogue fall short of such commitment.

NOTES

1. The publications that I am referring to are: S. Torres and V. Fabella, eds., *The Emergent Gospel* (Maryknoll, N.Y.: Orbis Books, 1977); K. Appiah-Kubi and S. Torres, eds., *African Theology en Route* (Maryknoll, N.Y.: Orbis Books, 1979); V. Fabella, ed., *Asia's Struggle for Full Humanity* (Maryknoll, N.Y.: Orbis Books, 1980); S. Torres and J. Eagleson, eds., *The Challenge of Basic Christian Communities* (Maryknoll, N.Y.: Orbis Books, 1981); V. Fabella and S. Torres, eds., *Irruption of the Third World* (Maryknoll, N.Y.: Orbis Books, 1983).

2. J. Cone provides a good history of U.S. minorities' relationship to EATWOT with special attention being paid to the relationship between North American blacks and Latin Americans in "From Geneva to São Paulo: A Dialogue between Black Theology and Latin American Liberation Theology," in Torres and Eagleson, *The Challenge of Basic Christian Communities,* pp. 265–81.

3. Sojourner Truth, "Ain't I A Woman" (1851), in Miriam Schneir, ed., *Feminism: The Essential Historical Writings* (New York: Vintage Books, 1972), p. 95.

18

An Asian Perspective
on the Oaxtepec Conference

K. C. Abraham

1. The Oaxtepec conference was a moment of great celebration. Indeed the people who gathered there had a lot to celebrate. Although they came from different continents and situations, they had one thing in common — that is, their commitment to the struggles of the poor. This common commitment was the focus of their celebration. Different groups from different situations participated in the celebration. "Stories" of poor women of the basic Christian communities in Mexico, the blacks of South Africa, indigenous people in Latin America, and women in Asia were all acted out in daily worship services. Testimonies of their sufferings and hope loudly proclaimed that the ultimate reality is not death but life, not oppression but liberation.

2. A celebrative event like an international conference is hardly an occasion for serious theological reflection. And it must be acknowledged that at Oaxtepec we in EATWOT did not make any notable breakthroughs in our thinking. We, of course, set out ambitiously. We wanted to analyze our commonalities and divergences and then move on to a process of cross-fertilization. Some obvious points were repeatedly made about our commonalities and divergences, hoping that they would set the stage for a meaningful dialogue. But that has not taken place.

We agreed that an unjust economic system in the world continues to keep millions of our people in abject poverty. It is oppression, global in proportion and intensely experienced locally. As we continued to reflect on the situation of depravity in the Third World, we were also led to the problems of oppression that are specific to each of the three continents and minorities in the United States. Cultural and religious oppression, racism, and male domination were some of these specific forms of oppres-

180

sion that we examined. The perception of these immediate forms of oppression within the global system of injustice posed a new challenge to us. Could we evolve a more adequate framework of analysis that links specific forms of oppression in the world? That was the question posed when the conference focused on the process of "cross-fertilization." Regrettably that process of dialogue was not even begun in Oaxtepec.

We agreed long ago, and repeated at Oaxtepec, that liberational praxis is the theological methodology of EATWOT. The Dar-es-Salaam Declaration, August 1976, known as the Charter of Identity of EATWOT, stated, "We reject as irrelevant an academic type of theology that is divorced from action. We are prepared for a radical break in epistemology which makes commitment the first act of theology and engages in critical reflection of the Third World."

Liberational praxis gives Christians a basis for entering into partnership with radical movements influenced by Marxist ideology. Asians, in their background paper for the conference, made a plea for taking this as a framework for interreligious dialogue and cooperation. They argued that in the Third World—where all religions together face the challenges of oppressive social systems and the need to struggle for justice—religions should meet each other through a process of exploring and sharing their liberative elements. They pleaded for an interreligious dialogue which is concerned not so much with reconciling different doctrines as with mobilizing the religions for the struggle for freedom. Implications of this should have been taken up during the session on cross-fertilization. Regrettably that did not happen. One is justified in concluding that the reflective process of Oaxtepec did not achieve its avowed goals.

There are several reasons for the failure to have a meaningful dialogue between different partners of EATWOT at Oaxtepec. One can easily blame the structure of the conference and some obvious organizational lapses. But they do not take us to the root of the problem. In our day to day work of theologizing we hardly take seriously the concerns or the articulations of our partners from different contexts. If we can exist without them year after year then there is no compelling reason why they should be taken seriously once in five or six years when we meet together. We seem to be saying that Latin Americans are not vitally important for African liberation theology; Asians are of no consequence to Latin Americans in their theological articulation; U.S. minorities can be ignored when Asians do their theology.

True enough, Latin American theologians have made an initial impact on liberation theologians in other continents. EATWOT was formed with the hope that it will provide a forum for mutual listening and challenging of theologians from Africa, Asia, Latin America, and U.S. minorities. We need to deepen that founding vision and make it a reality in our theologizing.

3. From an Asian perspective, the Oaxtepec conference will be remem-

bered for its emphasis on the reality of religions and culture. This peculiarly Asian agenda, which had remained on the periphery in the earlier discussions in EATWOT conferences, is now occupying the central stage of EATWOT concern. One is gratified to note that this emphasis on religion and culture is no longer promoted solely by Asians but is now squarely on the agenda of the entire Third World and of humanity in general. This intertwining of religion and culture is the reality of the people of Africa, of Indians and other minorities in Latin America, and of the Amerindians, blacks, and Hispanics in the United States. Their movements of liberation are rallied around their cultural and religious roots. Religion is no more an opiate for these groups. It provides the inspiration and critical tool to forge ahead in their struggle for justice and freedom.

A distinct challenge provided by the Oaxtepec conference to EATWOT was how to take the dynamic face of religion as a necessary element of Third World theology. This question has to be addressed. A negative view of religion is understandable because religious institutions and rituals are sometimes a source of oppression. A relative indifference to religion and religious faith is also a legacy of the modern scientific culture in which all experiences of reality are reduced to definable and quantifiable commodities. Only what is usable and marketable is valuable. Reason is reduced to technology, and all levels of human experience are ruthlessly manipulated. Oaxtepec seemed to make a plea that faith, religion, culture, and other experiences of people should not be reduced to scientific and technological theories, but we should discover their wholesome character. A holistic view of religion is necessary if we are to take people more seriously. For too long we have been under the tutelage of Western rationality and have remained insensitive to the liberational potential of religion and culture.

To dispel any misunderstanding, let it be categorically stated that the goal of our action is liberation and, therefore, in a situation of abject poverty and increasing disparities between the rich and the poor, the focus of our struggle should be economic injustice. The acid test of our faith, religiosity, and spirituality is how they respond to poverty. The point, however, is that even in the struggle against economic injustice we need to harness the resources available to people in their culture and religion.

The experience of people's movements forces us to have a new look at religion and culture, and their relevance for an ongoing struggle. The people have discovered the potential of religious reality. In an admirable analysis of the fishermen's movement in Kerala, S. Kappen has drawn our attention to the positive role played by Christianity in the struggle. Of course this is not establishment-oriented Christianity, but the faith derived "from a re-reading of the Gospels this time from the point of view of the poor and the dispossessed." He concludes, "This radical upsurge within Christianity shows that religions are not just dead but have untapped reservoirs of energy which can be harnessed to humanizing society."[1] This discovery has come late into our consciousness and its impact is not fully realized. Therefore, we have difficulty in clearly articulating a full-blown concept of religion. But there seems to be a consensus that many traditional as well as modern theories of religion are inadequate and do not conform fully to our experience. People who are involved in justice struggles, for instance, find Marx's view of religion compelling and useful. They have used it to demolish superstitious beliefs that enslave ordinary masses to nature. It has provided weapons in their fight against oppressive religious structures. It has helped them to see how religions are used for exploiting masses, for protecting the vested interests of the high and mighty. The very idea of contemplation and silence was used to suppress the masses, and they were made to accept passively their suffering, expected to make other-worldly flights from social reality.

Yet, people know that there are positive elements in the religions. Sometimes they are prominently expressed in the protest movements and traditions within the dominant religions, in myths, stories, and legends. We need to rediscover this dynamic heritage of ours as a source of theologizing.

Religion plays a supportive role in the liberation struggle of the people in the Third World. But more important is the process by which people appropriate for themselves their own history, culture, and religion. Sifting through elite distortion of their religion and wading through the grandiose edifice of religion built by dominant classes, they have in response to their contemporary challenges rediscovered the authentic core and essential dynamism of their religious heritage. They have appropriated the scriptures and the symbols for themselves by giving new interpretations and have taken over some of the institutional structures for themselves.

The process of appropriation is seen in the way they sing their old songs anew, in their rites and symbols, even creating new ones, and in their myths and legends. The language they speak puts them in touch with the basic truths that every religion and ideology grapples with, but each in a new way—the meaning and destiny of human existence; human capacity to break through the forces of destruction; liberation, both human and cosmic; in short, the struggle for a fuller humanity.

4. What about the theological and missiological implications of this positive attitude toward the dynamism of religion? Here Asians feel that Oaxtepec did not go far enough. It preferred to remain in a Christian mode, making it impossible for people of other faiths to recognize the liberative message. For Asians who live in pluralist situations, Christian symbols and language are not self-evident. They are not only obscure but are often associated with an alien culture. Asian liberation theologians are today committed to a process of absorbing from non-Christian religions "the Asian style of being, thinking, and doing."[2]

Christian doctrines and symbols are to be interpreted in the Asian context. The horizon of the world which they project and the horizon of the religious symbols of the poor in Asia should be brought together. Asian theologians like C. S. Song are consciously using the myths, symbols, and stories of Asian religions—myths, symbols, and stories which are really part of the collective memory of the people—to reconstruct their theologies.

Asian liberation theology arises out of an *oikoumenē* which is multireligious. An EATWOT consultation that was held after Oaxtepec stated that in the Third World—where all religions together face the challenges of enslaving social and cultural systems and the need to struggle for justice—religions should meet each other through a process of exploring and sharing their liberative elements. It called for the development of a "liberative ecumenism, that is, a form of interreligious dialogue which is concerned not so much with doctrinal insights or spiritual experiences that different religions can offer one another as with the contribution to human liberation that each can make."[3]

Asians hope that in the years to come EATWOT will probe these concerns further and will thus deepen its commitment to theologizing from the perspective of the poor.

NOTES

1. S. Kappen, *Mission Today* (Bangalore), Jan. 1980, p. 4.
2. A. Pieris, *An Asian Theology of Liberation* (Maryknoll, N.Y.: Orbis Books, 1988), p. 74.
3. *Voices* 11, no. 1 (June 1988), p. 168.

PART VI

WORSHIP

19

A Reflection on Worship

Samuel Rayan

Our worship grew out of our theological concerns. Theology is a spiritual activity, a function of our faith in Christ, interior to our faith-union in God. Worship opens us up to the call of the Spirit who pervades history and empowers the poor. Built around themes of liberation, our worship reflected God's seminal question: Where is your brother? It was worship that orchestrated our diverse activities and concerns and the distinct accents of our theologies.

The opening worship was a celebration of hope for the peoples' resurrection and liberation. The message was delivered by Ezekiel 37 and Luke 4 and a meditative homily. Moving testimonies of resistance, faith, and courage came from some who had suffered imprisonment and torture in Brazil and South Africa for their stand for justice and freedom. They made us sad, angry, tearful. "In prisons and torture chambers the communists prayed with us and we with them," they said. "We are proud of such sisters and brothers," we responded.

This opening prayer is a call to hope.
A call from the Spirit who conveys us into the future.
  Will these bones come alive again?
  Do we dare nurse the hope of a resurrection
  for the dry bones? . . .
We live scattered in this valley of death. . . .
Do we really believe and hope . . . ?
  Hope is not fancy.
  Hope is hope only within our commitment
  and the action we initiate to realize the vision.
  We are being challenged to action. . . .
Summon the winds.

> Summon them from all corners of the earth,
>   from all the Third World countries
>   and all oppressed situations. . . .
> Deep in our heart do we believe and hope
>   that someday we and God will do it . . . ?

"Yes, I will do it, you and I will achieve it," says God. From then on did we not look forward to the daily worship? "It was wonderful," said one. "A beautiful experience," said another. "An inspiring moment," added a third.

The next morning we prayed for openness and for the courage to take risks. We listened to Acts 11:19–26. The Christian movement goes out of Palestine and gains a new dimension. It goes out into the Third World and discovers its own depth and vigor. A closed community is opened up and changed by persecution and fresh contact. Asia urged EATWOT to approach other religions as channels of revelation and liberation. The Kingdom of God is not church-centered; it is God-centered. Go out to the "non-Jews," to the "others." Africa asked: Where is our root and our identity? We seek it in our culture. Our cultures have been and still are our most effective weapon against our destroyers. Negritude is powerful. Negritude is our identity. Latin America confessed: the Spirit has raised up prophets and martyrs among us. Their death and liberation theology have strengthened our fight against impoverishment.

If God is for us, who is against us? The poor and the despised need to know and feel that God is on their side. How are we going to be liberating symbols and signs of God's partiality for the oppressed? These things we pondered on the third morning. An African woman spread her arms and prayed:

> God, our God, why have you forsaken us?
> We have cried and cried, you have not heard us.
> Should we continue to cry?
> Jesus cried, and you heard him by raising him up.
> Will you resurrect us to new life,
>   and new womanhood, and true humanhood?

Another woman prayed:

> That your body may become our body,
>   your blood, our blood,
>   your Spirit, our own.

The morning after that we wove a yearning for the contemplative eye. We listened to an Upanishad: "As He shines, all things shine after him." And to a Filipino interpretation of the political change Filipinos had brought about: "The reign of God is here in the Philippines because the people have accepted responsibility." And to a re-rendering of John 4 by Sun Ai Park: It spoke about woman, seeker of companionship and communion. "I met men, but they were interested only in the sex role I can play," said this woman. "They would not have with me a real talk at a deeper level. They would not talk with me about God or a life or people or world happenings." With Jesus, however, a woman could "talk theology, philosophy, and the justice of God." Men fix on money and sex, and refuse contemplation.

One morning worship celebrated the Virgin of Guadalupe. A group of women from a basic Christian community from Guadalupe told the story and interpreted it in terms of Revelation 12:1–16, about the serpent who eats children and commits genocide.

> From heaven on a beautiful day came the Virgin.
> Her face was Mexican.

The account of it written by elders of the people is a liberation theology. The uncle is the important person in the family; he represents the tribe. The uncle, Don Diego, is ill with diseases the Spanish had brought with them. That means the whole tribal family is ill with all the ills the Spanish have inflicted on them. The Virgin comes to heal the small, powerless man, and to build up faith. . . . In the palace of the bishop and in the city there is mistrust. Persecution is unleashed. Outside the city, outside Spanish control, faith and trust blossom and roses bloom in winter. Mary had said to the little one, the little, powerless people: "Listen, my son, my little one, let nothing cause you fear. Don't be distressed, I am your health and protection."

The women, young and old, married and single, all very poor, said:

—We are beginning to walk a little each day.

—We are learning from the community what it means to live our life for others.

—We follow Mary, we orient our children, we wish to help repressed women.

—When husbands oppress us, we have this message of Mary. She came to the poor. With her we walk, seek to motivate our husbands, and liberate them.

—I am a mother of ten children. All of us were battered by my husband. I threw myself before a car. This sister here took charge of me, brought me to the basic Christian community, taught me to read the Bible. Thus I learned to walk with the word of God.

—We prepare people for the sacraments, for common action, for strikes. Our inspiration comes from the Bible and from Bishop Sergio Méndez.

—The apparition has been taken over by businessmen. They take over everything to make money from. We shall not let the rich take the Virgin away and use her for profit.

—[An Asian participant, Marianne Katoppo]: I am overwhelmed by the enthusiasm of the Mexican people: by their intellectual interest as they throng into the university to hear us speak; by their religious feeling as they walk at night in countless numbers toward the shrine. Some crawl on their knees. At the shrine, I contemplate the picture. Mary's message has not been understood by the leaders. This indigenous woman asked for a shrine of the people. She asked that the people stand up in freedom, and crawl no longer. The serpent is the landgrabber, the colonizer, the rapist of the Third World and its women. The real serpent has to be destroyed so that the people may rejoice.

We pray that we might understand Mary's message of evangelization and emancipation. The message is that the people's indigenous worth be recognized, and their culture, values, and languages be taken up. We wish to know how we might do this, and put an end to the poverty and illness of the people. Giving us the final blessing an elderly woman said:

We are one church with you. Life below, among the poor, is beautiful. I visited a poor family. The mother was serving tortillas with chili. They invited me. How was I to eat that? Not to make them feel bad, I sat down. The chili tasted so good, I had never eaten such food before. I hope you will have the luck to eat the food of the poor. I invite you to walk with the poor. I ask the Virgin to pray for the men who imagine they are superior. They are learning. Let us send a blessing to Nicaragua.

Resurrection was the theme when the U.S. minorities led us in prayer. They spoke of moving from oppression through struggle to victory:

> God of the poor, God of Africa at home and in diaspora. . . .
> God who is little and black. . . .
> Nobody knows the trouble I see,
> Nobody knows my sorrow. . . .

Slavery meant being treated as commodities, like horses and things. No family ties were recognized. After slaving for fifteen to twenty hours you were beaten for feeling the fatigue. Within three weeks after childbirth slave women had to go back to work.

> Oh freedom! Oh freedom! Oh freedom! Over me!
> And before I be a slave

> I'll be buried in my grave
> and go home to my Lord and be free.

To enslave is to dehistoricize black people. Only, they did not let this happen. They made history. Their masters failed. The Jamaican blacks sang:

> Up, you mighty race,
> break the fetters,
> — away with shame, doubt, and fear.

Martin Luther King, Jr., stood for justice for black people and for the oppressed everywhere. The convergence of the particular and the universal. "Injustice anywhere is a threat to justice everywhere." Jesus was God's black slave come to end human enslavement. His resurrection is the guarantee that the future of the blacks is in the hands of the conqueror of slavery. . . .

That is how we worshiped. Third World worship. Worship by the oppressed. Worship bursting with memory and with hope, vibrant with protest and with struggle. Worship that subverts and liberates, like the death of Jesus.

PART VII

FINAL REFLECTION

20

Commonalities, Divergences, and Cross-fertilization among Third World Theologies

A Document Based on the Seventh International Conference of the Ecumenical Association of Third World Theologians, Oaxtepec, Mexico, December 7–14, 1986

INTRODUCTION

1. We were glad to be together again. It was the Seventh International Conference of the Ecumenical Association of Third World Theologians and its Second General Assembly. Some fifty-five EATWOT members participated, a third of the number being women. Attending the assembly as observers were ten other persons from the press and from EATWOT's partner organizations and friends.

2. We met in Oaxtepec, Mexico, from December 7–14, 1986. Mexico, a point of confluence of ancestral, colonial, and modern cultures, was an appropriate place for the many cultural and theological currents of all the continents to flow into. Oaxtepec itself was particularly rich in memories of Aztec gods and their worship.

3. An intercontinental conference of women theologians preceded our seventh conference and was held at the same place on December 1–6, 1986. The twenty-three delegates discussed the general theme, "Doing Theology from Third World Women's Perspective."

4. We were thankful for EATWOT, which is now over ten years old and has grown and developed in remarkable ways. We have remained united

---

Note: This document is not an official statement of the Seventh International Conference of the Ecumenical Association of Third World Theologians. It was drafted by a participant who had been commissioned by the executive committee to do so. However, because it could not be completed on time, it was not possible to present it to the conference for approval. The following document has been abridged and edited by the executive committee.

across tensions and conflicts. We came to respect each other in each one's otherness, to see what is different as an enrichment for all, and to hold our diversities within a comprehensive commitment to the liberation of people from every kind of oppression.

CONTEXT

5. EATWOT was born in 1976. In contrast to the years 1976–1981, which were boom years for the Third World and provided much cause for hope, the years 1981–1986 were difficult ones for most countries in Asia, Africa, and Latin America. The First World nations have regained their control of the international situation. In the Third World the outlook has turned grim; the previous hope has slowly been dampened.

6. The program for transfer of certain resources to the Third World had been scuttled; the move for a new economic order, stalled; UNCTAD (United Nations Conference on Trade and Development), stultified; the debt trap, made more sophisticated and set up far and wide; and repressive regimes, foisted on people. The First World's greatest success is the hold it has on an elite group right at the heart of the Third World, a group which believes in First World ideologies and schemes and runs repressive states for the benefit of a world oligarchy. The result is deepening and massive poverty, large-scale oppression, and the vicious noose of external debts.

7. Theologians working for the liberation of the oppressed have had to confront the threat of the powers that be on two levels: (a) the secular powers from centers of domination have decided to attack liberation theology and basic church formations; (b) the administrative powers of Christian institutions have concurred. They are suspicious of Third World movements and liberation theologies. In the churches ecumenism and dialogue have weakened, and a wave of neoconservatism and fundamentalism threatens to engulf the gains of recent struggles and insights. Attempts are being made to exercise repressive control over theological thought and over religious thinkers and organizations.

8. What is under threat is the joyful freedom to be faithful to the living word of the God of life. We realize that it is not easy to be a prophet or theologian in the Third World. But opposition to our work also means that the voice of the Third World is beginning to be heard at the centers of domination. That voice can no longer be ignored.

THE THEME

9. Our work centered on commonalities, divergences, and cross-fertilization among Third World theologies. Its goal was precisely to examine the common and diverse aspects in the theologies developing in Asia, Africa, and Latin America in terms of theological issues, orientation, and meth-

odology, as well as the possibilities and need of mutual enrichment and cross-fertilization.

10. This attempt was only partially successful. Our conference reflected some aspects of the crisis of the Third World. There have been some divisions among ourselves; the preparatory committee was unable to steer the conference to accomplish its goal fully. The host committee also had difficulties in the organization and preparation of the event at Oaxtepec. Although the quality of the position papers and the experience and competence of the participants were ample basis for an enriching and fruitful dialogue, the interspersing of general assembly business, such as elections and amendments of the constitution, precluded a more in-depth analysis of the conference theme and frustrated some of the participants.

11. It was clear again that we have to continue talking about Third World theologies. Being together it was easy to perceive both our commonalities and divergences. At the same time, through formal and informal discussion, we were able to understand how we can learn from each other and to enrich our own perspectives. We want to present here the actual development of our theologies, as it has been expressed in different conferences, books, and dialogues previous to the Oaxtepec encounter and as it was expressed in the discussions at our tenth anniversary conference.

COMMONALITIES

12. Oaxtepec was another occasion to reaffirm our unity and to explore the commonalities of Third World theologies. Despite the moments of tension and polarization between some Africans and some Latin Americans, and the sense of marginalization experienced by some representatives of the minority groups of the United States, it was possible to overcome those differences and to reaffirm reconciliation in truth and love.

13. Perhaps the most significant and unifying aspect of the Third World reality is the people's resistance to oppression, racism, and dictatorships. The fundamental common factor on all our continents is people in search of dignity, meaning, and fuller humanity. People's resistance to oppression may be silent or expressed in protests, organized movements, or armed revolts. The struggle continues in South Africa, Namibia, Korea, Chile; it is carried on by Native Americans and Afro-Americans in the United States and in Brazil; and it is advanced by the landless, the bonded laborers, students, and women everywhere. Traditional religions have become centers of popular resistance and a source of inspiration to sustained struggle. Traditional cultures strengthen people for the combat. A new sense of equality and dignity, a passion for freedom, and the searing memory of having been wronged and humiliated cement the movements of resistance across nations and continents.

14. Liberation is the common theme and central concern for all of us, because the central and common experience of all has been domination

and oppression, whether colonial, racist, sexist, or capitalist. Basically this calls for a theology of the other—the other race, sex, culture, dignity, honor, and land. That will include a theology of conversion to the other and to the God of the other.

15. Third World theologies are born of suffering and humiliation on the one hand and the will to dignity on the other. They are rebellion and protest against personal and social sin and against all forms of domination. They start from the people's painful experience of poverty and death. Commitment to and practice of liberation come first; praxis is pregnant with theory; theology articulates the truth of praxis. The starting point is the faith experience and description of historical reality understood analytically/intuitively as well as struggles for change in favor of the oppressed. The event of Jesus and the tradition of his movement are accepted and reread in the light of our sufferings, struggles, and faith experience.

16. We have common experiences as peoples facing socio-economic and political challenges. We EATWOT members have noted the role of foreign ideologies in our countries. We are aware of the economic dependency syndrome and the "per capita" income idea which serves only to mask the abject poverty in which the vast majority of Third World peoples live—with the exception of a few of the newly developed countries. This is the most striking commonality of the Third World. It raises the question of what humanity worships: the God of life or the idol of gold.

17. We hold in common the need to retain our church base, in spite of our churches' differences both as denominations and as regional expressions of their stance on the realities in which they find themselves, of their involvement in theology and the liberation process, and of their responses to the situations on which we agree. We belong to these churches. For some situations this is an asset, for others, it is a challenge. However, we agreed that the church of Christ is God's instrument for the liberation of the human spirit and for demonstrating the first fruits of God's Reign. On this commonality we root ourselves in our churches and we pray that we, together and as individuals, become instruments of God's Reign on earth.

DIVERGENCES

18. EATWOT has defined itself in relation to and in contrast with First World countries, cultures, and theologies. Because of the missions, old and new, our own regions have been influenced by those theologies and ideologies. But it is clear that Latin America is the most Westernized of the three Third World continents and serves as an example of how complex this Euro-Christian takeover has become.

19. Looking at the regions of EATWOT, one is struck by the similarities between Africa and Asia on the question of doing theology in a multireligious context. Religio-cultural realities are strongest where traditional religions and cultures have resisted the European attempt to Westernize the

whole world. Latin American theologians have ignored for a long time the native and Afro-American expression of religiosity and have been influenced by the middle-class culture, which is a minority in a vast and multiracial continent.

20. From the very beginning there has been a different emphasis on the use and the quality of analysis for theologizing. This is an aspect in which we have perceived real progress in understanding the other's point of view. But still Asia and Africa are more challenged by their cultural and religious realities while Latin America is more taken up with the socio-economic situation of the people. In the last conferences (especially in 1981 at New Delhi and in 1983 at Geneva) it became clear that there are nuances in the understanding of poverty and the poor, which are the starting points of our theologies.

21. One of the most striking developments in EATWOT has been the challenge presented by some members to our common Judeo-Christian tradition. The living religions of Africa and Asia call for a conscious incorporation of theologies other than Christian into our thinking. This is especially true about Christology. It is impossible to accept that the majority of humankind would be deprived of the benefits of redemption and salvation. The Jesus of Nazareth should be expanded and considered also as the total and cosmic Christ.

22. We speak of our differences as wealth meant for sharing. We saw that we had not always been open and ready to be challenged by what is other and unfamiliar. We were touched by voices of confession and conversion. "We acknowledge now that we have learned a great deal from other continents and experiences." "We recognize that we have been arrogant." "We are thankful for the enrichment we have received." "Dialogue is a long and painful process. It calls for mutual trust and for courage to accept the other's challenge."

23. We should continue and deepen our dialogue on all sides and at all levels. Dialogue is both a source and a method of theology. The aim of EATWOT from its inception has been the promotion of dialogue and the development of contacts with other ecumenical organizations. We must, therefore, keep comparing notes and studying, with respect and openness, the commonalities and divergences in our situations as these unfold, and in our theological approaches and accents on all our continents.

24. A "fish-bowl" session surfaced the concept of a theology of hospitality: make the others (persons, races, cultures, religion, sex) welcome, and celebrate them in all their socio-cultural and theological otherness while not omitting to pose an honest critique and a gospel challenge. Our project is to tell the truth about life, about oppression, and about hope. We wish to be converted by truth and justice, and to be reconciled in them.

CROSS-FERTILIZATION AND NEW CHALLENGES

25. Our third step at Oaxtepec was to explore cross-fertilization and mutual enrichment among Third World theologies. Even though it was not

possible—as it has been said here before—to have an in-depth analysis of all aspects, there were enough indications of a common search and the arising of new challenges in the preparatory papers, the working groups, and informal discussions among participants.

26. We want to explore some of these new theological challenges and to begin a dialogue about them. We are glad to discover that life, risk, and love are signs of the Spirit, who, like the wind, blows where it will. We ourselves have been surprised by the questions and challenges. The Asian participants are raising new issues and are not afraid to open new paths in their responses. We don't yet have the answers, but we want to be faithful to John when he says that the truth shall make us free. We also believe that the charism of theologians is to read the signs of the times and to explore new models and responses. Yet, as members of our Christian communities and churches, we are accountable to the charism of the pastors, who are committed to unity and orthodoxy. In a spirit of fellowship and freedom we present some of these perspectives.

METHODOLOGY

27. It is in struggles for life that we encounter the God of life and discover a theological method. Our methodologies are not principles to be applied to reality; they are a guide to clarify our commitment and praxis. Our aim is not new doctrines, but new relationships and lifestyles. Method implies a direction, and liberation is the direction.

28. Third World theology is theology as if people mattered. Its concern is not the neatness of a system but the liberation of the people. It is not elaborated in the academy but developed by the communities of the poor. Through a spiritual experience the community makes the word of God its own and rereads it. It is the people who also have the authority of the word.

29. Theology is a constitutive part of the faith life of the community which keeps reflecting on the meaning for the here and now of its faith and life. Professional theologians are the communities' servants in interpreting events and in systematizing the communities' experience. Their fidelity and responsibility to the community are essential to the concept of theology.

30. Two main directions are to be found in Africa's theological responses. One relates Christian theology to African culture and spirituality and raises radical questions about Africanization. The other, found in South Africa, places the accent on liberation from socio-political oppression.

31. In Asia the oppressed people, the poor, the *minjung*, are the theological actors or subjects of theology in the measure in which they struggle against domination, and in the struggle discern God's supportive, imperative presence. Not all who do this are identified as Christians. Up to 97 percent of the poor of Asia are not Christian. The place of theology therefore is not only the church and its praxis but also the human community

striving for liberation and life where the Spirit is at work.

32. Minjung theology expresses itself in people's stories and biographies as against Western, logical, systematic presentations. Western classical theology is highly academic, like chemistry, and highly technical. Emerging Third World theology is of and for the vast masses of illiterate people. It will, therefore, be mostly unwritten, spoken, articulated in symbols, in folk songs, poems, myths, plays, art forms, dance, and celebration. God is expressed in flesh and mystery.

33. Theology is latent in people's struggles; it has a period of gestation in the heart of the people. Its primary expression is the transformation we see in the life of women and men committed to justice and liberation. It is women's viewpoint that theology must be done with passion and compassion, with the heart, the body, and the mind; it calls for a new language, one very different from the language of the academic. There is no need for Third World, nonliterate theology to be apologetic. It need not be on the defensive. But it has to justify itself before the exigencies of the situation and before the masses of the poor, the children and the women.

34. In EATWOT, right from Dar-es-Salaam, there has been a long and sometimes conflictive discussion on social analysis. Now the different positions have become less rigid and more supple. Latin Americans tell us that they have become more discerning. Analysis now is less dogmatic. Religiosity is integrated into analysis. Racism and sexism are recognized as distinct sources of oppression, not wholly reducible to economic factors.

35. Africans find Marxist analysis helpful in clarifying some aspects of reality, but add that African experience is different from Western capitalist society within which Marxism developed as a critique of its horrors. What we have in Africa is not merely capitalist alienation but historical annihilation and genocide. For Asia, Marxist analysis is not taboo provided it is contextualized and reinterpreted from a richer human perspective. A certain Marxist option is necessary to give to theology a new sharpness and concreteness. The U.S. minorities admit to a new realization that in order to understand their oppressed reality they must take more than racism into account. Color and race are not the only relevant factors. The economic factor must be taken into account as is clear from the fact that an emergent black middle class refuses solidarity with the struggles of the community.

36. In sum, all of us have learned to show more respect and concern for people than for systems. Turning to people we have become more cautious of scientific theories. People's wisdom is a far safer guide. We have seen a second, nonanalytical level of people's liberation theology spring up and flourish, and we have witnessed protagonists of the scientific analytical approach to theology becoming converts to the theological method of the people.

THEOLOGY, POVERTY, AND POLITICS

37. Third World theology is bound with the life and death of the poor. Death and pain of the poor come from evil and sin, personal and structural.

A new emphasis on the impoverished as theological and pastoral actors has emerged. An emphasis we discover at the heart of the gospel. It is through political struggles against sinful situations that the poor become theological actors. It is in the area of politics that the poor are seeking to create something new with space for all to participate. Their action is prophetic; it is open to the future. In their political awakening and social mobilization, their faith in God is becoming a central element. A faith bound up with the wisdom of workers, and the culture of the rural poor; a faith expressed in the liturgy of life, in people's pain, prayers, songs, and symbols. The theology of the poor breaks with the Western model of theology seen as the religious component of a whole way of domination; it roots itself in the people's culture of suffering and resistance and indomitable hope.

38. Most of us live in capitalist countries. Our experience is conditioned by this mode of production. For over five centuries capitalism has operated on our continents as a culture of death. It has taken religion captive to use it as a tool of death. It has been thriving on a global holocaust stretching from colonial conquest, plunder, genocide, and enslavement to Auschwitz and Hiroshima and the carnage of World War II and continuing in the politics of death in South Africa, Central America, Western Asia, and other theaters of oppression. Religious reflection worth the name is bound to engage in a theological, and not only ethical, critique of this culture of organized greed and this cult of Mammon-Moloch.

39. That should prepare us for a theologico-critical hearing of the claims of socialism, which has appeared on our continents as a hope-giving and enabling dream and as we step away from the death-system. Socialism has its failings which should not be minimized or overlooked, but its proven power to engender hope, its successful resistance to imperialism's armed might, and its alternative social thinking deserve to be theologically considered.

40. Racism is a distinct form of oppression, insolently rampant in South Africa with the support of the West. Racist oppressors maintained our physical labor power while attempting to destroy us psychically, economically, culturally; to annihilate our identity, personality, and dignity; and to reduce us to the status of animals and tools. This anthropological pauperization was carried in Africa and the United States to the point of paroxysm. Anthropological impoverishment represents the tragic condition of black people, but it is applicable to all the Third World poor.

41. Racism is active in other parts of the Third World as well—in the form of caste and untouchability in India, discrimination against Koreans as fourth-class people in Japan, harrassment of tribal populations all over Asia, and marginalization and humiliation of minority groups in the United States and Europe. In the Americas, the native peoples have the memory of massive physical destruction by European Christians. They have been nearly exterminated; they are the most oppressed of minority groups, pushed off their land, ignored, and made invisible. Afro-Americans remem-

ber that racism has been the fundamental justification for enslavement and oppression. Racists have sought to inject in the oppressed a feeling of inferiority and ineptness, and to stigmatize them as slaves in the depth of their personality, as a group meant by nature to be no more than a productive mass for the benefit of other races.

42. Part of our theological critique will bear upon the mechanisms of domination and pauperization. The Third World, impoverished and trapped in debt, is bound to raise the moral and theological question of repayment and restitution. In a straightforward and honest historical view of things, we must ask: Who indeed owes what to whom? The vast sums owed to Western banks and governments is but a tiny fraction of the enormous wealth transferred from our continents to the West in the colonial period and that continues to be transferred in this neocolonial era through a variety of socio-economic mechanisms. The masses of the people everywhere are likely to see the point that the Third World is the creditor. It is to the religious sense and feel for fairness of the common people of the world that theology should make its appeal.

43. A crucial theological issue is the relationship of churches and religions to socio-political realities and the organization of power. The relation between faith and justice is a critical question of theoretical and practical import. So is the question of love and the use of force in defense of a people's rights. Such problems must be placed in real historical contexts like the use of religion by the South African regime and by the U.S. administration; or state opposition to liberation theology; or the persecution of the church in some Latin American and Asian countries for working to create a just and peaceful world; or the censure of Christian participation in revolution in Nicaragua and Zimbabwe; or the Latin American Bishops' Conference's program for a theology of reconciliation of conflicting classes.

44. The concrete question is how the life and liberty of the masses of the people are to be defended against exploitation and brutalization by the powerful and their official and nonofficial armies. The reconciliation of Jesus passes through the cross. The poor have their cross, and Jesus recognizes them as his own. Will the rich also accept the cross and give up domination, and share with the people all accumulated wealth and power?

DIALOGUE WITH CULTURES AND RELIGIONS

45. We are wounded cultures. Our cultures have been colonized, attacked, devalued, distorted. Assimilation, negation, segregation, vandalism, school systems, technology, and the invasion of the media were the weapons used to uproot, degrade, and depersonalize our peoples.

46. But it is precisely in this area of culture that Third World peoples have refused to succumb. Africa and Asia have a keen sense of the vital role of culture. The dominant culture in Latin America is white and Western, but today Latin Americans are becoming more conscious that they

come from a mestizo race and are "discovering" the existence and values of blacks and indigenous cultures in their midst. Culturally, the U.S. minorities are Third World, but they are forced to be First World citizens in imposed Third World conditions.

47. Colonialism has not been able to subvert our cultures but has succeeded in hurting them deeply and distorting them through an imported educational system and the capitalist process. A noteworthy factor common to our continents is that those who oppress and exploit the masses, who militarize and misuse power, who get our countries into debt and subscribe to frontiers, divisions, and laws established by colonialists are people formed in a colonialist system of thought and values, analytical rationality, and conceptions of economics and politics.

48. These persons molded by the West's ethos and instructions have benefited from them and are anxious only to preserve them and the whole state of affairs as left behind by the colonialists, instead of starting afresh from the people and their resources, needs, perceptions, decisions, and possibilities. The battle between capitalist and socialist ideologies is a relatively new cultural phenomenon on all the continents.

49. To overlook the religiosity of Third World peoples would be to miss essential dimensions of reality. Religion governs the subconscious life of all social classes. Traditional religions speak to the problems and needs of everyday life — they deal with food and health, droughts and floods, hunting, fear, fertility, while Western Christianity appears to be too mental, abstract, juridical. Religions must not be disconnected from socio-political situations and problems. The fact is that they have often served to justify oppression, but have also acted as powerful critics of injustice and inequality. They have great liberative potential, but also a tendency to foster fatalism and passivity.

50. In the colonial era Third World religions and cultures were marginalized and attacked. Jesus Christ of the colonial churches came as a religious Julius Caesar, not to dialogue, invite, enable, give life, and help grow, but to conquer, destroy, and supplant. Things have changed; traditional religions are reviving; the hegemony of Christianity is being challenged; a new sense of the divine in history is taking shape.

51. The process shows at times a tendency toward fundamentalism, and at times a genius for syncretism, which is not a fanciful religious salad, but a selective reading of religious reality approached with openness and respect, and organized around a faith-nucleus. We understand better than rationalist traditions do "the strange wealth of syncretist myths and rites."

52. Asia, the birthplace of all the major scripture religions of the world, has a wealth of sacred writings, and continues to produce more. It combines traditions of scholarship and systematic religious reflection with mysticism and experience. Nonscriptural primal religions, be they African, Asian, or American, express themselves not so much in words as in symbols and

rituals, the dance and the social organization being among their most original and significant religious realizations.

53. In Africa, Islam is reviving; Christian churches are multiplying and growing rapidly and Africanizing themselves fast. There is tension brewing between the African churches and the Vatican, which is refusing to face certain questions concerning the healing ministry, pastoral care of the polygamous, the matter of the eucharist, African liturgies, and canonization of real models of Christian holiness instead of its rare and bizarre specimens.

54. There is in Latin America a veritable irruption of the religiosity of the poor, popular religiosity, which was once criticized and rejected by a theological elite, but is now considered with respect. This has given rise to different religious experiences, the most significant among them being the basic Christian communities. Noteworthy are the rebirth of Afro-American cults, the black recovery of religion which is also a recovery by former slaves of their ethnic identity and human dignity, and a new appreciation of indigenous religious tradition. Emergent Pentecostal movements reject capitalist greed, fraud, and affluence. There exists a deepening reflection on the Cuban and Nicaraguan revolutions and on the relationship between politics and the faith. Mention must be made also of fundamentalist and apolitical religious movements coming from the United States; and of the use of religion by a U.S. leadership which opposes liberation theology and promotes conservative theologies and counter-insurgency religions.

55. We listened to the U.S. minorities' story of how they found themselves in the midst of a new Americanism marked by political and religious fundamentalism and whose leadership tends to support apartheid in South Africa, seeks to destroy the hard-won freedom of Nicaragua, and is itching for a war to boost the profits of the ruling U.S. oligarchs. We heard with pain their understanding of themselves as victims of a system rather than as citizens of a democracy; and their description of America not as a dream but often as a nightmare. They spoke passionately of the ordeal of being black in a white racist society.

56. EATWOT has devoted through the years special efforts to the understanding of and to the dialogue with non-Christian religions and cultures. But we have not explored their traditions and symbols in relation to liberation and human promotion. We feel that we lack a methodology for such an exploration. Is it right to interpret other religions only on the basis of the Bible?

57. We want to develop such a methodology. At Oaxtepec some insights and tools of interpretation were proposed. We asked ourselves: Is the revival of ancient faiths a threat or an opportunity? The problems involved here will be appreciated differently depending on whether one's point of view is "evangelistic" or liberational, church-centered or people-centered. The theological implications of the following facts will have to be explored. These religions have played a major role in inspiring and sustaining resis-

tance to colonial imperialistic oppression though not in questioning patriarchy and sexist domination. In limited ways they have affirmed human dignity and defended God's image on our earth. But, at the same time, they have supported all forms of enslavement and oppression. The question is how to discern what is liberating and what is repressive. It is also necessary to develop tools of analysis for this discernment and a pedagogy for the transformation of religions and cultures into instruments of service and liberation.

58. Some of the old religions have their own and ancient scriptures. Asia speaks of the Bible as one among many sacred books, one of several revelations, and asks: Could a live historical process and spiritual quest be ruled forever by fixed texts born of particular, limited experiences of one ancient group of people? Are nonscriptual religious traditions necessarily inferior to those with scriptures? In the dialogue with these old religions, we are challenged and we raise new questions for ourselves. Is it not the witness of the scriptures that God is present not in books but among the people and in their struggles for justice and dignity? Should we not be converted from books and from oppressing one another with texts to the Spirit of the living God and of the questing people? How do sacred texts relate to one another, and to God's presence and word and activity in the human heart, in significant events, in the signs of the times, in the unfolding of history?

59. These lines of inquiry spring from our conviction that the Spirit of God carries our history and moves in its depths. We have come to discern the Spirit in every context and culture. Theology must revive the name of the Spirit and of the Risen One. The Spirit is not confined to the incarnation; it goes on to operate the resurrection, which brings all particular incarnations into the Realm of God, and makes a universal incarnation possible. The Spirit sets in motion a dialectic of incarnation-death-resurrection. The task of theology is to recognize the embodiments of the word in the history of freedom; the passion of Jesus in the struggles of the people; and the resurrection in their growing emancipation and fellowship.

THE GOD OF LIFE AND TOTAL CHRIST

60. A theology of life and of a God of life lies embedded in many a primal world view. The African understanding of human existence as a battle for life against the forces of death is a case in point. South African issues are issues of bread and life. Afro-Americans have resisted enslavement from the first day to this day. That they are passive is a convenient myth. They have resisted individually, collectively, violently, and nonviolently, using both religious and secular weapons. The eighteenth-century black churches played a significant role in the abolitionist and insurrectionist movements; and revolutionaries found inspiration in biblical religion.

The Hispanics too have struggled against injustice, challenged institutions, and managed to survive.

61. Asian peasants have a long history of silent resistance and of open rebellion. In most cases these struggles are experienced as having religious significance. God is experienced as partner in every striving against forces of death and domination. Concern for life is the key to the theological process. "I have come that they may have life and have it in abundance" (John 10:10), said Jesus. Was it not his sensitivity and commitment to live at all levels beginning with the basic and the physical that made him such a master of God-talk?

62. In Latin America there is also a battle going on between the forces of repression and death and the forces of life and freedom. Starting from that dramatic and painful experience, Christians have been led to proclaim God as the God of life. They have rediscovered this traditional title to name God in the midst of persecution and suffering. They have also been confronted with a new challenge, i.e., to deal with the evil of idolatry. The national security state and the capitalist system are asking from the people a religious commitment. The principles of military order and the free market appear as new idols competing with the true God, the lord of Jesus Christ.

63. Women, in particular, deeply convenanted as they are with life, with the giving and the protecting of it, carrying it literally and physically in their bodies, their arms, on their backs, are bent on helping to birth the theology of life with which people's struggles are pregnant. For the women of the Third World spiritual experience means being in communion and solidarity with all those who fight for life.

64. We confess Jesus as the son of the living God and the main source of revelation. But some Asian theologians look for new ways of interpreting the presence of God in non-Christian populations and raise critical questions. They say that Jesus came from the working class and a colonized people. Christology has to deal with racial discrimination, militarism, pauperization of the people. To Christologize also means to be committed to the struggle for a new social order and to participate in the pains of its birth and in the joys of the new creation. In the context of the Spirit and the earth's travail we ask: Is not the reality of Jesus larger than the particular flesh-history he lived? Is Jesus of Nazareth the whole of the Christ, the whole word of God? Should we not join the historical Jesus and the cosmic Christ in a rich pneumatic Christology and a cosmo-theandric vision of reality?

65. Jesus reveals God, but does not limit or exhaust the divine. In the light of the risen Jesus and the cosmic Christ, nothing prevents God's self-revelation to all God's people. It is liberating to confess that God is not confined to Christian traditions, churches, and scriptures. Wherever God makes self-disclosure and self-gift, the word enters the earth, becomes embodied in history, participates in people's struggles for justice and free-

dom, and helps propel them toward their (up)rising and liberation.

66. The Bible too has become a theological issue. There is among the poor a growing appreciation of the Bible as a book where God and people interact and as a book of stories of the struggles, frustrations, and triumphs of the poor. It is to be read and interpreted from the perspective of the oppressed. Third World women have decided that instead of rejecting the Bible wholesale as hopelessly patriarchal, they should "mine" deeper into it, and accept as authoritative what promotes life and its fullness.

WOMEN'S THEOLOGICAL PERSPECTIVE

67. EATWOT has made some real progress in the matter of women's participation and is genuinely concerned for the promotion of women. In this theological community women's presence is becoming visible. Women are making a new contribution and discovering a new methodology, for they have their own way of sensing the meaning of the faith.

68. Women theologians of EATWOT had their own theological conference at Oaxtepec. That was an important moment from the program launched at Geneva in 1983. There were national consultations held in preparation for their intercontinental meetings. This program is intended to create space for women theologians to meet and share their experiences and views, to discuss the patriarchal elements in theology today, and to reformulate theology from the perspective of full humanity for all.

69. At Oaxtepec the women discussed several important issues; they underscored the oppression of women and affirmed the existence of liberation movements. Among the efforts toward liberation, theologizing emerges as a specific manner in which women struggle for the right to life. It was said that the Bible plays a vital role in the lives of women and in their struggle for liberation. Christology appeared to be central to women's theology. In the person and praxis of Jesus Christ, women find the grounds of their liberation from all discrimination. The passionate and compassionate way in which women do theology is a rich contribution to theological science. Finally, the women made several recommendations to the leadership of EATWOT in terms of organization, content, and publications.

70. The women were asked by the planners of the EATWOT conference to make a critique of the association's programs and theological content. They made a presentation during the conference. They recognized some progress in the increase of the number of women theologians, in their growing credibility, and in the increasing respect by the male theologians. They underlined the vital contribution of women to theology, and they asked for more freedom and creativity.

71. But it is not enough to be satisfied with numbers. They said the question is this: How are women's issues dealt with in EATWOT? What difference does our presence and the listing of our concerns make to the process of theologizing? Should not a different kind of theologizing happen

because we are present? To the suggestion that men do theology in a deeper way "because we are here," the answer was that "we should not only complement men's theology but change the whole style of doing theology."

THE MISSION OF THE CHURCH

72. From EATWOT's founding at Dar-es-Salaam until the present we have reflected on the meaning of evangelization as the task of the church. In that first dialogue we said: "The church, the body of Christ, needs to become aware of its role in today's reality. . . . Jesus identified himself with the victims of oppression, thus exposing the reality of sin. Liberating them from the power of sin and reconciling them with God and with one another, he restored them to the fullness of their humanity. Therefore, the church's mission is for the realization of the wholeness of the human person" (from the final statement).

73. Today, as we continue trying to define the mission of the church, we are more aware that evangelization is linked to human promotion. Evangelization is to share the gift of Jesus, but at the same time it is an opportunity to learn from others. Evangelization cannot be arrogant, as in the past. It has to be considered as a modest and friendly presence on the part of the churches to discover for themselves the wonder of God's grace in every history, culture, and people, and to celebrate that grace and give thanks; to be open and accept the other's specific gift of truth and God-experience for their own enrichment and growth; to make available to the other their own specific experience of God, love, and hope as these have entered human history in the reality of Jesus of Nazareth; and to join hands with all who stand for human dignity and struggle together for the liberation of all.

74. Evangelization can no longer be a matter of spiritual conquest or religious colonization. The church can be only a disciple among disciples, and a seeker after fuller and finer participation in God's truth. Everywhere the need is for the church to be local, real, autonomous, responsible. Everywhere the question is about the church's official stand on Third World realities. Everywhere it is a question of recognizing and promoting real models of holiness in the women and men who live out their fidelity to Christ in day-to-day life despite suffering, poverty, temptations, risk, and danger instead of holding up rare models of unreal and artificial sanctity.

SPIRITUALITY

75. The concept of spirituality is broad and encompasses different meanings according to the context and people's positions. The whites in South Africa claim to be living a biblical spirituality. Among the oppressed, we find an other-worldly type of spirituality. The spirituality which is at the source of Third World theology consists in a passionate commitment to

God's Reign on earth, and therefore to the earth and to its liberation and transformation. It is a spirituality which challenges the oppressed to throw off their yoke and be free.

76. We seek to identify the presence and action of the divine both in creation and in history, in the cosmos and in significant events and movements. We discover God and the Christ of God in oppressed peoples, despised races, marginalized cultures, and humiliated histories. Jesus saw God at work in the life of bird and flower; he saw God as lovingly partial to the lowly and the unlearned; he saw his own suffering self in the broken and the dispossessed of history.

77. Jesus denounced oppression; he programmed liberation, made a whip and wielded it, and indicated the abolition of all oppressive power, be it altar, be it throne. We want our approach to reality to be not atomizing and dichotomizing but holistic, unitive, intuitive; beyond the merely rational-logical. There is a spiritual and mystical understanding of reality prior to reflection and analysis. Such is the grasp of reality natural to "little ones," the unsophisticated masses of the people. It is the source of symbol, language, dance, poetry, liturgy, as well as of institutions; it lies at the basis of artistic and scientific inventiveness. Such people in quest of meaning and fuller humanity are themselves the rich source of Third World theology.

78. Spiritualities come alive in liberation movements. In the struggle for life there unfolds a history of lived heroic holiness. Liberation struggles express God as the God of life striving against death in the concrete situations of existence. The struggles represent God's dealing with the crucified of history. Spirituality must never be abstracted from history and its particularities and conflicts; it must be concretized within given socio-political contexts, and tested in a historical process in the crucible of burning human problems.

79. Feminist spirituality, people-oriented and relational, life-giving and peace-bringing, includes struggle against systems of death and domination and against discrimination in church and society. Woman's care to remake her body for fresh life sums up her spirituality, and represents her specific contribution to the creation of a new earth, socially and ecologically sound and whole.

80. EATWOT provides a forum for different spiritualities to meet and be enriched within the experience of the Holy Spirit and through the mediation of concrete socio-political involvement.

81. We are thus working toward a spiritual theology which will encompass the cosmos, the people, the Christ of God, and God; will integrate nature and history, word and silence, action and contemplation, the mystical and the logical; and will overcome the dichotomies between earth and heaven, between doctrine and devotion, a teaching church and a taught church.

82. We witness to the presence of the Spirit in the Third World and among its poor; we witness against all lies and calumnies, against all antilife

forces and processes of death. We repudiate the insinuation that our theologies are camouflaged Marxism. Ours is a Christian confession. And in the name of that confession we reject all ahistorical idealisms, all alienating and soporific spiritualities, and all theologies without home and homeland, without a passionate love for land and people.

83. We name our martyrs and draw strength from the thousands of children, women, and men who have been insulted and killed because they cared for the poor, for people, for justice and God. We ask the martyrs of yesterday and of today, the martyrs of colonial and slave systems, the martyrs of South Africa, Central America, Korea, and the Philippines, to stand here with us.

WORSHIP AND PRAYER

84. Our worship grew out of our theological concerns. Theology is a spiritual activity, a function of our faith in Christ, interior to our faith-union in God. Worship opens us up to the call of the Spirit who pervades history and empowers the poor. Built around themes of liberation, our worship reflected God's question: Where is your brother? (Gen. 4:9). It was worship that orchestrated our diverse activities and concerns and the distinct accents of our theologies.

85. The opening worship of the conference at Oaxtepec was a celebration of hope for the people's resurrection and liberation. The message was delivered through the readings of Ezekiel 37 and Luke 4. The next morning we prayed for openness and for the courage to take risks. We listened to Acts 11:19–26. The third morning we were asked to reappropriate the question: If God is for us, who is against us? Another day we wove a yearning for the contemplative eye. We listened to an Indian Upanishad. We were also invited to celebrate Mary, under her title of Guadalupe, by a group of Mexican women. They sang: "From heaven on a beautiful day came the Virgin. Her face was Mexican." When the U.S. minorities led us in prayer, resurrection was their theme: from oppression through struggle to victory.

SELF-EVALUATION AND PLANS FOR THE FUTURE

86. Oaxtepec became an important moment in the short history of our association. EATWOT has grown and has gained credibility among ecumenical circles as a group engaged in contextualization of theology. It has made a contribution to the clarification of the mission of the church and has emerged as a channel for the voices and aspirations of people oppressed and marginalized in the Third World.

87. Our seventh theological conference celebrated our tenth anniversary. It was a moment of gratitude to God and to all who have helped us to develop. But at the same time it was an opportunity for self-criticism as a praxis of liberation and growth. Several self-critical observations were made

on the conference floor or in informal conversations or in written notes.

88. The new executive committee, elected for a period of five years (1986–1991), has assumed the responsibility of leading the association, correcting the mistakes, and deepening our vision. At the end of our conference a program of action was proposed for the next five years. The program includes general criteria and orientations and concrete projects and proposals.

89. Some of the orientations refer to the meaning of our theologizing and the identity of EATWOT. We committed ourselves as persons and as an organization to deepen the following criteria.

90. Our theology will work with faith understood as collaboration with God's plans for our world—collaboration with God active in the totality of world history no less than in our particular histories. Oppression will then be seen as an expression of Godlessness, a denial of faith in God. The process of liberation will be experienced as a joint venture of God and the people. Such theology will be expressed in the language and art of the people, and especially in their free, cooperative, egalitarian social organizations and celebrations.

91. The identity of the Third World theologian has to be defined in terms of political tasks, commitment to liberation struggles, and sustained reflection on God's stake in history. Room must be found in EATWOT not only for the presence of women but for a distinctly feminist way of doing and articulating theology. The place of Marxist analysis has to be determined. A thorough debate is in order to make our socialist option clear instead of speaking vaguely of a third way.

92. Dialogue with other religions as God's partners and ours in the human-religious task of liberating the oppressed and constructing a new world is a felt need at all levels of EATWOT. The presence and participation of followers of other faiths (and of secular ideologies) in our future meetings must be seen as normal, natural, and necessary. Equally important is the presence and participation in our ongoing discussions and theological activities of nonacademic people, of workers, and of the poor.

93. Our work should aim at defining a total human perspective. Asians have challenged our Christian theology almost at every point: Christology and the "uniqueness" of Christ, evangelization, mission, church, the Bible as normative, theology as reflection on church practice, etc. They have led us to an appreciation of revelation and grace on the basis of the Spirit. We must open up to the massive challenge and promise of these vaster horizons. Our ecumenicity and our central concern for the poor demand this of us.

94. At the same time, we affirm and wish to strengthen the route we have already taken in our theological journey and to integrate the insights gained into our future tasks. In Latin America, the people in the basic Christian communities read the Bible and social reality through their experience of struggle and hope, and grasp things with the intuition of faith and common sense. We admire the spirituality of Africa: its courage to stand

up to oppression, its resourcefulness to survive, the strength with which it has maintained its culture and creativity. We admire the spiritual strength and clarity of Native Americans who have so consistently spurned the glamor of Western culture and upheld their dignity and claims to sovereignty. Important for the future is the capacity, which we should nurture and develop, to dream dreams and see visions and nurse utopias. We make our own the U.S. minorities' concluding message: there is no blueprint . . . and the minorities seem to have no real effective power to bring about change. Yet it is precisely out of this apparently impotent situation that we dare to dream and risk the efforts of creating something really new.

95. We wish to invite the Caribbean and the South Pacific Islands into EATWOT and to make room in it for their concerns. The Caribbean is at the crossroads of many races and cultures and has a cruel history of enslavement and suffering. The South Pacific Islands are concerned about nuclear testing and nuclear waste dumping on their beautiful shores. We need the presence of these two regions to share with us their struggles and their religious interpretations.

96. At Oaxtepec it was decided to expand within EATWOT the concept of "minorities." So far, we have had three distinct regions: Africa, Asia, and Latin America, and a fourth region or group called "the minorities of the USA." The assembly decided to make the concept of minorities more inclusive. We will invite the oppressed minorities from Europe and other groups like the Maori tribes of New Zealand to be part of the association.

97. It was also agreed upon to form a task force on "Dialogue with Socialist Countries," which will follow up the dialogue already initiated with China and will establish new contacts with other socialist countries.

98. In terms of programs, EATWOT decided to continue with the work of the four regions/groups: Africa, Asia, Latin America, and the minorities. Each group will develop and implement its own programs. We will also continue the interregional work and dialogue through the existing working commissions (Church History and Women's Theological Perspective) and through the newly formed Theological Study Commission.

99. Oaxtepec was a beautiful moment of celebration of our anniversary, a moment of evaluation and projection toward the future. EATWOT has come out of this assembly strengthened and resolved to overcome external attacks and its own shortcomings. We feel that we reflect the general situation of crisis in the Third World and, at the same time, the hope of the poor who know that God will liberate the oppressed. The conference expressed all these feelings in dialogue, prayer, worship, and sometimes in our differences and our fears. We are grateful to God and to all those who through ten years have been partners and friends. Together we pray for the coming of the Spirit.

Contributors

K. C. Abraham is vice president of EATWOT and Professor of Theology and Ethics at the United Theological College in Bangalore.

Tissa Balasuriya is director of the Center for Society and Religion in Sri Lanka. He is the author of numerous books, including *Planetary Theology*.

Mary Rosario Battung is a religious Sister from the Philippines who works with the Zen Center for Oriental Spirituality in Manila.

Maria Clara Lucchetti Bingemer is professor of theology at the Pontifical Catholic University of Rio de Janeiro in Brazil, and co-author of *Mary, Mother of God, Mother of the Poor.*

Kelly Delaine Brown is Assistant Professor of Systematic Theology at Howard University Divinity School.

Emílio de Carvalho is the Methodist bishop of Luanda, Angola and president of EATWOT.

Frank Chikane is General Secretary of the South African Council of Churches and the author of *No Life of My Own.*

James H. Cone teaches theology at Union Theological Seminary in New York. He is the author of *A Black Theology of Liberation, For My People,* and numerous works in black theology.

Patrick Kalilombe is the Catholic Archbishop of Malawi and lecturer in Third World Theologies at Selly Oak Colleges, Birmingham, England.

José Míguez Bonino is a Methodist theologian from Argentina who has been widely active in the ecumenical movement, serving on the Faith and Order Commission of the World Council of Churches. His books include *Doing Theology in a Revolutionary Situation* and (as editor) *Jesus in Latin America.*

Mercy Amba Oduyoye is Deputy General Secretary of the World Council of Churches in Geneva. A native of Ghana, she is the author of *Hearing and Knowing: Theological Reflections on Christianity in Africa.*

Sun Ai Park is from Korea, an ordained minister of the Disciples of Christ, coordinator of the Asian Women's Resource Centre for Culture and Theology in Hong Kong, and co-editor of *We Dare To Dream: Doing Theology as Asian Women.*

Samuel Rayan is an Indian Jesuit and principal of the New Indian School of Ecumenical Theology in Bangalore.

Pablo Richard is a Chilean theologian who serves on the team of the Departamento Ecuménico de Investicaciónes (DEI) in Costa Rica. He is the author of *Death of Christendoms, Birth of the Church.*

Elsa Tamez teaches at the Biblical Seminary in San Jose, Costa Rica. She is the author of *God of the Oppressed* and editor of *Through Her Eyes: Women's Theology from Latin America.*

Sergio Torres is a Chilean priest who teaches systematic theology at the Alfonsin Institute of Pastoral Theology in Santiago, Chile. He is the co-editor of four previous EATWOT volumes, including *The Challenge of Basic Christian Communities* and *Doing Theology in a Divided World.*

Also from Orbis

PRAYER IN WORLD RELIGIONS
by Denise Lardner Carmody and John Tully Carmody
A much-needed, clear, and practical book that surveys prayer in Hinduism, Buddhism, Judaism, Islam, African, and Native American traditions. After an introduction demonstrating the relevance of prayer to current interreligious dialogue, the Carmodys look closely at each tradition, describing the historical context, rituals, stories, and prayers typical to each. The conclusion reveals the overall import of prayer in religious living, providing a better appreciation of the depths and riches of the prayer lives of those who are not Christian, for the sake of both greater tolerance and understanding and the enrichment of Christians' own religious lives. 144pp. Index.
ISBN 0-88344-644-8 Paper

CHRISTIANITY THROUGH NON-CHRISTIAN EYES
by Paul J. Griffiths
This anthology of twentieth-century analyses of Christianity by representative non-Christians provides new perspectives for thinking with theological seriousness and historical sensitivity about the reality and challenges of religious pluralism. Griffiths introduces the concepts and problems of relationships between religious communities, then devotes a section each to Judaism, Islam, Buddhism, and Hinduism. The essays themselves—by such figures as Masao Abe, Abraham Joshua Henschel, Seyyed Hossein Nasr, Mohandas K. Gandhi, Bibhuti S. Yadav—cover a wide range of opinions and arguments, from the polemical to the irenic.
"A much-needed book. . . . A most valuable resource."—*John Hick*
300pp. Notes, bibliography, index.
ISBN 0-88344-661-8 Paper

LIBERATION THEOLOGY: A DOCUMENTARY HISTORY
Edited by Alfred T. Hennelly
This book is the quintessential reference work on liberation theology—its background, origins, development, and surrounding controversies. Not only an archive of fifty-nine vital historical documents (many in English for the first time) *Liberation Theology: A Documentary History* provides a compelling first-hand look at dramatic confrontations such as the silencing of Leonardo Boff and Pope John Paul II's visit to Nicaragua.
"Should be on the shelf of everyone who wants to understand the evolution and etiology of liberation theology—the most significant development in the Catholic Church since Vatican II."—*Robert F. Drinan*
564pp. Notes, index.
ISBN 0-88344-593-X Paper

LIBERATION THEOLOGY AND ITS CRITICS
Toward an Assessment
by Arthur H. McGovern

Liberation theology has provoked a wide and diverse range of responses from a multitude of critics — theological, methodological, political, ecclesiastical. This book provides a comprehensive and systematic explication of these diverse criticisms, as well as a reasoned and rigorous defense of this new way of doing theology.

"I applaud this sympathetic defense of liberation theology, which at the same time treats its critics with civility and seriousness. . . . It broadens common ground — the primacy of faith, the need for true democracy, and the urgency of economic vitality. . . ." — *Michael Novak*

304pp. Notes, index.
ISBN 0-88344-595-6 Paper